The Army and the Navajo

The

ARMY
and the
NAVAJO

Gerald Thompson

THE UNIVERSITY OF ARIZONA PRESS
Tucson, Arizona

About the Author . . .

GERALD THOMPSON has concentrated his historical investigations largely on American Indian and military activities in the Southwest. His research interests have led to extensive travel in the area, presentations at historical conferences, scholarly articles in historical journals, and membership on the special research project team that prepared *Arizona's Heritage: Today and Tomorrow*. Thompson, a member of the staff of *Arizona and the West,* received his Master's degree in history from the University of Arizona and is focusing continuing studies on the career of Edward F. Beale.

THE UNIVERSITY OF ARIZONA PRESS

Copyright © 1976
The Arizona Board of Regents
All Rights Reserved
Manufactured in the U.S.A.

I.S.B.N.-0-8165-0541-1 cloth
I.S.B.N.-0-8165-0495-4 paper
L. C. No. 75-8457

For my family and friends

Contents

ILLUSTRATIONS

Preface

DURING MUCH OF THE NINETEENTH CENTURY the United States government struggled to cope with the dilemma of the American Indian. What should be the government's policy toward the Indian? How could it "civilize" the Indian and bring him into the realm of American society? These questions were pondered repeatedly by succeeding administrations and a multitude of humanitarians. Through trial and error, by 1860 the government had developed what it hoped would be a viable institution — the Indian reservation — to deal with these problems and objectives. Protected by a military garrison that kept the settlers and Indians apart and attempted to maintain the peace, the reservation would become a vehicle for the transformation of wild, nomadic, American natives into productive members of society. The passage of time proved that the reservation system was at best only a temporary feeble solution. Still, the leaders of the United States in the 1860s and 1870s regarded the institution as a humanitarian and enlightened approach to an ancient problem.

This present volume comprises an administrative study of the Bosque Redondo — one of the largest Indian reservations ever created in the United States. Laid out beside the Pecos River in New Mexico Territory in 1863 by Brigadier General James H. Carleton for the Navajo Indians, the Bosque was maintained for five years before being abandoned. Its successes and failures provided American leaders with valuable insights into the Indian problem. It also taught the Indian Bureau and the army which pitfalls to avoid in starting and operating a large reservation.

Many myths have developed about the Bosque Redondo Reservation. Some writers have called the reserve an American concentration camp; others have referred to it as a giant contracting scheme. Navajo folklore has nurtured the view of the Bosque Redondo as a place of horrible suffering and misery, with stories being handed down from generation to generation. Although no study of the Bosque Redondo can discount the suffering that occurred at the reservation, the situation should be viewed in a broad context and in the light of cold reality. The army did not create the Bosque Redondo to punish the Navajos but rather to prevent these Indians from being exterminated by New Mexican militia. It was also an attempt to teach the Indians the ways of the

[ix]

white man, so that ultimately they could join his world. This meant a radical alteration of the Navajo culture, but few individuals of that day regarded Indian culture as worth saving. Enlightened, humanitarian thinking argued for total assimilation, not the preservation, of Indian identity.

Was the Bosque Redondo simply a contractor's scheme? A cursory study of rising commodity prices in New Mexico during its existence might indicate that the reservation had been created to make certain merchants and contractors wealthy. However, on the whole, the fact that prices steadily rose during these years was largely due to supply and demand. There were several instances of outright contractual fraud and of deliberately juggled prices, but on the whole the cost of breadstuffs and meat was determined by the marketplace. The role of the marketplace in determining commodity prices was clearly visible in the beef contracts. As demand for cattle increased, prices rose. Then a new market was discovered in cheap Texas beef, which dramatically drove down the price of beef. The financial operations of the Bosque Redondo Reservation, which constitute a major aspect of this book, were a very important but seldom examined aspect of Indian history.

This study is primarily an administrative history of the Bosque Redondo Reservation. Consequently, other aspects of the reservation — for instance, its political impact on New Mexican politics — have been minimized. Nor does this history of the Bosque include a study of military affairs in New Mexico during these years. Other works have covered this aspect. As a military reservation, however, the Bosque cannot be discussed without dealing with the military officers who administered its operations.

General James H. Carleton, the architect of the Bosque Redondo Reservation, reflected clearly the ideals of a mid-nineteenth-century humanitarian. He believed that men had a duty to uplift the native Americans from their "savage" ways. He spoke and acted with a sense of the White Man's Burden, equalling any Englishman in India or Africa. Like most humanitarians, Carleton believed that Christianity had fostered the achievements of his superior civilization, and he urged that the "savages" be taught the revealed truths of God, which would put them on the path to assimilation. The Indians' way of life must be totally transformed. For the proud Navajos, the Bosque Redondo became the crucible for this drastic change.

Only faint voices called for the preservation of Indian culture during these years. The widespread belief that Indians possessed a life-style and culture that should be preserved as a valuable part of mankind's total heritage has developed only since 1930. In the West of the 1860s most settlers favored outright Indian extermination; in the minds of many citizens the Indian's position in society was lower than that of the black.

Other writers have mentioned the unique role of the military on the frontier, but it bears repeating. The army constantly found itself in an awkward position, protecting both the Indians and the settlers from each other. At the same time the military voiced the most vigorous pleas for humanitarian treatment of the Indians. Prominent officers urged kind Christian treatment for Indians, protected reservations, and eventual assimilation.

The Bosque Redondo Reservation was the scene of a lengthy cultural confrontation between whites and Indians. After daily contacts with the Indians, and working side by side with them, the white men grew to realize that the Indians were human beings (although perhaps not considered as equals) who basically desired to live in peace and relative comfort. The Navajos, on the other hand, learned many of the values and shortcomings of the white man's world. This knowledge, on the part of both groups, proved valuable in later years. In contrast to the Navajos, the Mescalero Apaches at the Bosque Rodondo experienced a greater cultural shock. They found farming a great change from their strictly nomadic life-style. Yet even the Mescaleros tried to adopt the values imposed upon them.

The idea of preparing a history of the Bosque Redondo was conceived in the fall of 1968 by Harwood P. Hinton, editor of *Arizona and the West* and Professor of History at the University of Arizona. The primary material available for reservation studies was truly overwhelming. As the Bosque Redondo was a military reservation, War Department records proved extremely important. The Consolidated Fort Sumner File at the National Archives was invaluable. This file had been mis-shelved for many years, after which it finally was discovered with other New Mexican material. It contained extremely crucial material relative to the last three years of the reservation. Other interesting commentary on the Bosque Redondo came from the U. S. Grant Papers in the Library of Congress.

A great many persons and institutions have earned my deepest gratitude for their assistance in this work. To Harwood P. Hinton, who has read and adroitly criticized this work, I am extremely indebted and very grateful. The staff of the National Archives deserves special commendation. They went far beyond the call of duty in assisting me. I also wish to thank the staffs of Special Collections, University of Arizona Library; Arizona Historical Society; Bancroft Library; Huntington Library; Denver Public Library; Colorado State Historical Society; California State Library; Smithsonian Libraries; Museum of New Mexico; Yale University Library; University of Chicago Library; and the Library of Congress. Additionally, I would like to acknowledge the help of Henry P. Walker, assistant editor of *Arizona and the West,* Herman E. Bateman, Chairman of Graduate Studies and Professor of History at the University of Arizona; Myra Ellen Jenkins, State Historian and Chief of Historical Services at the New Mexico State Records Center; and Richard Salazar, archivist, New Mexico State Records Center.

To Margaret, my wife, I wish to express my loving gratitude for her patience during the years that I have studied the Bosque Redondo. She not only endured listening to countless discourses on Indian policy but tolerated such eccentric behavior as exploring old Fort Sumner in windy freezing weather on New Year's Eve.

Finally, I wish to express appreciation to the University of Arizona Press for publishing this work.

G. T.

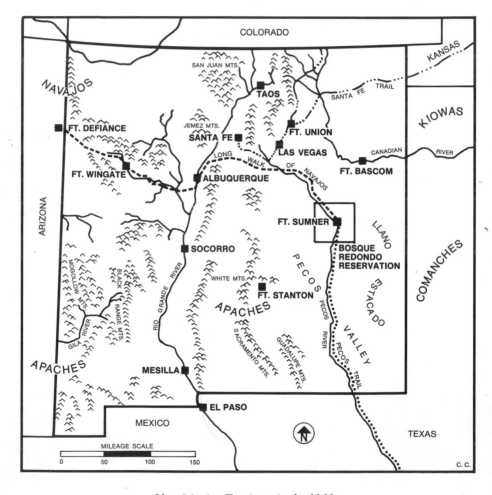

New Mexico Territory in the 1860s

1

The Navajo Problem

"From time immemorial these Indians had subsisted upon the
flocks and herds of your fathers; had times without number,
even in one single hour reduced whole families from com-
parative wealth to poverty. Your ancestors, under the Spanish Government, made many campaigns against them, and
many treaties of peace with them. But the Indians soon
forgot the obligations to which they had pledged themselves,
in each successive treaty. Then came other campaigns and
other treaties, under the Mexican Republic. Again the Navajoes forgot the punishment they had received, and over and
over again, broke their treaties. After the annexation of New
Mexico to the United States, by the Treaty of Guadaloupe
Hidalgo, the troops from the north commenced *their* campaigns. And what now was the result? Why, the treaties were
broken, and on some occasions, even before the troops had
been entirely withdrawn from the Navajo country. To cure
this great evil from which your territory had been so long
a prey, some new remedy must be adopted."

General James H. Carleton

FOR FIVE YEARS (1863–68) the sprawling Bosque Redondo Reservation on
the Pecos River in eastern New Mexico was the scene of a unique experiment.
Here the federal government struggled diligently to find a humanitarian solution to the vexing problem posed by the depredations of the Apache and Navajo
Indians. Many governmental officials believed that the basic life-style and culture
of these Indians could be changed by religious and vocational education, under
the guiding hand of the military. They looked upon the Bosque Redondo as a
vehicle for this transformation. However, from the start, management errors,
conflicts in administration, and bad fortune plagued the experiment. Within
three years conditions on the reserve had become unbearable (the Mescaleros
had long since fled). In 1868 the government wisely resolved to return the
Navajos to their homeland. The reservation had failed, but many of the goals
of its founders had been realized. The Navajos had learned a new way of life,

[1]

and they never again posed a serious threat to Rio Grande settlements. Thus, the Bosque Redondo experiment provided a significant precedent for future reservations.

In the mid-nineteenth century the Navajos and the Apaches had inhabited the Southwest for at least four hundred years. In the sixteenth century, when the Spaniards made contact with the two tribes, both had similar cultural traits and were hunter-agriculturalists. The Navajos (meaning people with planted fields) claimed the high plateau country of northwestern New Mexico and northeastern Arizona. Their homeland was extremely varied, containing forested hills, plunging canyons, rainbow-colored sands, and towering buttes. Cutting through the heart of their country, the San Juan River flowed from the western flank of the Rockies in a northwesterly direction to the Colorado River. Most of the Navajo country appeared barren, covered with sage and low brush. Towering mesas, like brooding gods, seemed to watch over the Navajos. In time the nature of the land took on a special, deeply religious, meaning for the Indians. To the south, their Athapascan cousins, the Apaches (a Zuni word meaning the enemy), roamed the mountain country of western New Mexico and eastern Arizona, penetrating into Mexico. When the two tribes acquired the horse from the Spaniards, their cultures were permanently altered. Instead of traveling and hunting on foot, they began moving rapidly from place to place and satisfying their wants through raiding.

Living in clans scattered throughout the region, the Navajos enjoyed an abundance of game and edible plants. In their forested mountains they hunted deer, elk, and wild turkey as skillfully as any tribe of the Plains. From the sophisticated Pueblo Indians living to the east along the Rio Grande valley, the Navajos acquired many new ideas. They witnessed the wealth and prosperity which grew from tilling the soil. They knew the grain that filled the Pueblos' storerooms could be eaten in winter, or when a game shortage developed. Consequently, Navajos began to farm on a small scale at the mouths of washes, their fields watered by summer rains. Their lives gradually became more stable, more fixed. As they matured and settled, the Navajos placed more importance on stories, songs, chants, and ceremonials. Although not as elaborate as the Hopis in their rituals, the Navajos borrowed some of the religious beliefs of their neighbors, as they had borrowed the idea of farming from the Pueblos.[1]

Navajo life gradually changed. As seminomads who hunted, farmed, and raised livestock, the Navajos fell prey to their neighbors, the Utes. During the 1600s the Utes probably pushed the Navajos farther south and east into greater contact with the Pueblo Indians. The great Pueblo Revolt of 1680, which temporarily expelled the Spanish from New Mexico, had a decided impact upon the Navajos. Fearing the retribution of the avenging Spaniards, many Pueblos fled west, where large numbers intermarried with the eastern Navajo clans, and were absorbed into their culture.[2]

In marked contrast to the Navajos, the Apaches retained traditional cultural patterns. Although separated into many bands throughout the Southwest, all pursued a nomadic way of life and lived by hunting, gathering, and raiding. One group, the Mescalero Apaches, who would eventually be brought to the Bosque Redondo, lived in southern New Mexico. Calling the mountain ranges east of the Rio Grande their home, they climbed during the summer into the cool Sacramento and White mountains to hunt game; in the winter they sought homes in the canyons and foothills. Here they killed elk and deer; they spent a great deal of time gathering berries, fruits, nuts, and mescal, a staple from which they derived their name. Unlike the Navajos, the Mescaleros did no farming and had no desire to do so, preferring the freedom of the nomadic life.

From the first, the Spaniards exhibited a curiosity about the Indians they encountered on the northern border. The Franciscan and Jesuit missionaries regarded the Indians as an untapped source of spiritual wealth. They expended their efforts on the more civilized tribes, such as the Pueblos, and did not come squarely into contact with the Navajos and Apaches until the late seventeenth century. In the years that followed, they wrestled mightily with these wild peoples, who responded by raiding the Spanish settlements and outposts with impunity. The Spanish built presidios in the Indian country and repeatedly launched expeditions to punish the responsible parties; they also concluded numerous treaties, destined to be short lived. In making these agreements, the Spaniards apparently believed that they were dealing with single united tribes, when in reality they were making peace with simply a clan or two, who had no power over the others.[3]

By 1720 the Spaniards managed to arrange an uneasy peace with the Navajos. By this time the Indians had acquired livestock to supplement their farming endeavors, and could subsist reasonably well without raiding. Moreover, the Spaniards had conducted several punitive expeditions during which they captured Navajo women and children whom they took back to the Rio Grande villages. Here the captives served as laborers or household servants. The peace, however, did not last.

In the 1750s Spanish settlers received land grants and began invading Navajo country in northwestern New Mexico. The Indians, in turn, started stealing livestock, and another series of military expeditions followed. Navajo raids and depredations increased, and many settlers abandoned their isolated ranches. In 1786 Governor Juan Bautista de Anza of New Mexico reached an agreement with the Navajos. Indian farmlands in the disputed region would be protected, provided that the Navajos did not molest Spanish livestock. In general, both parties observed the treaty, and within a decade the New Mexicans regarded the Navajos as wealthy settled people. The Indians raised extensive crops of corn and wheat, and possessed enormous flocks of sheep, as well as herds of cattle and horses.[4]

After 1800, New Mexicans again attempted to extend their holdings into Navajoland — and again the Indians retaliated. Spanish troops took the field, and in January of 1805 Antonio Narbona's soldiers inflicted a defeat on the Navajos in Canyon de Chelly. Although a paper peace followed, lasting nearly twenty years, the Navajos increasingly placed a greater importance on raiding and warfare in their culture. Repeatedly they seized Mexican women and children, and a pattern of Navajo–New Mexican intermarriage developed. By the 1820s the Navajos were the most feared Indians of the Southwest. Warfare and raiding now had evolved into a way of life.

The Mexican government, which came into power in 1821, continued the old Spanish treaty system with the Navajos. The Indians, however, were aware of the military weakness of the frontier governors. Whenever a Mexican army campaigned against the Indians, they quickly pleaded for peace, and the Mexicans would accept. Treaty followed treaty, with no enduring peace. Then, suddenly, the Mexicans departed, and a new type of white man came on the scene.[5]

In 1846 an American army under Brigadier General Stephen W. Kearny took control in New Mexico. The new conquerors adopted the old Spanish-Mexican policies of expeditions and treaties, and, like their predecessors, had no success in securing peace. By the time of the outbreak of the Civil War in 1861, Indian affairs in New Mexico were in a tumultuous state. The army withdrew the garrisons that had maintained a semblance of order in the 1850s, and the soldiers were sent east for the coming struggle. Indian tribes throughout the Southwest took advantage of the situation; they began plundering at will. New Mexicans needed decisive measures to solve their Indian problem.

By the early 1860s the federal government had evolved certain Indian policies. These included military campaigns, treaties, removal, and the construction of forts to maintain the peace. Unlike the Spaniards, who regarded the Indians as heathens possessing a valuable soul, the Americans thought of the natives as a part of the landscape who should retreat before civilization — just as the frontier itself retreated. The Indian Removal Act of 1830 marked the high tide of this type of thinking. During the decade of the 1830s the government moved most of the Eastern tribes to lands west of the Mississippi River. During the harsh winter of 1838–39, the army escorted the Cherokees and other so-called "Civilized Tribes" from the Georgia country west over the "Trail of Tears" to a new home in the Indian Territory, where a number of Plains Indians were settled. The arrival of these nations among the Comanches and Kiowas caused great problems. The government established forts in the Indian Country, but difficulties continued. By the 1840s federal Indian policy had entered a transitional period.[6]

General Kearny in 1846 believed that a strong American force placed in the Navajo country could compel the "savages" to obey the law. On September 18 he sent out two detachments, one under Major William Gilpin, and the other under Colonel Congreve Jackson, to scout the Indian land. Kearny then left the Territory, heading for California. The Navajos apparently interpreted Kearny's departure for California as a retreat; they continued to raid, even stealing cattle from the herd accompanying his column. When informed of the loss, the angry general on October 2 ordered Colonel Alexander W. Doniphan to march his regiment into Navajoland. Sending orders to Gilpin and Jackson to meet him at Ojo del Oso (Bear Springs, near present day Gallup), Doniphan marched from Santa Fe in late October with three hundred men.

The three American columns met a large number of Navajo leaders in mid-November at Ojo del Oso. Doniphan told the Navajos that if they continued their raiding they would be killed. Reportedly the Navajos replied that the Americans were now fighting the Mexicans, and, as for themselves, they wished only to continue their long-standing raiding on the Mexican settlements. Doniphan promptly warned that all Mexicans in New Mexico were now under American protection. On November 22, the Americans concluded their first treaty with the Navajos, with fourteen Indian leaders placing their marks on the document. Three days later Doniphan forced the Zuñis and Navajos to sign a peace treaty with each other. The Americans naively believed that they had settled the Indian difficulties.[7]

Peace did not come. Navajo depredations on the upper Rio Grande settlements continued, and many citizens lost their lives. By the summer of 1849, the military organized another expedition to strike the Navajos. Led by Colonel John M. Washington, military governor of New Mexico, and Indian Agent James S. Calhoun, this large force left Santa Fe in August. Within two weeks they were scouring the heart of the Navajo country, west of the Pueblo Bonito ruins, one hundred miles northwest of Albuquerque. In early September the soldiers marched into Canyon de Chelly, where Colonel Washington held a council with the several local clan leaders. When he presented the Indians with figures concerning livestock losses, and accused them of being responsible for those losses, they denied making raids or stealing livestock. After several days of argument, on September 9 the Navajos signed another treaty.

Under this treaty the Indians granted large concessions to the United States. The Navajos agreed to surrender all stolen property to the government and promised free passage to all persons through their country. Also, they permitted the government to establish in Navajoland such military posts or trading posts as it believed necessary to keep the peace. Both sides pledged a perpetual peace. For obeying the treaty, the Navajos would receive presents and annuities from time to time. The Senate ratified the treaty on September 9, 1850, one year later.[8]

By 1850 Governor James S. Calhoun had formulated a reasonable policy for handling Indian affairs in New Mexico. Calhoun divided the tribes into two groups: the sedentary (Pueblo) Indians and the wild tribes (Navajos, Apaches, Utes). He urged the government to give the Pueblos full status as citizens, including the right to vote and own property. The wild tribes, on the other hand, would require more attention before they could fit into American society. He proposed that the military curb Indian raids and collect the Indian groups on reservations. There, under skilled Indian agents, the natives could be taught the ways of husbandry.

Calhoun's ideas proved too visionary for the time. The majority of his agents became more interested in "lining their own pockets" than in helping the Indians. Governmental officials in Washington proved indifferent to New Mexico's Indian problems; they failed to supply the quantities of food, seeds, and equipment necessary to transform the Indians' life. Calhoun's major problem, however, proved to be the new military commander, Colonel Edwin V. Sumner, a man noted for his stubbornness.[9]

Sumner had his own plans for subduing the wild Indians of New Mexico. He built a chain of new military posts, brashly planting one of them in the middle of the Navajo ancestral domain. Erected in 1851 and named Fort Defiance, it lay approximately one hundred ninety miles west of Albuquerque. Sumner also pursued a hard line toward the Navajos. When they began depredating again in the Rio Grande valley, he led a force from Santa Fe in August of 1851 to Navajo country. His column contained four companies of cavalry, two of infantry, and one of artillery. The massive expedition completely failed, for Sumner even had difficulty in finding the Navajos. But Fort Defiance, established as a symbol of federal authority, would be a constant target for the Navajo anger.

Officials held another meeting with the Navajos in late January of 1852 at Jemez Springs, on the extreme eastern edge of Navajoland, to determine why the Navajos refused to cooperate with the government. The ranking Navajo leaders boycotted the gathering, and those attending possessed little authority. The council produced no results whatsoever. Having reached a point of acknowledged defeat concerning New Mexico Indian affairs, Sumner wrote the Secretary of War C. M. Conrad on May 27 that the government probably would be better off if it gave New Mexico back to the Indians and Mexicans.[10]

Elsewhere in New Mexico, Indians posed a similar threat and were handled with equally unfortunate results. In the southern part of the territory, the settlers lived under the constant fear of Apache raids. The Mescaleros, for instance, engaged in intermittent warfare during the 1850s. On three different occasions during the decade the government concluded treaties with the tribe, only to see them broken. On one occasion the representatives signed a treaty with the Mescaleros living in the White Mountains, only to learn that the agreement did not bind the Mescaleros living in the Guadalupe Mountains farther to the south. Furthermore, the Indian agents experienced great difficulties in obtaining the promised annuities and gifts for the Indians, which caused further dissatisfaction. On still another occasion, the Mescaleros were blamed for depredations committed by the Jicarilla Apaches.[11]

The Indian agents assigned to the Navajos found they could exercise little authority. The Navajo agency was at Fort Defiance, and with no authority other than persuasion, the agents tried to control the Indians. Charged with the responsibility of distributing government gifts to the Navajos, agents found it difficult to explain why presents for the Indians did not arrive or were sidetracked en route between the East and Fort Defiance. The military still held the actual responsibility for Indian affairs, but the Navajos were scattered by clans, and the nature of their life made it impossible for the army to keep a constant watch upon their activities.

In mid-July of 1855, American officials concluded another treaty with the Navajos at Laguna Negra, fourteen miles distant from Fort Defiance. Zarcillos Largos and Manuelito, two leaders who had gained tribal stature by resistance to the Americans, represented the Navajos. Governor David Merriwether, General John Garland (commanding the military district), and Henry L. Dodge (the Navajo agent), represented the United States. The agreement provided for the usual annuities and guarantees of perpetual peace. Manuelito, whom the Americans designated the "official chief," received the symbolic peace medal and cane. Other powerful Navajo leaders attending included Barboncito and Ganado Mucho, who shortly thereafter became the war leaders against the Americans.[12]

The Laguna Negra Peace soon broke down. In 1858 Manuelito served notice on the commander of Fort Defiance, Major William T. H. Brooks, that the Navajos would no longer obey the rules concerning pasturage. The treaty permitted the military to graze their horses, mules, and cattle on the land surrounding the fort, the best pasturage in the vicinity. Manuelito stated that his people needed this lush grass and water for their own herds and flocks. The government owned many wagons and mules and could haul hay to the post from distant parts of the territory, but the Navajos would be forced to leave their homeland without the grazing area. Manuelito's band then proceeded to move its herd closer to the fort, and Brooks promptly ordered his men to drive off the Indian stock. In chasing the animals, the soldiers skirmished briefly with the Indians and killed many of the cattle. The military refused to make restitution for the losses.

Another expedition left Fort Defiance in August of 1858 to punish the Navajos. Major Brooks' Negro servant had apparently molested the wife of a Navajo, and Indian custom demanded his death. The Indians killed the black man but refused to surrender his murderer. The incident was an excuse to start another campaign. Colonel Thomas Fauntleroy, now commanding in New Mexico, also was under great pressure from enraged citizens of the territory to strike the Navajos. In the ensuing campaign, Lieutenant Colonel Dixon S. Miles made a surprise raid on Manuelito's camp in early October, but the elusive leader managed to escape. Over the next several months, Miles killed some fifty Navajos and in December forced the Indians to conclude a peace.[13]

Relative quiet prevailed in the Navajo country for nearly a year. Manuelito tried to persuade his people to attack Fort Defiance, but Zarcillos Largos counseled against such a rash move. In Santa Fe, the Territorial Legislature wanted to know if the Navajos had complied with their latest promises to the government. The answer, unfortunately, was "no." While raiding had declined significantly, it remained a problem, and the legislature called for the raising of a regiment of volunteer troops. The citizens of the territory wanted a large well-armed militia, and they wished to determine for themselves the need for expeditions against Indians. Moreover, the volunteers would sufficiently chastise the Indians before making peace with them. Many individuals in the Indian Department and in the army worried that a large volunteer campaign against the New Mexican Indians could result in a war of Indian extermination.

By 1860 the Navajos were ready for war. Through constant harangues and arguments, the war leaders convinced many Navajos that the time was ripe to drive the white man from their country. Several skirmishes took place at Fort Defiance in January and February, and the post commander Major Oliver L. Shepherd reported fears of another full-scale Indian war. Just before dawn on April 30, a large Navajo war party struck the hated fort. Under the leadership of the embittered Manuelito and Barboncito, an eloquent speaker and powerful medicine man, about 1,000 Navajos nearly overran the post before being driven back. The attack on Fort Defiance immediately prompted preparations for another expensive campaign against the Navajos.[14]

For several fruitless months, the military combed the Navajo domain. In August, Major E. R. S. Canby arrived at Fort Defiance to cooperate with Colonel Fauntleroy in the campaign, but they achieved no concrete results. Canby spent months in the field trying to reach a peaceful solution to the problem; he negotiated with the various tribal leaders at numerous times. However, the complex problems existing between the military and the Indians remained unsolved.

Meanwhile, citizen groups and prominent politicians in Santa Fe urged Governor Abraham Rencher to put the volunteer militia into the field. Rencher, in turn, appealed to Secretary of War, Lewis Cass, requesting that the army wage an effective war against the Indians. In early October of 1860, he noted, a Navajo raiding party had struck within eight miles of Santa Fe, driving off more than two hundred mules. He added that New Mexico's delegate to Congress, Miguel Otero, recently had spoken before the House of Representatives and ominously declared that the New Mexicans themselves could resolve their Indian problem if the government allowed them to do so.

The militia finally refused to wait any longer; four hundred men took to the field, against the wishes of Governor Rencher. Manuel Chaves, elected lieutenant colonel, headed the volunteer battalion of five citizen companies. In a veritable tour de force of the Navajo country, the militia punished the Indians severely. Giving no quarter, the volunteers openly murdered a great many Indians and took women and children captive. They drove off Indian cattle and sheep or simply butchered them. When their ammunition ran out, the militia regrettably returned to their homes. Thanks to the efforts of the volunteers, Canby managed to secure a short-lived armistice with the Navajos. To the political and military leaders of New Mexico, the recent events made it clear that unless a lasting peaceful solution to the problem could be found, the end result would be a rash of volunteer expeditions and the eventual extermination of the Navajos.[15]

In early 1861 repercussions of the secession crisis in the East were felt in New Mexico. With the firing on Fort Sumter, South Carolina, commanders issued orders for the abandonment of Fort Defiance along with many other posts in the far Southwest. The frontier troops were desperately needed in the East. To the Indians throughout the territory, especially to the Navajos, the withdrawal of the troops seemed to indicate that their resistance finally had gained success. In short order, Canby's southern colleagues resigned their commissions and headed for the Confederacy. Canby soon found himself in sole command of the Department of New Mexico.

As the troops left New Mexico Territory for the Eastern theater of war, the Navajos and Apaches took advantage of the situation and began terrorizing the countryside. Raiding and killing became the order of the day. In isolated settlements, settlers cowered, fearful of death if they dared to venture into the countryside. Ranches, mines, and farms were abandoned in ever-increasing numbers, as the Indians kept up their ceaseless warfare.

Canby lacked the power to make a decisive move against the Navajos. Preoccupied with the Confederate invasion up the Rio Grande River from Texas, he wrote in November that the tumultuous state of Indian affairs demanded drastic action. The Navajos should be separated into two groups — friendly and hostile — and given the choice of extermination or removal. If they chose the latter, Canby believed the Navajos and other hostile tribes should be removed to locations "so remote from the settlements as to isolate them from the inhabitants of the Territory." For the time being however, he must cope with Confederate invasion, a large task in itself. Canby needed every soldier in the territory, including volunteer forces from New Mexico, Colorado, and California, to prevent the South from gaining control over New Mexico.

In the spring of 1862, Union forces halted the Confederate invasion and began to push the Texans back down the Rio Grande and out of the Territory. Canby turned back to the Indian problem. Once more he suggested to Washington that the Navajos be removed to a point so far from the New Mexican population that neither the New Mexicans nor the Navajos would cause trouble.

New Mexicans recently had taken up their old habit of sending expeditions into Navajo country to attack the Indians indiscriminately, slaughtering and enslaving them. Stability would come, Canby believed, only when the government placed the Navajos on protected reservations. He suggested that they be removed to several, small, isolated reserves, where they could be instructed in agricultural pursuits and learn to become self-sufficient. For Canby, however, these ideas seemed to have the quality of dreams. He never proposed a systematic scheme for Navajo removal. However, he sowed an idea that would have a significant bearing on the future of the Navajo nation.[16]

In early September, Canby issued orders to mount another Navajo campaign. He directed that a new military post, called Fort Wingate, be established in the Navajo country, near the head waters of the Gallo River. In addition, Fort McCrae would be built near Las Cruces to control the marauding Mescaleros. Canby ordered Colonel Kit Carson to occupy Fort Wingate with four companies of the First New Mexico Volunteers. On September 21, Carson wrote to Canby requesting a conference with him in Santa Fe before Carson himself should depart for Wingate. He had heard rumors that the New Mexico volunteers would launch a large assault on the Navajos, and he wanted to know his specific orders should there be such an expedition. Carson never received a reply. Canby had been replaced.

On September 18, Brigadier General James H. Carleton, commanding the California Volunteers, relieved General Canby as departmental commander in New Mexico. Carleton had led an army across the Southwestern deserts in midsummer from California to the Rio Grande.[17] Canby informed Carleton of his planned campaign against the Navajos and of his ideas about reservations. He surely indicated the dismal record that the military had experienced in trying to secure peace by negotiating treaties. Canby had reached the conclusion that the Navajos had to be removed from their homeland to a location in the Territory, where they could become self-sufficient. He had made no precise plans for their removal, nor had he formulated a detailed campaign strategy. In fact, he had never considered a location for a reservation. Carleton agreed with Canby's general assessment of the state of Indian affairs in New Mexico, and he soon began a program to implement his predecessors' plans.

2

"Fair Carletonia" on the Pecos

"Say to them: 'Go to the Bosque Redondo, or we will pursue
and destroy you. We will not make peace with you on any
other terms. You have deceived us too often and robbed and
murdered our people too long — to trust you again at large
in your own country. This war shall be pursued against you
if it takes years, now that we have begun, until you cease to
exist or move. There can be no other talk on the subject.' "

Carleton's orders to Kit Carson

UPON ASSUMING COMMAND of the Military Department of New Mexico in
October of 1862, General Carleton faced an Indian problem of great dimensions. The withdrawal of troops from the scattered garrisons in the territory had
emboldened both the Navajos and Apaches to strike mercilessly at the settlements and to interrupt regular travel on the highways, thus causing great destruction to life and property in New Mexico. A close observer of the local scene,
William F. M. Arny, a former Indian agent and now Territorial Secretary, estimated that property losses to the Indian raiders in 1862 amounted to $250,000.
Settlers had lost over 30,000 sheep to the Navajos alone. In southern New
Mexico, the Mescaleros plundered with great ferocity. Indian Superintendent
James L. Collins attributed some of the unrest to the fact that Confederates had
promised the Mescaleros a reservation and large annuities if they would create
havoc among the small settlements and ranches. All prominent New Mexicans
urged that the military subdue both tribes and place them on reservations.[1]

The location of new reservations generated great interest. Secretary Arny
suggested that the Navajos be given a reservation in their own country. The
tribe had raised sheep, horses, and cattle, and had farmed extensively, which
testified to the practicality of their remaining there. However, Superintendent
Collins, through his Santa Fe *Gazette*, opposed any plan that would allow the
Navajos to remain in their ancestral lands. The experiences of the 1850s had
shown the impossibility of controlling the Navajos in a distant desolate country.
Furthermore, Collins stated that General Carleton believed the Navajo country

[10]

"as rich if not richer in mineral wealth than California." Arny agreed that valuable minerals might be there, but he did not feel that moving the tribe was necessary to exploit the wealth. Arny's views, however, were temporarily ignored. Territorial Governor Henry Connelly and Superintendent Collins, both powerful advocates of removal, found a friendly supporter in General Carleton.[2]

Soon after reaching Santa Fe, Carleton began laying plans to stop Indian depredations. On September 30 he wrote Adjutant General Lorenzo Thomas in Washington that during the Confederate invasion of New Mexico the Navajos and Apaches had swept into the settlements, stealing large numbers of stock and killing many inhabitants. To open communication lines and highways and protect the citizens in the southern part of the territory — a critical region because of its proximity to Confederate Texas — Carleton announced that he was launching a campaign against the Mescalero Apaches. Colonel Kit Carson and five companies of the First New Mexico Volunteers would reoccupy Fort Stanton in the Mescalero heartland and would punish the Indians for their recent aggressions. At the same time, the General sent four other companies of that regiment to build a new garrison, called Fort Wingate, on the outskirts of Navajo country. After the completion of Carson's operations, Wingate would be a base for a full-scale campaign against the Navajos.[3]

For several reasons, Carleton chose to move first against the Mescaleros rather than against the Navajos. The Mescaleros were a relatively united tribe, their three bands contrasting sharply to the innumerable Navajo clans. More importantly, the Mescalero population was estimated at between five hundred and one thousand, while the Navajos numbered nearly ten thousand. Undoubtedly the Navajos constituted a greater threat to life and property, but Carleton believed the expedition against the Mescaleros would be concluded swiftly. The Navajo campaign promised to be an arduous prolonged affair.

Carleton kept his plans for removal to himself at this point. Although a Mescalero reservation might be created in the Fort Stanton region, the General gave much thought to a larger farming area where the Mescaleros might be self-sufficient. If the Mescalero reservation proved a success, then the Navajos possibly could be located on either the same or a similar reserve. Should the experiment fail, Carleton could consider still other solutions to the Navajo problem before committing the government to a costly, long-range program. By proceeding against the Mescaleros, he was following what appeared to be a wise, cautious, and pragmatic course.

On October 12 Carleton sent Carson detailed instructions. He directed that his soldiers give no quarter in their campaign. "All Indian men of that tribe [Mescaleros] are to be killed whenever and wherever you can find them," Carleton ordered. Carson was to tell the Mescaleros that they were being punished for breaking their treaty of peace, for their treachery, and for their crimes. Carson, however, had no power to conclude treaties. If the leaders begged for peace, they must journey to Santa Fe where Carleton personally would dictate the terms. Relaying these instructions to his commanders, Carleton added: "Slay them until you receive orders to desist from these headquarters." The Mescaleros must learn that peace was infinitely preferable to war.[4]

Confident of Carson's capabilities, Carleton made detailed plans for the peace. On October 31 he ordered the establishment of a military post on the Pecos River at a point known as the Bosque Redondo (Round Grove), one hundred ten miles southeast of Las Vegas. The site contained a round-shaped grove of towering cottonwood trees scattered along the river bank, which gave the spot its name. The new post, called Fort Sumner, honored Carleton's former commander in New Mexico, General Edwin V. Sumner. At this fort the army could offer protection to New Mexicans who wished to open farms that winter in the upper Pecos valley, and also to those who wanted to graze their flocks on the lush grama grass stretching north ninety miles to Anton Chico. Carleton regarded Fort Sumner as a barrier blocking Kiowa and Comanche raiders from the Texas Plains, and Mescalero incursions from the south. Yet, his real reason for establishing the post was to provide a reservation for the Mescaleros.[5]

Carleton approached the task of solving the Indian problem of New Mexico with great vigor. Born and reared in New England, he joined the regular army, fought in the Mexican War, and was assigned to Fort Union in New Mexico in the 1850s. Most of his subsequent career had been spent in the West. A man of great energy, deeply religious, righteous, and moralistic, he was a model Christian warrior. As New Mexico was under martial law in the fall of 1862, he saw an opportunity to solve the age-old Indian problem there.

In his years on the frontier, Carleton grew intimately acquainted with the difficulties surrounding Indian-white relations. During the early 1850s, while commanding Fort Union, he had taken part in several Indian campaigns in New Mexico where he gained a firsthand knowledge of the frustrating operations against the Navajos and Apaches. In the late 1850s he had commanded Fort Tejon, fifty miles north of Los Angeles, California, and watched with interest the development of the neighboring Tejon Indian Reservation.[6]

During the Gold Rush of 1848–49, hordes of settlers had flooded into the hinterlands of California, attacking the Indians at will. Gradually hemmed in, the Indians began retaliating. With unrest mounting, an Indian Peace Commission between March and January concluded eighteen treaties. The Senate, however, promptly rejected the treaties, due to the sizeable expenses involved.

Edward F. Beale, the first Superintendent of Indian Affairs for California, became greatly concerned about the plight of the Indians. He hit upon the idea of a reservation where the Indians would be taught to become self-sufficient farmers. In this way the public could not complain about the expenses of annuities and supplies. Beale's system harked back to the days of the Spaniards in that he insisted that a military post be located near the reservation. Journeying to Washington with his plan, he received backing from several prominent politicians.

In September of 1853, Beale established an experimental reservation in the Tejon Valley. The army built Fort Tejon nearby. The fort and reservation were in a strategic position to restrain the Southern California tribes. More importantly, the Tejon Valley contained fertile land capable of being irrigated. Beale put the Indians to work opening extensive farms, which soon proved a great success, and the Indians became self-sufficient. Many persons pointed to the Tejon experiment as an example for the Indian Bureau to consider in the future.[7] Carleton believed that he could accomplish in New Mexico what

James H. Carleton, architect of the Bosque Redondo experiment.

Beale had achieved in California. Navajos and Apaches placed on closely supervised reservations could learn the arts of husbandry and in time become equally self-sufficient.

Carleton ordered a board of officers to meet at the Bosque on or about November 15, 1862, to fix the exact site for Fort Sumner. The board included Lieutenant Colonel Theodore H. Dodd, First Lieutenant Cyrus DeForrest, Second Colorado Volunteers, and Surgeon James M. McNulty. DeForrest and Dodd were unable to serve on the board and were replaced by Captains Joseph Updegraff and Allan S. Anderson, both of the Fifth Infantry.

Updegraff and a detachment of cavalry and infantry from Fort Union reached the Bosque on Sunday, November 30, and pitched their tents. The weather was intensely cold. For the next several days, he, Anderson, and McNulty scouted the riverbanks on horseback for a post site. At first the officers decided that the best place would be on the east bank of the Pecos about seven and a half miles from the head of the Bosque. However, they soon had second thoughts. Hauling building materials from Albuquerque or Fort Union would be a long, difficult operation. Moreover, the Pecos River at this point was very salty and unpalatable. Finally, marshes and mudflats indicated that the Pecos often overflowed its banks at this point in the spring.

Abandoning their earlier choice, Updegraff and his companions on December 4 formally recommended that the best site for Fort Sumner was at the junction of the Agua Negra with the Pecos, roughly forty-five miles upriver. At this point abundant wood existed, the water flowed sparkling clear, and the area appeared less prone to flooding. Perhaps most important, it was closer to the settlements and to Fort Union, the major supply point. In every way, the Agua Negra site was "preferable to the Bosque Redondo."

Carleton fumed when he read the board's report in December. On two different occasions in the 1850s he had visited the Bosque and had suggested it to his superiors as the perfect location for a cavalry post. In February of 1852, after thoroughly examining the Bosque Redondo, he had reported that the majestic cottonwood grove constituted an almost endless supply of wood. The soil was very rich, a dark chocolate color, and water abounded the year round. Two years later Carleton again extolled the location. However, a survey made in 1859 by Thomas Claiborne of the Mounted Rifles disagreed with Carleton's findings. Claiborne declared the Bosque site "altogether unfit for a post." Carleton, however, possessed great faith in his own ability and ideas. Brushing aside the board's report, he announced that Fort Sumner would be built at the Bosque Redondo.[8]

Meanwhile, Carson's campaign against the Mescaleros had ended. Captain William McCleave had inflicted heavy losses on them in an encounter in Dog Canyon near Alamogordo in November. Sorely pressed by other detachments, the Mescaleros, with the troops in close pursuit, fled to Fort Stanton and surrendered to Carson. On November 12, Carson sent Indian agent Lorenzo Labadie and three chiefs — Cadette, Chatto, and Estrella — to Santa Fe to meet with General Carleton. Carleton dealt with the Mescalero chiefs in a stern manner. He stated that his troops would continue to attack the Mescaleros until they agreed to removal to a new reservation on the Pecos River. The chiefs indicated that they had suffered severely in the campaign; they were worn out and had exhausted their provisions. Soldiers guarded the waterholes in their country, and their warriors had expended all their ammunition. As braves they would have preferred to fight, but warfare was no longer possible. Sadly, they agreed to Carleton's terms. They would go to the Bosque Redondo.[9]

At first, Carleton may have envisioned that the Mescaleros would be at the Bosque only for a short time. He had not made a final commitment to launch the experimental reservation. Sending that part of the tribe which had surrendered to Fort Sumner was a means of separating the hostile from the peaceful members of the tribe. Carleton informed both the chiefs and agent Labadie that once the entire Mescalero tribe had surrendered they would be given a reservation in their own country near Fort Stanton. Labadie and the Mescalero chiefs returned to Stanton to await the march to Fort Sumner.

In December of 1862, Fort Sumner consisted solely of tents. Commanded by Updegraff, the garrison consisted of six officers and one hundred thirty-three enlisted men. Three companies resided at the post: Updegraff's Company A, Fifth Infantry, commanded by Second Lieutenant Samuel L. Barr; Company B, Second Cavalry, California Volunteers, under Captain John C. Cremony; and Company M, First New Mexico Volunteers, under Captain Charles Diaz. Other officers included Surgeon George Gwyther, and Second Lieutenant Jacob Stinzer, Company M, First New Mexico Volunteers.[10]

National Archives

Old Post at Fort Sumner, where the soldiers lived during the first cold winter on the Pecos.

Updegraff entrusted Captain Cremony with the responsibility of selecting the best spot to lay out the post. Taking ten men, he scouted up and down the river for several miles, finally choosing a site on the east bank approximately five hundred feet from the river near the southern end of the Bosque. The location had three advantages: it was close to water, it had grass near at hand, and it could furnish firewood. In the freezing weather, soldiers immediately appropriated the numerous stakes and timbers from an old corral at the site. For years sheepherders had grazed their flocks there, and in the mid-1850s a licensed trading post had operated at the Bosque. Updegraff confirmed Cremony's site and ordered the troops to begin construction of temporary quarters. The first buildings consisted of crude adobe jacals which offered only windbreaks and little warmth. As winter temperatures in the area occasionally dropped below zero, everything was done in haste.

Labadie reached the Bosque with the first small group of Apaches in early December. The journey from Fort Stanton had been an arduous one. Many Indians suffered from a shortage of food and inclement weather. Apache women and children rode in the backs of wagons, generously provided by the Quartermaster of Fort Union, but the men had to walk. Updegraff put the Indians to work constructing shelters. When the huts were completed, the troops turned to constructing stables, warehouses, a hospital, and other vital buildings.[11]

Within a few days after their arrival at the Bosque, the Apaches found themselves without food. Labadie notified Cremony that the Indians had consumed their last rations several days before and that it would be another two days before additional food would arrive. The Apache men asked if they could be permitted to go hunting. Indian agent Labadie warned Cremony that if the Indians began starving they might try to escape from the reservation; however, Cremony pressed Updegraff for permission, saying he would accompany them and insure their return. By remaining at the Bosque, the women and children would serve as hostages to secure the arrangement. The next day the Apache men rode out to hunt, with Cremony the only white man in the party. The officer later claimed that he carried four pistols and a large Bowie knife. The Indians had only bows and arrows, having been required to leave their rifles and pistols in camp. The thirty-six hour excursion proved successful, the Indians killing eighty-seven antelope. The hunt undoubtedly created a feeling of mutual trust between the troops and Apaches.[12]

General Carleton meanwhile had decided that the Apaches should stay permanently at the Bosque Redondo. The site of the reservation was well suited to farming. Along most of the Pecos channel, low bluffs generally hugged the riverbanks, preventing farming in the bottom lands. However, at the Bosque Redondo, the bluffs were approximately eight miles apart at the widest point and gradually tapered for a fifteen-mile stretch along the river. The fort was located at the southern terminus of the prospective farming area. Throughout the valley, grama grass grew profusely, providing forage for livestock. To Carleton it seemed the perfect site for enormous farms, which would make the Indians virtually self-sufficient.[13]

In early January of 1863, other Mescalero bands arrived from Fort Stanton. By February 1, Carleton had congratulated Colonel Carson, stating that his campaign had been a complete success. Approximately three hundred fifty Apaches were encamped at the reservation, drawing rations from the army. More of them were en route.

Sometime in early 1863, Updegraff learned from Carleton that a rationing crisis was in the offing. Commissary stores had fallen low throughout New Mexico, making it necessary for the army to reduce its rations until new purchases could be made. Updegraff notified agent Labadie that he must cut the Mescaleros' rations. Labadie, who got along well with Cremony, went immediately to his friend and expressed great concern over the order. Cremony passed on the agent's views to Updegraff, who informed General Carleton that full rations for the Apaches were an absolute necessity to keep them at the Bosque. Cremony argued that as long as the Apaches had sufficient food they would be reasonably content. Convinced by the logic of the argument, Carleton ordered that full rations be continued for the Indians.[14]

In March, General Carleton arrived at the Bosque with a party that included Superintendent Collins, Surveyor General John A. Clark, Bishop John B. Lamy, and Dr. Michael Steck, former Mescalero agent. The presence of Bishop Lamy indicated the great importance that Carleton placed upon the religious and moral education of the Indians. Carleton had long believed that if the Indians could be instilled from early youth with the Christian concept of right and wrong, the problems existing between Indians and whites would vanish. He did not feel that Indians attacked white men because they were a foreign invader but rather because they possessed a heathen concept of right and wrong. If the Apaches at the Bosque Redondo showed any inclination toward Christianity, he wanted Bishop Lamy to send a priest from Santa Fe to instruct them in rudimentary subjects and also the Gospel. Carleton reasoned that the Catholic Church with its pageantry, pomp, and ceremony would be more attractive to the Indian mind than the less colorful sects of Protestantism.

After visiting the Mescalero camps and holding a council, Carleton ordered Updegraff to begin instructing the Mescaleros in planting crops and constructing homes like the Pueblo Indians. A collection of agricultural implements brought by Superintendent Collins for the Mescaleros to use in farming was unloaded. Regarding housing, Carleton in his zeal apparently overlooked the fact that the Apaches had taboos against permanent houses and had led a nomadic life in the past. As the tribe was no longer considered hostile, he placed Labadie in control of rationing the Apaches. Before returning to Santa Fe, Carleton stated that he believed the Apaches would quickly adopt the more civilized life and optimistically forecasted great success for the venture.[15]

Superintendent Collins did not share Carleton's view. Believing that the Mescaleros could not be trusted, he directed Labadie to supervise carefully the farming operation, for he feared this task would not "be attended with success." In conversations with tribal leaders, Collins sensed a deep sadness and felt that many desired to flee the reservation at the first opportunity. A sizeable number of the band were irreconcilable, and if they should escape it would be "well enough if a good part of the old warriors were killed off, for the task of reforming them was a hopeless one." Carleton agreed with Collins in reference to the old warriors, but he put great faith in the young Indians and believed they could be changed.[16]

In the middle of April, after the Apaches had been given rations for a month and a half, Superintendent Collins commented on the mounting expense of feeding them. Four hundred fifty Indians lived at the Bosque, and they required full rations. They had not been able to leave the reservation to hunt since January, when they had murdered a sentry. Furthermore, Collins felt that to feed them it would be necessary to make purchases outside New Mexico. Throughout 1862 corn had been freighted to New Mexico from the States, and the requirements of the Bosque certainly would increase shipping costs. Flour in the territory sold for six dollars per hundred pound sack. When the high shipping costs ($2.50) from Fort Union to the Bosque were added, the price of the staple reached $8.50. The base price for flour really was not too steep, since the same commodity sold in Denver for $10.00. However, the shipping expenses were quite steep, nearly twice the rate required for the freighter to make an adequate profit. Wavering in his support of Carleton's policy, Collins suggested that perhaps the newly created territory of Arizona should handle the Navajo problem, as most of the tribe resided west of the New Mexico-Arizona line.

Carleton supporters persuaded Collins to change his mind. Before taking over the Santa Fe *Gazette,* Collins had been a prominent merchant in the city, and his business associates doubtless persuaded him that the large government contracts necessary to supply the reservation would boost the economy of New Mexico. Moreover, Carleton and Collins both supported the Democratic Party, and Union Democrats would profit from the army contracts.[17]

Through the spring and early summer of 1863, Labadie supervised the Mescaleros in laying out farms at Bosque Redondo. In the mesquite-covered ground near the Pecos, the Indians struggled to clear roots so they could plow and seed the land. They also labored on an irrigation ditch to divert water from the river to their fields. The Mescaleros apparently disliked the labor, having rarely engaged in the pursuit of husbandry. They would work only when under the supervision of military overseers. Those who did labor had to do so without proper tools. Many of them worked the soil with the bare hands. Therefore, soldiers and civilians had to perform much of the work at the reservation farm. Despite these problems, by June the Mescaleros had cleared, plowed, and planted over two hundred acres in corn, beans, and melons. Labadie wrote Commissioner of Indian Affairs William P. Dole on June 30 that the Indians were gradually becoming interested in farming. However, much of their accomplishment stemmed from the restraint the troops exercised over them.[18]

In June the Mescaleros complained vehemently that the flour they received was making them sick. They believed that someone had deliberately tried to poison them. Upon inspection, Labadie discovered that the flour contained large quantities of nonedible substances: bits of slate, broken bread, and something that resembled plaster of paris. It was an old ploy of western contractors to load up their flour sacks with such foreign junk in order to make an even greater profit. Labadie wrote Superintendent Collins about his discovery; he stated that twenty-five Indians had fallen ill from eating the adulterated flour. Collins immediately directed him to stop issuing the flour, which had been purchased from William H. Moore, a prominent New Mexican contractor and mining speculator. A short time later an army board, appointed to examine incoming shipments to the Bosque, reported that 48,608 pounds of flour was of "livid quality." * Tactfully, Labadie, who had the confidence of the Mescaleros, calmed the Indians and the crisis passed.[19]

Throughout the summer of 1863 food shipments continued to arrive at the Bosque. In July a military board inspected a wagon train of foodstuffs from Fort Union and found the shipment short fourteen pounds of ham, three bushels of beans, and nine bushels of salt. In August a herd of seven hundred sixty head of beef cattle arrived at Fort Sumner under a contract with Charles S. Hinckley, who formerly owned Hinckley and Company's Mail Express in Colorado.[20]

Carleton's plans for the Bosque stressed education and religious instruction for the Indians. Warmly endorsing the General's ideas, Bishop Lamy was pleased to receive Carleton's request on June 12 for a priest to work with the Apaches. The General happily explained that Fort Sumner had been approved as a chaplain post, and it only remained for an energetic man to be appointed. Lamy recommended that Father Joseph Fialon be sent to the Bosque Redondo. This young vigorous priest was then studying in France and would reach New Mexico in the early fall. Carleton heartily approved the selection, saying that another aspect of "this great work" would soon begin.[21]

At the reservation, the Mescaleros completed their corn planting in early July. In contemplation of the harvest, Labadie wrote Commissioner of Indian Affairs William Dole that several buildings were required for the storage of crops. He also pointed out the need for a blacksmith shop, a carpenter's shop, and a house for the agent. Part of Labadie's request was granted. The Indian Bureau authorized the erection of one simple adobe building, a rectangular structure with two rooms. Labadie and his family occupied one room, and the other served as a storehouse.

Carleton grew impatient with Updegraff's lack of progress in building the fort. The permanent substantial buildings were still unfinished. Carleton was aware of the hardships the men had endured during the winter, and he vowed that both soldiers and officers would have adequate shelter by that fall. He urged Updegraff to increase his efforts and reminded him that three companies of soldiers were stationed at Sumner, more than enough to finish the job. To rush work, the General authorized employment of fifty additional civilians. But Updegraff could not readily find laborers and searched far up the Pecos for them. When he finally had collected the new work force, he placed every able-bodied soldier on detail to help in the building. Only twenty soldiers remained for guard duty. Still, construction of the post remained at a standstill, as frequent summer rains came, preventing the manufacture of adobes.[22]

On August 29, Updegraff informed Carleton that tiswin drinking had become a serious problem among the Apaches. The corn had begun to ripen, and Mescaleros were sneaking into the fields to steal corn for the manufacture of the illicit brew. Drunkenness was rampant among them. As a large scouting party had been sent north to the vicinity of Agua Negra, many Apaches had the chance to escape if they became so inclined. He needed more troops to guard the Indians.[23]

---

*John Watts stated that the flour was not spoiled and that he had eaten bread made with it. William H. Moore, friend of Carleton and son-in-law of J. D. Tipton, was an associate of Lucien Maxwell and William Kronig, and the founder of Elizabethtown. He was murdered on May 1, 1873, over his questionable financial transactions.

In the early fall of 1863 Carson's campaign against the Navajos, which had started in midsummer, was well under way. On September 5, Michael Steck, who had replaced Collins as Territorial Indian Superintendent, wrote Agent Labadie that Carleton was sending the first contingent of Navajos to the Bosque. This group of fifty peaceful Cebolletan Navajos lived in the Mount Taylor region near Fort Wingate and belonged to Sandoval's band. In the past the Cebolletans had often served the army as scouts, first for Mexican and later Anglo expeditions against the major portion of the Navajo people. Although other Navajo clans disliked the Cebolletans intensely, Carleton insisted that all Navajos, regardless of past loyalty, go to the Bosque Redondo.

From William Keleher, *Turmoil in New Mexico*
Michael Steck, Superintendent of Indian Affairs for New Mexico,
who vigorously opposed the Bosque Redondo Reservation.

Steck indicated to Labadie that the Navajos were technically prisoners of war and directed him to refuse to take charge of them. If he did so, the Indian Bureau would become responsible for the entire tribe, once it had been rounded up and placed on the reservation. Steck said that his Indian Department was virtually without funds. Adequate provisions were not available for the Mescaleros at the reservation, and the additional burden of the Navajos was ridiculous.[24]

Unaware of Steck's instructions, Carleton instructed Updegraff to see that Labadie fed Sandoval's Navajo band. Informed of this order Steck immediately wrote Carleton that the Mescalero agent would be responsible for the Navajos, only if the military supplied them with provisions. As he already was preparing to feed the Navajos, the General postponed a decision on this important question until the entire tribe had been placed on the reservation. He may have felt that if the Indian Bureau showed that it could not afford to feed the Navajos, a strong argument against moving them to the Pecos might be raised. Steck foresaw that the sustenance of the tribe required enormous funds, and he believed that such high costs would cause the grand plan to fail.[25]

Carleton, on the other hand, radiated confidence. He wrote Adjutant General Lorenzo Thomas that *all* captured Navajos and Apaches would be sent to the Bosque Redondo, and the army would feed and take care of them until they became "able to support themselves, as the Pueblo Indians of New Mexico are doing." The Mescaleros were contented and happy at the reservation, he said, failing to indicate the problems that Updegraff was having. He then previewed his plans. Little by little the Navajos would be brought to the reservation and treated with Christian kindness. The children would be taught to read and write. The arts of peace would be instilled in them, and the truths of Christianity would be revealed. In time, the Navajos would become a new people. They would acquire new habits, a new life-style, and most importantly new beliefs. Gradually, as the old Indians died off, the young Indians would grow up without their ancestors' affection for robbery and murder.[26]

Although Superintendent Steck opposed bringing the Navajos to the Pecos, he was well pleased with the progress the Mescaleros had made. Even though four hundred acres had been planted and the harvest was small, he believed that the Mescalero farms could produce more the following year. In late September, he came to the Bosque and held a council with the Apaches. He explained that he could no longer furnish them with full rations. Under proper restrictions, he suggested that Labadie permit the Mescaleros to leave the reservation to visit their old hunting grounds where game flourished.

When he learned of Steck's suggestion, Carleton balked at the idea of the Indians leaving the reserve, even though he had permitted a similar venture the previous December. He assumed that Steck had declined to feed the Apaches, hoping to block the Bosque experiment. Although the Indian Department possessed foodstuffs, he was convinced that the superintendent took this stand because he knew that the army would "not see them starve." Finding himself powerless to influence events on the Pecos reserve, Steck in November left for Washington to give a complete report to Commissioner Dole. He intended to discuss the changes which Carleton contemplated for Indian affairs in New Mexico, and the obstacles he himself faced in trying to operate under military rule.[27]

Carson's campaign in the Navajo country dragged on into the early winter of 1863. Although his soldiers destroyed large amounts of Indian provisions, he still could not gain a decisive victory. Occasionally small bands of destitute Navajos turned themselves in at Fort Wingate and with a soldier escort left for the Pecos. For example, Delgadito, one of the most important clan leaders, and one hundred eighty-seven of his followers, surrendered in late November. Carson sent them to Santa Fe where Carleton met and talked with them; on November 22, the party started for the Bosque Redondo. When the Indians reached the reservation, the army immediately provided the women and children with worn Sibley tents, poor shelter against the freezing rain, snow, and chilly winds, while the men constructed more substantial huts. By December, the number of Navajos at the Bosque stood at over two hundred fifty.[28]

Carleton knew that if Carson's campaign proved successful, the Bosque reservation would soon be crowded with Indians. Anticipating this expanding population, he advertised in the New Mexico newspapers for bids to furnish the quartermaster at Fort Sumner with shelled corn, the basic staple in the Indian diet. He requested a delivery of 1,000 fanegas (a fanega equalled one hundred forty pounds) as early as December 25; he indicated that additional shipments of 1,500 fanegas and 1,000 fanegas were required on January 31 and March 15, 1864. These supplies were expensive, but Carleton hoped the Indians would be able to support themselves from the Bosque farms within a year. Andres Dold, a leading merchant in Las Vegas, obtained one of the army contracts — in fact, the largest. Dold agreed to deliver 20,000 pounds of corn-meal at Fort Union, for distribution to various points, including Fort Sumner, for a price of five and three-quarter cents per pound. Months later, because of the increasing needs at the Bosque, such a price would be more than doubled.[29]

Everything seemed to be going smoothly at the reservation. In November, Captain Updegraff, who had failed to show the proper dedication to the "great" work, was replaced by Major Henry D. Wallen, Fourteenth Infantry. Carleton liked Wallen. The forty-five-year-old Georgian had spent many years on the Western frontier. Unlike Updegraff, he stopped the tiswin drinking, and pushed ahead on constructing the post buildings.[30]

Labadie reported to Steck that the Mescaleros were clearing new land and enlarging the irrigation ditches for next year's crops. He predicted that the Mescaleros would double their harvest in 1864. The agency now held 10,000 pounds of corn in storage, and the Indians seemed content. Labadie also received complete cooperation from Major Wallen. He loaned the agency ten yoke of oxen to pull the plows, and he instructed the quartermaster to purchase from the Apaches a large amount of their unripened corn for livestock fodder. Following this transaction, $458 in credit was given the Indians at the sutler's store. Labadie felt the payment served as an incentive to labor harder in the coming year.[31]

In mid-November, a hostile Navajo band passed near Fort Sumner and drove off most of the sheep owned by their peaceful kinsmen. Captain Cremony, commanding the cavalry detachment at the post, organized twenty troopers, and with Labadie and forty Mescaleros, rode in hot pursuit. The chase was difficult. The loose sandy soil tired the horses, and after a fruitless day Cremony decided to turn back. The renegades managed to get away with the

Major Henry D. Wallen, Seventh Infantry, commanded Fort Sumner from November 1863 to April 1864.

flock as well as twelve Mexican captives. The cavalry failed to distinguish itself, Labadie reported. It could not overtake the Indians who were driving the slow-moving sheep.[32]

In Washington, in early December, Superintendent Steck reported to Commissioner Dole on the Bosque Redondo Reservation. Steck agreed that the area possessed certain advantages in location and arable land. However, the site contained only enough land for a limited number of Indians; in fact, it was about the right size for the three Apache bands — the Mescaleros, Gilas, and Jicarillas. Together, these bands totaled approximately 2,500 individuals, with the average family containing five persons. If the total arable land were divided among these Indians, Steck argued, each family would receive twelve acres, more than adequate to provide for its needs. The Navajos, however, numbered about 12,000 and owned several hundred thousand sheep, besides large herds of horses. The impracticality of locating such a large group of Indians on a limited land base was obvious.

Steck referred to Surveyor General Clark's report on the arable land at Fort Sumner. Clark, a friend and supporter of Superintendent Collins, had attended the March council at the Bosque and on October 21 had sent a report to Steck on his inspection of the reservation.* He also had traveled seven or eight miles both above and below the post and had estimated that 4,000 acres of arable land existed in a strip one hundred fifty yards wide on each side of the river. The potential farm lands ran for approximately thirty miles along the Pecos.

According to Steck, 4,000 acres were totally inadequate for the Navajos, regardless of the Apaches. Furthermore, the two tribes had fought each other in the past and were traditional enemies. Managing two powerful tribes posed a big task, even if the tribes were friendly. Carleton's contention that the Apaches and the Navajos formed one great family had no basis in their current relations; the basis was somewhat similar to the linguistic connections between Spaniards and Italians. Adding the traditional hostility of the two tribes, the grandiose reservation idea seemed to have originated in the mind of a fool. Steck urged that the Bosque be used as an Apache reserve and that the Navajos be settled in their own country.[33]

Steck also discussed the potential supply problem at the Bosque when the Navajos arrived on the Pecos. The army would feed the Indians while the Indian Department attempted to furnish clothing and other essential nonedible articles. Steck requested nine hundred yards of blue and red cloth, and as the Indians dressed mainly in blankets, he needed 1,000 red, 700 blue, and 1,500 white blankets. His list also included hickory shirts (750), needles, awls, sheep shears, axes, fry pans, beads, mirrors, and small brass buttons. In many ways Steck's recommendations did not suit the wants or needs of the Indians. Although the Navajos were to be taught the arts of husbandry, Steck did not place agricultural implements on his list.[34]

While Steck remained in Washington, in early December in Santa Fe Governor Connelly delivered his second annual message, praising Carleton's

*Clark had urged the reinstatement of Collins as superintendent after he had been dismissed in June for fiscal irresponsibility.

Indian policy. A remarkable transformation had taken place within one year, he declared. The Mescaleros had been reduced to a state of peace and were now located on the Pecos reservation where they would present no further danger to the citizens. They would soon forget their nomadic pursuits and become "one of our industrious and thrifty Pueblos." The Apaches had shown great industry in applying themselves to agricultural works, and they possessed a "spirit of existence" that would eventually lead them into a civilized mode of life. Connelly predicted that a new day was dawning for Indian affairs in the territory.[35]

Shortly after Connelly's speech, a Navajo band, numbering some one hundred and fifty, ambushed Labadie's supply train en route from Albuquerque to the Pecos. Striking the wagons near the mountain village of Chilili, thirty miles southeast of Albuquerque, the renegades received a brisk short volley of fire from the wagoners, which killed one Indian. While Labadie and his men tried to reload their weapons, the Indians swept in, hoping to capture two Mexican boys with the train. Only the heroic stand by Jose Carrillo, one of Labadie's employees, halted the attack and prevented the death or capture of the youths. Several Navajos were wounded, and one driver was killed. The Navajos destroyed all of the wagons along with the supplies for the Mescaleros. During the battle, the Navajos also managed to steal the oxen from the train, and fled east.

Following the Chilili fight, observers reported Navajo renegades in the Red River country in northeastern New Mexico. They stole a large flock of sheep there, killed the sheepherders, and took several Mexican captives. They were believed to have been the same group that Labadie had encountered a few days before. While the hostile band crossed the Red River, a detachment of soldiers had a severe fight with them. Several Indians fell under the troopers' fire, and two of the captives were rescued, but the soldiers could not retake the stolen stock.[36]

When Labadie reached the Bosque Redondo he found other problems. An outbreak of smallpox seemed imminent among the Mescaleros, and he hastily wrote to Steck in Washington for serum. Steck asked Dole for $300 to vaccinate the Indians. If the disease spread, the Apaches would all bolt the reserve and head into the mountains. Steck obtained the money and secured the serum. While the vaccination was carried out, Carleton sent fifty bed-sacks and one hundred blankets to Major Wallen for use at the Bosque. These supplies were the beginning of an Indian hospital.[37]

Other problems occurred in December. In the early morning hours of December 16, a group of over a hundred Navajos, probably the same marauders ranging the countryside, struck the Mescalero agency. In the darkness they silently drove off 5,200 agency sheep, as well as thirteen burros and several horses. They also broke into a storeroom and stole blankets, provisions, one hundred fifty moccasins, and four rifles. In fleeing the Bosque, hurrying the sheep before them, the Navajos startled several Apaches, who ran to inform their leader, Ojo Blanco. Ojo Blanco was furious and quickly notified Labadie.

At 5:00 A.M. Labadie reported the theft to Major Wallen. The commander immediately roused two infantry companies and a cavalry detachment from their slumbers, and drew two days' rations. The cavalry detail was small because most of the company were out scouting for Navajos. Labadie and Carrillo collected and armed thirty Apaches to ride at the head of the column. Traveling with them was Reverend Fialon, who had arrived in the fall. At 5:30 A.M. the combined force headed north following the trail of the Navajos — with Labadie, Fialon, and the Apaches soon outdistancing the infantry and cavalry.

About thirty miles northwest of Fort Sumner, near Ojo Borrico, the Apaches sighted the Navajo band, which was moving slowly, hampered by the large flock of sheep. The Apaches halted and waited for the cavalry to catch up. The infantry, seeing their march was useless, had long since turned back to the post. The Apaches, however, became impatient, for the fleeing Navajos increased their pace. Labadie decided to attack, and with the trusted Carrillo and Reverend Fialon, the group moved forward. Only ten Navajos were mounted; the rest were on foot. Twenty Navajos were armed with rifles, and many others had bows. The Navajos could not withstand the fierce onslaught of the Mescaleros, who promptly killed twelve of their group; they abandoned the flocks and successfully made an escape. In the disorganized battle which had lasted over half an hour, only one Apache fell with a mortal wound. Labadie recovered all of the sheep and most of the provisions and supplies taken from the agency.[38]

Carleton was incensed by the poor showing of his soldiers in the chase. He sent Cremony, who had been off scouting with most of the cavalry and thereby missed the engagement, a withering blast for failing to get his men quickly into the field. In a vitriolic letter to Major Wallen on December 24, Carleton warned that if Cremony did not get his men into action with proper dispatch in the next emergency, he would be replaced. Cavalry were expensive to maintain and were totally useless if not effectively employed. Carleton declared that Labadie's Mescaleros should be rewarded for their meritorious conduct; he ordered that every one who took part in the fight be given an old uniform. Furthermore, five of the tribe were to be issued passes and asked to return to their old country and persuade the rest of the tribe to come to the Bosque.[39]

Still another raid on the Bosque occurred in early July. In the dark of night on January 4, 1864, Navajos crept to within a mile of the garrison, gathered sixty horses from the Mescalero herd, and several cavalry mounts. Ojo Blanco again reported the loss, saying the Navajos had fled south. Major Wallen rushed a large detachment of infantry and cavalry into the field. Labadie and sixty mounted Mescaleros accompanied the soldiers. The weather was bitter cold as a heavy snowstorm had raged through the night, but the troopers and Apaches managed to overtake the Navajos at 11:00 A.M. about twelve miles south of Fort Sumner.

In a brief skirmish, nine Navajos were killed. The band then broke into two groups, fleeing in separate directions. Accordingly, the pursuing forces also split and fought running skirmishes until sundown. In the freezing weather many soldiers had difficulty placing caps on their firearms, and several suffered frostbite. Private Peter Loser, Second California Cavalry, and former bodyguard of General Carleton, particularly distinguished himself by killing five Navajos. By the time the fighting had ended and they had retraced their steps to Sumner, the soldiers were suffering acutely from the intense cold. Labadie's hands had been partially frostbitten. However, the soldiers and Apaches were happy. Forty Navajos were known to have been killed, but the number may have been as high as sixty. The running battle had been waged for some ten miles along the riverbank.[40]

As his plan to subdue the Navajos fell behind schedule, Carleton began to worry. Less than three hundred of the tribe were at Fort Sumner, and it was reported that many had fled the reservation. Carson's campaign in the Northwest, however, was clearly taking a toll. Equally important, the Navajo leader Delgadito was in the Navajo country trying to convince other clans to go to the Bosque. Because many Navajo women and children at the Bosque were "suffering from the extreme cold," Carleton informed Adjutant General Thomas, he needed authorization to buy cheap blankets and to issue condemned clothing. He spoke bitterly about the Indian Department. If the Department did not manifest more interest "in this important undertaking of getting these Indians onto a reservation it would be better if that Department had nothing to do with them."[41]

By January of 1864, Carson had hemmed in many Navajos in northeastern Arizona. Due to the military pressure, they had been unable to store grain for the winter. Some of their fields had been burned and livestock scattered. When a heavy winter storm blanketed the domain with snow, Carson decided to launch a daring two-prong attack against Canyon de Chelly, the traditional Navajo stronghold. While one force struck the west entrance, another attacked the eastern gateway. Literally surrounded, many Navajos residing in the canyon area decided to surrender. By February 1, large groups of Navajos came into Forts Wingate and Canby, the latter having been established some thirty miles farther west of Wingate.* The Santa Fe *Weekly New Mexican* glowed ecstatic over the defeat of the ancient enemy. "Daylight is dawning," wrote one reporter, adding that Carleton was "accomplishing much."[42]

While Carson tried to crush Navajo resistance, Carleton became aware of Steck's resistance to placing the Navajos on the Bosque Redondo. In a letter to Francisco Perea, New Mexico's delegate to Congress, the General on January 12 stated that virtually every important person in the territory had endorsed the policy of relocating the Navajos, and he hinted that Perea should use whatever Congressional influence he possessed to prevent Steck from altering that policy.[43]

By February of 1864, large numbers of destitute Navajos had begun the difficult "Long Walk" to the Bosque Redondo. Their presence would cause the character of the reservation to change. The problems of providing food, shelter, and clothing overshadowed everything and proved to be even more taxing than the opponents of the policy had predicted. But despite almost insurmountable difficulties, Carleton was determined to make the Bosque a success. The reservation on the Pecos, he believed, would stand as a model of the proper way in which to control and civilize the native American.

---

*Frequently, historians have stated that Carson destroyed the Navajo orchards in Canyon de Chelly in January 1864. This destruction, as well as the burning of extensive maize fields, did not occur until the expedition of Captain John Thompson, First New Mexico Cavalry, in July of 1864.

3

Navajos Reach the Bosque Redondo

"To gather them together little by little onto a Reservation away from the haunts and hills and hiding places of their country, and there be kind to them: there teach their children how to read and write: teach them the art of peace: teach them the truths of Christianity. Soon they will acquire new habits, new ideas, new modes of life: the old Indians will die off and carry with them all latent longings for murdering and robbing: the young ones will take their places without these longings: and thus, little by little, they will become a happy and a contented people, and Navajoe Wars will be remembered only as something that belongs entirely to the Past."

"The only peace that can ever be made with them must rest on the basis that they move onto these lands and like the Pueblos become an agricultural people, and cease to be nomads."

General James H. Carleton

CARLETON, ON FEBRUARY 7, 1864, jubilantly informed Adjutant General Thomas in Washington that Colonel Carson had won a decisive victory over the Navajos in Canyon de Chelly in northeastern Arizona. The campaign was the "crowning act" in the life of the famous scout and Indian fighter. "I believe this will be the last Novajoe War," Carleton declared. His next task was to provide support for these destitute Indians. In the long run, he said, "we can feed them cheaper than we can fight them." Over the next several months, however, administrative difficulties hampered the new reservation.

In his official corrspondence, Carleton failed to mention the role played by the Navajo chief Delgadito in ending the campaign. In early February, this Indian leader had persuaded more than 1,200 of his people to surrender at Fort Wingate and start the long journey to the Pecos. Delgadito told them that he had seen the rich valley of the Pecos and believed that the Navajo farms and flocks would flourish at the new reservation. In a more practical vein, it was better to go to the Pecos than to fight Carleton's troops. The General had informed him in person that resistance meant the extinction of the Navajo people, but if they submitted to his terms, the United States government would spare no effort to make the reservation a success. Delgadito had little choice, and he probably contributed more than any other individual in convincing the Navajos to make the move to the Pecos.[1]

Navajo warrior, unidentified

Denver Public Library

Delgadito's influence particularly was obvious in the surrender of several Navajo groups at Los Piños. These Indians were *ricos* (wealthy) who arrived with large herds of horses and flocks of sheep and presented themselves in a friendly and agreeable manner. They were a completely different class of Indians from those surrendering to Carson. Most of the Navajos surrendering at Wingate lacked any worldly possessions and were virtually naked and starving; they had suffered greatly from the campaign. The *ricos*, however, possessed the economic base to continue their resistance for many months or perhaps years. Wisely, they saw that resistance was futile, and the end-result would be the loss of their wealth.

In mid-February, Major Wallen, commanding at Fort Sumner, wrote Carleton that the Navajos needed an Indian agent. Three hundred seventy now resided on the reservation, and they were "without clothing or farming implements." They were anxious, said Wallen, to begin cultivating the soil and building "a Pueblo" for themselves. The Navajos envied the Apaches and complained that they seemed to have all of their wants satisfied. Most importantly, the Apaches had an agent to look after their needs. In response to Wallen's letter, Carleton appointed Captain William Calloway, First Infantry, California Volunteers, as the Superintendent of Indian Farms. It was impossible to obtain a Navajo agent, the General said, for the Indian Bureau refused to take charge of the Navajos.[2]

General James H. Carleton and friends, 1865. Standing (left to right):
Col. E. H. Bergman, Col. C. P. Clever, Gen. N. H. Davis, Col. H. M.
Enos, Dr. Basil K. Norris, Col. J. C. McFerran. Sitting (left to right):
Gen. D. H. Rucker, Gen. Christopher Carson, Gen. J. H. Carleton.

Carleton became increasingly irritated by the Indian Bureau. In late February he informed Adjutant General Thomas that 2,000 Navajos soon would be at the Bosque, most of them destitute. "If the Indian Department *will not* do anything for them it should be so understood definitely," he stated. Once that had been made clear, the military would assume full responsibility for furnishing their food, clothing, and farming implements, and for directing their labor. He concluded with the hope that an agent could be appointed for the Navajos.

After weeks of exhausting travel with army escorts from Fort Wingate, one Navajo group after another settled at the Bosque Redondo. Here, the military assigned them camping areas north of Fort Sumner and the Apaches, until more permanent home sites could be selected. Within a short time, Captain Calloway divided them into work details. Their major project was to enlarge the irrigation ditch dug by the Mescaleros in 1863. Although the ditch was soon extended to the point that it could irrigate 1,500 acres, the amount of irrigable land remained insufficient to provide for the Navajos. To open additional land, Calloway drafted plans for another ditch to circle for six miles in a big loop around the arable land on the east bank of the Pecos.[3]

In Santa Fe, Carleton, anticipating Navajo needs, had advertised in the Santa Fe *Weekly New Mexican* for bids to supply the Bosque. The quartermaster agreed to pay $6.50 per fanega for 6,000 pounds of shelled, sacked corn, and four cents per pound for loose corn. The usual policy in contracting for a reservation was to solicit bids months in advance of need. Clearly, however, Carleton faced an emergency situation, with the Navajos starving at the Bosque. They had to be fed immediately. As a token gesture, William Baker, who handled Superintendent Steck's affairs while he lobbied in Washington, sent a small shipment of goods in mid-February to the Bosque. He also announced that the Indian Department had no additional supplies at that time.

While in Washington, Michael Steck seized every opportunity to attack Carleton's policy. As in the past months, he urged that the Navajos be located on a reservation in their homeland, specifically mentioning the Little Colorado River area in Arizona. Writing to Commissioner Dole on February 15, he stated that General Edward R. S. Canby, who formerly commanded in New Mexico, agreed with him. In fact, Canby had made an agreement with several Navajo chieftains for their bands to settle on the Little Colorado, but the Confederate invasion had forced cancellation of the plan. By the spring of 1864, Dole needed no additional pressure; he already was a staunch opponent of Carleton's reservation project.[4]

From his headquarters in Santa Fe, Carleton carefully watched every development at the Bosque. On February 25, he informed Wallen that 1,300 more Navajos would soon reach the Bosque and that Wallen was to keep a close watch on rations. He wanted Wallen to make frequent estimates of the quantities of bread, meat, and salt required by the Indians. There should always be enough food on hand to supply the Indians for fifty days. The Navajos, especially, must always have sufficient food. They will be given rations, Carleton wrote, even if he had to slaughter government mules and horses to feed them. He would do everything possible to fulfill Wallen's requisitions. Then Carleton instructed Wallen to count the number of Indians receiving rations twice a month, and to keep an exact record of arrivals, births, deaths, and desertions. He must have eight plows constantly running in the fields from March 1 to June 10 for the planting of corn, and until July 10 for beans and other crops. Perhaps the most important project, he told Wallen, was to dig Calloway's *acequia madre,* or main irrigation ditch, to run for six miles east of the river, to provide an adequate supply of water. He realized that Wallen's responsibility in starting the Indian colony was enormous, but he promised that the government would appreciate and notice his tireless labors.[5] Carleton neglected nothing. He even personally ordered seeds to be shipped to Fort Sumner.

The problem of feeding the Navajos preyed incessantly on Carleton's mind. In late February he telegraphed Adjutant General Thomas urging that 200,000 rations be shipped to New Mexico from Fort Leavenworth as soon as possible. His request indicated that Carleton feared a food shortage in the New Mexican market. The same day, he advertised in the local newspapers for subsistence bids for the Bosque Redondo. The army required deliveries on April 10, April 30, and May 25 of the following items: 150,000 pounds of wheat meal, 100,000 pounds of cornmeal, and 900 head of beef cattle. On still a separate contract, he requested an additional 1,000 head of cattle. Little did the General realize that the beef purchases would spur the development of New Mexico's languishing cattle industry.[6]

At the end of February, the eastern mails brought copies of the New York *World* and the *Journal of Commerce,* which charged that Carleton was

guilty of favoritism in awarding military contracts. In response to the allegations, a large number of the General's supporters met in Santa Fe and adopted
a resolution condemning the charges. Among those attending were Chief Justice Kirby Benedict, a War Democrat; Governor Connelly; former Superintendent Collins; Anastacio Sandoval, a leading merchant and former judge;
and Ceran St. Vrain, a legendary trapper and explorer who owned several
of the largest farms in New Mexico. Both St. Vrain and Sandoval held sizeable contracts for supplying the Bosque Redondo. The accusation that Carleton had let the contracts to his friends perhaps had some basis in truth, but
his backers, including those with contracts in hand, signed a petition which
was published in the *Weekly Gazette*, denying that he had ever been guilty of
favoritism. Supplying the Bosque with such enormous quantities of foodstuffs
eliminated all but the largest New Mexican contractors. For obvious reasons,
these individuals staunchly supported the reservation concept and became
"friends" of Carleton.[7]

As the Navajos now were arriving in large numbers, Carleton created
the position of Military Superintendent of the Navajo Indians. He appointed
Captain Henry B. Bristol, Fifth Infantry, a young officer from Michigan, to
the position and instructed him to report directly, not going through the commanding officer of Fort Sumner. The appointment somewhat appeased the
Navajos, who had been asking for an agent. Bristol's duties were unrelenting.
When the Navajos became sick from eating food made from flour, Bristol
wrote directly to Carleton. In reply, the General disputed that the flour was
the cause of the illness. He believed the Indians were not cooking their food
enough and were eating raw flour. However, he was shipping in cornmeal and
unbolted wheat meal, and Bristol must instruct the Indians to make matates
and grind the meal like the Mexicans. In a side note Carleton stated that every
commander in the territory had been ordered to reduce military rations, insur-
ing that a sufficient amount of foodstuffs would be available to keep the
Navajos alive.

Back in Santa Fe, the *Weekly New Mexican* began urging the farmers
in New Mexico to expand their agricultural lands. A total of 2,500 Navajos
either lived at the Bosque or were en route there, and the government needed
corn, flour, and other provisions for quite some time. Moreover, the crops
would bring high prices due to the large demand and small supply.

In addition to securing subsistence, Carleton also endeavored to provide
the Indians with shelter from the freezing cold. As the supply of condemned
army tents rapidly ran out, Carleton suggested that the Navajos make wigwams
or teepees like those of the Plains tribes. He promised to construct a pueblo-
style town at the earliest possible moment, believing that the old ruins found
in the Navajo homeland testified to a basic Pueblo character. The Pueblo
Indians had always been the white man's model native American. In outward
appearances their life-style, with its highly developed agriculture and apart-
ment-like buildings, seemed more "civilized" to the white man. Carleton sent
Wallen his views regarding such a community. He wanted the Indians to erect
buildings, one story high, around an open courtyard; the roofs having low
parapets for easy defense. In a few years, Carleton said, "no Indian village in
the world would compare with it in point of beauty." The Navajos, however,

balked at living in adobe houses, particularly if a death had occurred there. Eventually, the military prepared a compromise. The Navajos kept their traditional "huts" (hogans), but they had to arrange them in an orderly manner. They located their hogans in uniform rows. When a death occurred, a family could destroy the hogan and go to the end of the row and erect a new one. This program proved impossible, but it indicated the extent that Carleton was prepared to go in order to change the Navajo.

When they reached the Bosque, many Navajos brought their livestock with them. The military generally purchased the animals, paying cash for them. This exchange gave the Indians another important lesson on the road to being civilized. The army was scrupulously honest, and many Indians soon learned the relative value of stock and money. Their livestock purchases helped to defray the expense of importing cattle, while the hides and pelts from the cattle and sheep served as clothing.[8]

Although Carleton's command was New Mexico, the scale of his Indian policy frequently forced him to turn his attention to Washington, D.C. In March of 1864, ex-Superintendent Collins traveled there to lobby for a special one-year appropriation for the Navajos. He carried letters from Governor Connelly, Kit Carson, and Carleton. The Bosque, wrote Carleton, was "the best pastoral region between the two oceans." Within ten years the Navajos would be the "happiest and most delightfully located pueblo of Indians in New Mexico, perhaps in the United States."[9]

At the same time that Collins lobbied for an appropriation, Indian Commissioner Dole attacked Carleton's Bosque scheme. In a letter to John P. Usher, Secretary of the Interior, Dole voiced Steck's attitudes and views about the undertaking. The Bosque lacked the arable land to support a tribe the size of the Navajos, and even if the reserve were extended farther down the Pecos River, the water to the south was far too saline for agricultural and drinking purposes. Apparently, Collins had been telling prominent persons in Washington that Steck opposed the entire concept of a reservation system. Dole made it clear to Usher that Steck avidly supported the concept of reservations. The Superintendent disagreed with Carleton about this reserve, the Bosque, because Carleton had concentrated two powerful tribes on the same reservation with an inadequate land base for the population.[10]

While the question of the Bosque was argued in Washington, additional problems developed on the reserve. Mexican traders began sneaking into the Indian camps to sell whiskey, and disturbances naturally followed. The military seized two men, Ramon Lopez and Mateo Sena, and charged them with violating the trade intercourse act. Informed of the incident, Carleton ordered Wallen to put the two traders under guard and force them to work on the Indians' farms, planting and digging, until the next meeting of the district court.[11] No one, except authorized persons, were permitted on the reservation, nor were the Indians allowed to sell any clothing or food that had been issued them.*

---

*Steck believed that the illegal trade could not be prevented at the Bosque, for the reserve was located too close to the avenues of commerce. However, if the Navajos lived on a reserve in their own country, trade could be controlled.

Carleton tackled the problem of rationing for the Navajos and Mescaleros with vigor. In early March he held a conference at Santa Fe to determine the size of the ration. Governor Connelly, Carson, and Major John C. McFerran, Third Infantry, attended. Carleton stated that food rather than guns would keep the Indians on the reservation. So far the army commissary department had been unable to procure enough food to feed the Indians. But if they were placed on starvation rations, many Indians would bolt the reservation. The only solution was to give the Navajos rations previously designated for troops. At all military posts in New Mexico soldiers would be placed on half rations.

After much discussion, the board agreed to distribute one pound of flour or meat as a daily ration to each Indian man, woman, and child. If possible, the ration would be one-half pound each of meat and corn-flour meal. Rice or beans were an acceptable substitute for the latter. The Indians were directed to cook the ration as soup, in which manner it would certainly sustain them. Carleton, however, anticipated continuing difficulties in feeding the Indians until either the supplies arrived from the states or the corn in New Mexico ripened. It distressed him to cut the rations of his troops; and he appealed to them to recognize the need of the moment and the humanity of the act.[12]

By mid-March, Carleton concluded that the military must feed the Navajos for many months. In a letter to Adjutant General Thomas he requested that a supervisor be appointed at a salary of $3,200 to manage the needs of the Navajos. He also suggested the services of an assistant supervisor with a salary equal to that of an Indian agent, a practical and knowledgeable farmer, and a general mechanic. Most of all, he wished the supervisor to avoid spending his time "grinding axes" — a reference to Labadie and Steck.[13]

On March 17 Captain Bristol petitioned William Baker, Steck's assistant in Santa Fe, for all of the Indian goods his department held. There were 5,000 Navajos at the Bosque, or shortly expected, he said, and they were "entirely destitute of everything." The military needed immediately all spades, hoes, candles, shears, plows, wool, leather, tin cups, kettles, knives, awls, axes, hatchets, and articles of clothing that could be shipped to the Bosque. The army would reimburse the Indian Department, when other shipments reached New Mexico from the states. Baker refused Bristol's request, saying the supplies on hand were destined for the Pueblos. Informed of this situation, Carleton became incensed. The Indian Department not only had failed to feed the Mescaleros, he asserted, but now refused to furnish supplies for the Navajos. When Baker attempted to communicate with Carleton on the subject, the General ignored him.[14]

During March, Carleton quarreled with Captain Amos F. Garrison, his district commissary officer, over subsistence contracts. Writing his superior, General L. P. Taylor, Commissary General, in Washington, Garrison stated that Carleton had let contracts in violation of army regulations and had ignored completely the commissary office in these arrangements. Citing one particular instance, Carleton asked Garrison to make some minor purchases for the Indians, in effect compelling him to leave Santa Fe for eight to ten days. Upon his return to headquarters, Garrison found that the General had let large contracts while he was absent. These contracts had been made on the open market, without the usual proposals and bids as required by regulation.

Garrison also charged that a contract for 1,000 head of beef cattle had been made at a price of twelve and a half cents per pound on the hoof. In the past beef had always been purchased at Fort Union from the wagon trains at eight cents per pound. Garrison did not feel the situation was as urgent as Carleton feared. The officer then referred to a contract for shelled corn to be delivered to the reservation in July and August. Plenty of time remained for the taking of bids for the corn, he declared. Carleton had never consulted him in contract matters since the Navajos had been located at the Bosque. Garrison's office had become merely a rubber stamp to approve contracts the General made. Garrison concluded his lengthy diatribe against Carleton with an offer to resign his commission. He could not be held responsible for the good or bad management of the subsistence department in New Mexico. "If the present officer *remains* in command of the Dept.," Garrison stated, "my usefulness here to the service is at an end."[15]

Carleton believed the emergency at the Bosque required drastic action — which included bypassing Garrison in letting contracts. In a telegram to Adjutant General Thomas, the General explained that by making personal appeals he had been able to secure more cattle and breadstuffs than he previously thought available. Originally, he had requested two million pounds of flour and corn from the states. He now felt only 500,000 pounds were needed. Instead of 4,000 head of cattle, only 2,000 were required at the Bosque. Even so Carleton underlined the urgency by asking that annual supplies, as well as his special requests, be shipped as soon as possible.[16]

About this time Carleton focused his attention on the Mescalero Agent Labadie. Perhaps at the instigation of Steck, Labadie had upset the Navajos by telling them that they were trespassing on an Apache reservation and that soon they would be forced to move elsewhere. Carleton angrily ordered Major Wallen to expel Labadie from the reserve if he caused further trouble. This order also applied to all Indian Department personnel. As long as the army fed the Indians, the Indian Department would not be allowed to meddle. When that department shouldered these responsibilities, it could conduct affairs in its own way. Until that day, the General would run the Bosque Redondo reservation.[17]

In late March Wallen sent Carleton a list of persons drawing or buying rations at Fort Sumner. Six of the persons were associated with the Mescalero agency. Carleton replied that only military personnel could draw supplies and that Labadie and his assistants were not to be granted this privilege. Officers, particularly, could make purchases in reasonable quantities for their families. In the past, this privilege had been abused, and if such irregularities occurred again the responsible parties would be arrested and perhaps court-martialed.[18]

On March 26, the army accounted for its first month of large-scale rationing — actually half rations — to the Navajos and Apaches at the Bosque. It distributed fresh beef totaling 126,000 pounds, with 3,029 pounds of beef pluck (heart, liver, and lungs) and also gave the Indians over 78,803 pounds of mutton. The wheat meal issue totaled 113,384 pounds, and corn 171,526 pounds. Other items included flour, coffee, sugar, and salt. The cost of these supplies came to $70,578. In the Santa Fe *Weekly Gazette*, ex-Superintendent Collins described the amount expended as negligible considering that the Mescaleros and Navajos had been "completely subdued" and were incapable of further mischief. The "beneficial results of that peace" could not be estimated in dollars and cents, he said.

The reduced rations given the Indians at the Bosque Redondo caused problems. Labadie wrote Carleton that the issue was too small and that Apaches and Navajos suffered greatly from hunger. The meager ration issued weekly was insufficient to sustain life. Possibly exaggerating, the Mescalero agent stated that several Indians had died from hunger and that others were near the point of death. The Indians consumed their total weekly ration during the first two days, and during the next three chewed on hides, and begged wherever they could.* If General Carleton allowed these conditions to continue, the Indians would lose what little confidence they presently had in government promises.[19]

Wallen agreed with Labadie. Since the issuance of half rations, Indian leaders had complained loudly and persistently about food. To stop complaints, Wallen on his own had distributed another small ration. Wallen told Carleton on April 1 that the ravenous manner in which the Indians gulped down their food led him to investigate the situation. With the post surgeon, he toured the Indian camps. "The suffering, even to actual starvation, was terrible," he said. Without consulting the General, Wallen thereupon handed out a full ration on his own responsibility.

Wallen also stated that he had altered the policy of distributing rations. When given food for a five-day period, the Indians could not save rations beyond the first day. He therefore changed the system so that rations were distributed every third day. In explaining these changes, Wallen informed Carleton that if half rations continued for another week, nearly all the men, and certainly those without families, would leave the reservation. With his small force, he would be powerless to stop them.

Fortunately, by April of 1864, Carleton had enough food on contract to provide full rations for both the army and Indians. He ordered all garrisons to return to full rations, and he reauthorized feeding grain to cavalry horses. Prices on foodstuffs in New Mexico soared. Sheep prices rose from $2.50 to $4.00 per head, while beef prices increased one hundred percent. These prices hurt the average citizen, who was now unable to afford mutton and beef.[20]

In Washington, the Indian Bureau softened its view toward the Bosque Redondo. Commissioner Dole had discussed the project with General Canby, Carleton's predecessor, who stated that the Navajos, if properly established at the Bosque Redondo, would soon become self-sustaining. Dole wrote Interior Secretary Usher on April 4 that he had no Indian Department personnel at the Bosque representing the Navajos and therefore could not really judge the merits of its location. Under the circumstances, it was not wise to look for a new home for the Navajos at this time.

Collins had also influenced Dole's thinking about the Bosque. Dole now believed that the Navajos could become self-sufficient within a year. The Indians were an agricultural and pastoral people, Collins argued, and a

---

*Half rations totaled roughly 1,000 calories per day, hardly sufficient for Indians who already were half-starved.

$100,000 appropriation would provide them with basic agricultural implements and clothing. As the Indian Department had little to lose by supporting the Bosque Redondo, Dole decided to give the program a chance. He recommended a $100,000 appropriation to Interior Secretary Usher, with the understanding that the army continue to handle the food distribution to the Navajos. With the backing from the departments of Interior and War, the Navajo appropriation was assured.[21]

Dole had reassessed his thoughts about the Bosque for other reasons. Two months earlier President Abraham Lincoln had placed his approval on the reservation system by signing an order creating a reserve of forty square miles for the Apache Indians in New Mexico. Moreover, Dole knew that Secretary of War Edwin M. Stanton and other powerful men in Washington supported Carleton's plan, and he did not wish to incur their wrath. Dole did not know how President Lincoln felt about the Navajos, but he decided to follow Stanton's advice because the army was in charge of the Indians. The Commissioner recommended that Carleton's plan be given a chance — perhaps personally hoping that it would fail.[22]

At the Bosque Redondo, both the Navajos and Apaches complained loudly about the ration of one pound of meat a day. To quiet them, Carleton on April 9 ordered Wallen to issue an additional pound of breadstuffs, suggesting that beans might be useful. As the Indians liked to eat the entrails of animals, these also were issued. Wallen and Labadie were instructed to reassure the Indians that everything possible was being done to feed them and that they must be patient. Wallen also might instruct his men to tell the Indians that many New Mexicans were jealous of their having "such a beautiful place" in which to live.[23]

Carleton continued to draw fire from the Indian Bureau. His criticisms of the New Mexico Indian Department reached Commissioner Dole by way of Steck, and Dole censured the General in a letter to Usher. Carleton, he said, had manifested a malicious spirit in his references to the past and future conduct of the Indian Bureau. Furthermore, his recommendation that a separate department be created in New Mexico to administer the Bosque Redondo Reservation was certainly unnecessary. The split between the military and the Indian Bureau over the Bosque was gradually widening.

In Albuquerque, the *Rio Abajo Weekly Press* on April 12 attacked Carleton's policies. The editor recommended that a general referendum be held to decide the proper location of the Navajo reservation. Sheepmen liked to graze their animals in the Pecos country becaues of its mild climate and rich grasses, but with the Indians in the region, they could not do so. Moreover, the Navajos really constituted an Arizona problem. A majority of that tribe lived in Arizona, and the new territory should be entitled to the advantages and disadvantages of a reservation for them. In conclusion, he stated that the people of New Mexico ought to have been consulted before the Navajos were moved to the Bosque. The paper called for public meetings and the exercising of the democratic process to decide the issue.[24]

Favorable reports started to pass across Carleton's desk. In mid-April he learned that rations he had requested were now on their way to New Mexico by a special wagon train from Fort Leavenworth. The food crisis seemed to be over. Conditions at the reservation continued to be peaceful.

Since the daily ration had been increased to one pound each of meat and breadstuffs, the Indians were content. They were turning out in sizeable numbers to work on the irrigation ditches. With easing of food restrictions, the leaders again received their special rations of sugar and coffee, and they encouraged their people to turn out their men for labor.

Wallen held frequent meetings with the tribal leaders, and he tried to maintain a strict sense of justice in dealing with both Navajos and Apaches. He explained to the chiefs the efforts and hopes of the Commanding General for them. They seemed to appreciate what the army desired to accomplish, "as far as Indians can," he wrote. He impressed upon the Indians that ex-Superintendent Collins had made a long journey to the Great White Father in Washington to obtain presents for them; alluding to the $100,000 appropriation, he said the presents soon would arrive. He spoke of the necessity of working the farms so that they would become self-sufficient. Unfortunately, the weather for the past month had been miserably cold, prohibiting regular field work. Catarrh and dysentery had broken out, and there was also a high rate of erysipelas, especially among the recent arrivals. The garrison doctor had treated some two hundred Navajos. Because the Indians worked better when small rewards were available, Wallen asked Carleton to ship a small quantity of tobacco and other small presents, for it might be used to great advantage.[25]

In April, Superintendent Steck left Washington for New Mexico. At Leavenworth, Kansas, he met several prominent persons who collectively had received nearly $500,000 in contracts to supply both the military and the Indians at the Bosque. Writing to Dole, Steck estimated that supporting the Navajos alone would involve an expenditure of $816,000 for the first year. In their own country, only a minimal expenditure was required, as they could live off their flocks. He again urged Dole to permit the Navajos to return to their homeland.[26]

More Navajos from Arizona arrived at the Bosque. The weather had been miserable during their overland journey. One group of 2,400 Indians, escorted by Captain John Thompson, First New Mexico Volunteers, had been caught in heavy snows, and many poorly clad Indians died from exposure and from dysentery. Altogether, a total of one hundred ninety-seven Navajos fell out and died between Fort Canby and Fort Sumner. Although by mid-April there were over 4,000 Navajos at the Bosque, many of the *ricos*, the wealthy stockowners, had not come in. The banks of the Pecos now presented a pathetic spectacle. The brush huts and mud hogans of starving half-naked Navajos stretched along the river for fifteen miles, the largest concentration of Indians ever to be gathered in the Southwest.[27]

Captain Bristol, the Navajo Superintendent, on May 2 sent Carleton a survey of the number of Indians at the Bosque Redondo. He had counted 4,414 Navajos: 1,296 men over eighteen years of age, 1,338 women over sixteen, 1,689 children, and 96 infants. Bristol reported thirty-six deaths among the Navajos, saying they had occurred among the young children due to "diseases of childhood." Only three births were known. The Apaches numbered 364, with 107 men, 130 women, 117 children, and 10 infants. Over a six-month period the Apaches said that there had been thirty-three deaths among their children, principally because of coughs. It was difficult to keep records of vital statistics on the reservation. For example, the Indians rarely, if ever, reported deaths or births.

Progress was being made on the reservation. The Apaches appeared content, showing no disposition to desert the reserve. Their farming efforts were commendable. Both tribes were engaged in planting. At Sumner construction of the post quarters finally moved forward. One set was completed and another started. Fruit trees had been planted but were not doing well because of the severe cold weather. Pasturage was poor, and the Indians had to wait for the first rain of the season to bring forth the grass. In all, Bristol noted that everything seemed fine, and with additional cavalry troops for security the "colonization bids fair to succeed."

Another group of Navajos arrived from the west on May 10. The new contingent, escorted by Captain Francis McCabe, 1st New Mexico Cavalry, contained 777 persons, which increased the total number to 5,182 Navajos.* Six Navajos reportedly had died recently at the Bosque, but Bristol thought the real number was higher. These deaths were attributed to the difficult journey to the Pecos. Yet on the whole, the Indians seemed content.

A shipment of grape cuttings that Carleton had ordered from Santa Fe had arrived, but many died on their way to the Bosque. The new shade trees, however, fared well. Carleton had ordered that trees be planted at the reserve both for shade and fuel; most of the old cottonwoods had been felled for construction or firewood. Bristol stated that "from all appearances the Post will soon wear truly the title of 'the Bosque.' "[28]

Labadie continued to encourage the Mescalero Apaches to farm. Although the Navajos were characterized as "honest workmen" who constantly endeavored to enlarge their fields, the Apaches lived in constant fear of them, quartered near in overwhelming numbers. Every night the Apaches posted guards around their land. In March they had expressed great resentment when land they had worked the previous year was given to the Navajos. Then, a second division of Apache land occurred. Labadie was powerless to prevent this, because the army controlled the entire reserve.

The Apaches completely rejected the idea of adopting a "pueblo style of life." In fact, Wallen wrote Carleton that the Apaches habitually changed their camping grounds nearly every ten days. Little progress had been made in teaching them the truths of Christianity. The Apaches had two gods — a good one and a bad one, but beyond that their religion was not distinctive. Wallen took steps to locate them in good substantial houses and to teach them a love of home and labor. The Apaches, he observed, were very chaste in their relations with Americans and Mexicans, a sharp contrast to the licentious Navajo women. The Mescaleros' love for gambling, however, was exceeded only by their love for intoxication. Viewed altogether, the tribes had a long road ahead to the white man's world.[29]

A great dissension flared when Wallen ordered Labadie to halt the Apache planting and send the Indians to work on a new irrigation ditch for the Navajo lands. The Mescaleros grumbled. They had placed 1,100 acres

---

*The Navajos numbered 1,497 men, 1,597 women, 2,010 children, and 96 infants.

under cultivation, and corn, melons, pepper, pumpkins, and beans were doing well. They also had planted fifty acres of wheat and seventy of corn for the use of the agency personnel. The Apaches grudgingly built the ditch but complained they lost thirty days of valuable time on their own land. Labadie wrote Steck that the Indian situation at the Bosque disgusted him. The Mescaleros said they would rather live with the Kiowas and Comanches than with the Navajos. This bitterness exploded into action. Ojo Blanco and forty-two Mescaleros, knowing that Chief Cadette was away, fled the Bosque on the night of April 25 and began terrorizing the countryside. In their rage they killed eleven persons and drove off sizeable quantities of livestock before disappearing to the south.[30]

Ojo Blanco, whose band had performed gallantly against Navajo raiders a few months before, left the reservation because the army had precipitously moved the Apache camps next to the post. The Apaches had been scattered on both sides of the river, for several miles. Believing that Labadie's control over them was much too loose, Wallen had ordered them gathered into a single camp, located within a mile of the post. Every morning at 7:30 A.M. an army bugler summoned them to labor on the ditch. No animals were allowed to roam at large. Whenever the Indians moved, they were counted. It was more than their free spirits would stand, and Ojo Blanco and his followers fled.[31]

During May more wagon trains loaded with supplies rumbled in from Fort Union. The commissary officer signed a voucher on May 19 for $15,635 for two hundred fifty cattle delivered by H. B. Denman, a merchant and former mayor of Leavenworth, Kansas, and a friend of Carleton. The purchase price averaged 12.5¢ per pound. On the same day, large shipments of wheat were received from Lucien B. Maxwell, who owned large farms on the Cimarron, in addition to being one of the wealthiest men in the territory. Several days later 19,938 pounds of wheat meal were purchased for $1,694 from William H. Moore and Company. Wheat meal sold for roughly the same price per hundred-pound sack as cornmeal. In less than a year's time, the price of corn and wheat meal delivered at the Bosque jumped from $8 to approximately $12 per sack.[32] During the two months of April-May, 1864, the military issued approximately $175,000 in supplies to the Indians at the Bosque. Included were over 150,000 pounds of corn, 371,000 pounds of meat, 3,000 pounds of flour, and 350,000 pounds of wheat meal. Clearly, contractors regarded the reservation as an enormous plum.[33]

By early summer many of the buildings at Fort Sumner were completed. Most were one-story adobes with high beamed ceilings and typical Southwestern architecture. The fort had been carefully planned, and the buildings sat along streets laid out in an orderly manner around the parade ground. On May 24 the flagstaff was erected; the next day, in the presence of the garrison and a number of curious Indians, the flag was raised. Captain Prince G. D. Morton, the assistant quartermaster, touched a tender note by singing "Rally Round the Flag." At isolated Sumner, one could easily forget the great struggle being waged in the East. Major Wallen, the post commander, then addressed the crowd, reminding those assembled that they had embarked on an historic and a great humanitarian task.[34]

At Santa Fe, Steck in late May learned from a delegation of Moqui (Hopi) Indians who visited him that many Navajos still remained in Arizona. The Hopis were pleased that their enemies, who were encroaching on their land, were being removed by the Great Father. They believed their prayers had caused the removal of the Navajos, and they wanted to make certain that the remainder also would be taken away. Supporters of Carleton's plan had predicted that by July the entire tribe would be at the Bosque, although they admitted that some *ricos* might not come in. Commenting on the Hopis visit, Steck indicated to Commissioner Dole that the remaining *ricos*, such as Manuelito, would be difficult to bring to the Bosque. The military was spending over $50,000 per month feeding the Navajos, a cost that precluded the Department of Interior from assuming control over them. Steck predicted that expenses must increase rather than decrease at the Bosque.[35]

Steck also had heard that Carleton planned to spend lavishly on constructing buildings and opening additional farms, hoping thereby to prevent the Navajos from being returned to their own country. If the government invested additional money in the Bosque scheme, Steck said, it might never be able to extract itself from the banks of the Pecos. The Navajos still opposed the reservation, and on several occasions various groups had fled and committed depredations en route to their homeland.

But despite the resistance of Steck, work at the Bosque went forward. Under the leadership of Captain Calloway, the Navajos cleared land for new fields, and by June they had planted and had 3,000 acres under irrigation. Considering the acute shortage of adequate farming tools, this accomplishment was considerable.[36]

An indicator of the size of the Sumner operations was the number of civilians employed in the quartermaster department there. In May, eighty-nine civilians were employed by that one department. This group included clerks, two interpreters, one yard master, three blacksmiths, twelve carpenters, six masons, nine adobe layers, one saddler, nine teamsters, forty-three laborers, and one messenger. The laborers averaged an income of about thirty dollars a month. The total number of civilians on the reservation amounted to an additional two or three companies of men.[37]

In June the Carleton-Garrison feud over contracts surfaced again. Carleton had been receiving reports from Washington that Garrison had severely criticized his contracting policies. The thin-skinned General wrote the officer an angry letter. He demanded to see copies of Garrison's correspondence to the Commissary General in which he had "alluded directly or indirectly to myself personally or officially or to my administration or policy with reference to Indians or to the Feeding of Indians." He desired to correct any misrepresentation that the Captain may have made through malice, ignorance, or forgetfulness. He was particularly distressed by Garrison's statement that it would cost the government over one-half million dollars to operate the Bosque.

Garrison replied that he had no copies of the letters because he had penned them himself on a Sunday afternoon when the clerks were off work. Regarding Carleton's charge that he had grossly over-estimated the cost of feeding the Navajos, Garrison retorted that from every reliable source he had heard that it would cost at least $500,000 to sustain them. If anything, he had under-estimated the figure. Time would show that he was right. Yearly expenditures came to exceed one million dollars.[38]

Garrison became increasingly bitter about Carleton's free-wheeling contracting procedures. He again wrote his superior in Washington, repeating his earlier charges. A handful of men, he wrote, "traitors to the flag of their country, their honor and their God, had banded together in New Mexico." They pursued contracts with an intent "more voracious, than a pack of wolves upon the scent of blood."

As criticism mounted, Carleton assembled a special board to investigate the contracts let in the past three months in his military department. The hand-picked board included Captain William H. Lewis, Captain William Bell, and Carleton's aide de camp, First Lieutenant Cyrus H. DeForrest. The members examined twenty-three contracts and found all correct with no evidence of irregularities. Two interesting beef contracts had been let to Lucien B. Maxwell and H. B. Denman. Maxwell's contract called for 8½ ¢ per pound, while Denman's return was 12½ ¢ per pound. The difference, however, was accounted for easily. The Maxwell cattle came from his Cimarron ranch, while Denman's herd was driven from the States. Price variances for corn also were noted and explained in a similar fashion. Furthermore, contracts let on the open market, due to the previous emergency situation, were always higher than those let through bids. The board adjourned, declaring that everything was in perfect order.[39]

The reservation on the Pecos was now the most important activity in New Mexico. In July, Carleton, well aware that his career and the careers of his friends depended on the success of the experiment, appointed Kit Carson to be Military Superintendent of Indians at the Bosque Redondo. He wanted Carson to investigate conditions there thoroughly. On July 12 the famous scout held a council with the Navajo leaders. They were perfectly content, he later reported, and seemed well pleased with their treatment at the reservation. They appeared to understand and appreciate the efforts that were being made to "render them comfortable and happy."

The crops were doing splendidly. Over 3,000 acres had been planted, principally in corn, and he estimated that the harvest would average between twenty-five and thirty bushels per acre, or a grand total of 84,000 bushels. The Indians also had planted a large quantity of beans and other vegetables. Considering the disadvantages under which the Indians labored, such as scarcity of tools and lateness in planting, the harvest seemed truly remarkable. Carson credited the success to Captain Calloway, Superintendent of Farms, and the men of his company who had showed untiring zeal in instructing and directing the Indian labor. Carson recommended that a small herd of sheep and goats be given every Navajo family, the former to supply wool for clothing, and the latter to supply milk. The money they had accumulated from fodder sales to the army should be expended for this purpose. If these funds were presented to the Indians in cash, they would purchase needless ornaments and trinkets. In conclusion, Carson felt the Navajos were making great progress.[40]

The condition of the Apaches, however, presented a stark contrast. The military found it almost impossible to get them to perform manual labor. The tribe had only one hundred and sixty acres under cultivation, and the work had been done mainly by hired hands. Carson neglected to point out that the Apaches had been taken from their land to work for the Navajos. Labadie, he felt, was not performing as well as he should have, and his rosy reports contradicted the sad reality. Carson held a conference with the Apaches, and they promised to try harder. They seemed satisfied with their treatment.

Carson declared that rumors were circulating on the reservation that the Navajos might be moved back to their own country. Fortunately, the Indians had ignored them. Civilians had started these false reports. Citizens had been sneaking onto the reservation to engage in illegal trade with the Indians. Certain rascals even had swindled the Navajos out of their farming implements. To prevent these incursions Carson recommended that pickets be stationed in the northwest corner of the reserve, near the road to the settlements, to prevent all unauthorized persons from entering the Bosque.

The Navajos and Apaches lived in "most perfect harmony" at the Bosque. Only a few minor complaints, easily resolved, had been made. Some minor stealing of corn occasionally occurred, but the amount involved was insignificant. Like a true military man, Carson noted that the Indians policed around their huts and enjoyed good health. Only sixty Indians were receiving medical treatment, and Carson planned to have the entire Indian tribe vaccinated as soon as possible. The Indian hospital which Carleton had started many months before was being erected, although heavy summer rains had hampered the construction. Carson also recommended that the army put up grist mills and give young Indian males practical instruction in such mechanical arts as blacksmithing and carpentry.

Carson concluded his lengthy letter with fervid praise for the reservation. He was quite pleased with everything connected with the Bosque. He congratulated Carleton on "the entire success which has crowned your efforts in ameliorating the condition of the Indians and in giving permanent Peace to this Territory."[41]

Captain Bristol, who had replaced Wallen as post commander, was also optimistic about the experiment. He had traveled over every foot of the farm and had never seen anything so grand. He congratulated Carleton, saying, "your selection of the Pecos for them is the very best the country affords." The site had the perfect climate, abundant grass, and fine water. Most of all, the location was perfect — as it was far "away from the Mexicans!" Bristol, however, admitted that rain was a serious problem. Precautions had to be taken to prevent buildings under construction from falling down. Water had melted over 50,000 adobe bricks. He forecast that the Quartermaster might not be able to complete construction of the post by the fall, as had been planned.[42]

Labadie's troubles became acute when the Apache crops started to ripen in the early summer. The Navajos made repeated raids on the fields and attempted to destroy the crops of their ancient foe. The Apaches, in retaliation, invaded the Navajo farms and fought battles with hoes and shovels among the tall green stalks. When these fights occurred, the troops at Sumner quickly moved in, rounded up the Indians, and threw them in the stockade. At times the fights became so intense that the soldiers opened fire, only to find that bullets would not stop the two tribes from trying to crush skulls with farm implements.[43]

In midsummer all eyes turned toward Washington when the news came that Congress had passed a law appropriating $100,000 for relief of the Navajos. The Indian Bureau was in charge of spending the money for non-edible supplies. Believing that the $100,000 could not sustain the Navajos, except in extreme suffering and destitution, Dole foresaw that his Bureau could act only as an auxiliary to the War Department, which now held the Navajos as prisoners. Dole appointed William Baker, Steck's assistant, and Jesse H. Leavenworth, a Chicago merchant and former colonel of the Second Colorado Volunteers, to make the purchases in New York and in the St. Louis area for the Bosque.[44]

About the time of the announcement, Steck and Baker were in Washington. In conferring with Commissioner Dole, Baker stated that a powerful group in the territory (probably meaning Carleton's supporters who held contracts for the Bosque) were working against the best interests of the government. Baker himself was "unwilling as well as unable to meet their opposition or incur their displeasure." Steck had hinted that the reservation appeared to be basically a scheme to generate lucrative contracts, particularly for suppliers of corn, wheat, sheep, and cattle. Amos F. Garrison, no longer the commissary for the Department of New Mexico, agreed. Steck also reminded Dole that the War Department had ordered a board of officers to convene at Fort Sumner to investigate expenditures. The board discovered that at the end of the four months beginning in March, expenditures for the Bosque totaled $510,000, a truly fantastic sum.*[45]

The Superintendent said that if each Indian on the reservation received forty cents per day, the $100,000 would last only two weeks. Actually, the Indians were receiving closer to twenty cents per day for individual rations, but even at this rate the $100,000 appropriation would last slightly more than a month.[46]

Steck was joined by Miguel Romero y Baca, the probate judge at Las Vegas, in condemning Carleton's experiment. On June 23 he wrote Dole that the large flocks the Navajos had brought with them to the Pecos had forced local sheepmen to remove their animals from the area. If their flocks became mixed with the Navajos' flocks, one risked his life in trying to reclaim them. Like Steck, Romero proposed that the Navajos be settled on the Little Colorado in Arizona.[47]

Despite the continuing criticism, Carleton forged ahead. In New Mexico the Catholic Church regarded the Bosque Reservation as captive audience for education and conversion. On July 17 Carleton wrote Captain Bristol that three priests and several sisters expected to begin instructing the Navajo chil-

---

*By June, the problems at the Bosque Redondo had created confusion in Washington. Stanton asked Usher to reimburse the War Department for the supplies that had been issued to the Indians in the absence of agents at several forts in New Mexico. Usher refused the Secretary's bid at trying to get the Indian Department to admit responsibility for the Navajos. In the past the army had issued rations to the Indians and was later reimbursed by the Interior Department, but in this instance the quantity was so overwhelming that Stanton must have known his request would be refused.

dren. He asked Bristol to have the Navajos make enough adobes for an eight-room building, capable of serving as both a school and a teachers' quarters. He wanted the school located near Sumner and built in the typical Spanish style with an open courtyard. If any Indians assisted in building the school, they were to be paid. Carleton also recommended that the site include a garden where the boys could be instructed in farming.[48]

Supplies poured into the Bosque almost daily. St. Vrain delivered 191,800 pounds of wheat meal and 57,500 pounds of flour for the sum of $22,053. Andres Dold, a Las Vegas contractor, sent wagons carrying 20,500 pounds of flour, 14,757 pounds of wheat, and 64,872 pounds of corn, for approximately $17,400. James Hunter and C. W. Kitchen delivered five hundred head of cattle on contract for $34,350. They also delivered 228,150 pounds of corn for $24,070. Another large delivery of corn came from Samuel Watrous, a prominent rancher and farmer in Mora County, who shipped 110,580 pounds for $12,163, and William Moore sent nearly $10,000 worth of corn and wheat meal. The Bosque Redondo was proving a great boon to business in New Mexico.[49]

Despite various problems which beset the Bosque experiment, considerable progress was made there during the first six months of 1864. Collins used his influence to persuade the Department of the Interior to give the reservation a chance, and Congress had passed a $100,000 relief bill. At the reserve, soldiers and Indians had planted several thousand acres, and a plentiful harvest was anticipated. Unfortunately, in the weeks ahead unforeseen circumstances clouded these bright prospects.

4

Insects and Fraud

"We had a field of nearly three thousand acres which promised to mature finely, when, after it had tasselled and the
ears formed, it was attacked by what they here call the cut
worm or army worm, *and the whole crop destroyed!*"

General James H. Carleton

"The distribution [of gifts to the Indians] presented an interesting scene and if those who had grabbed no inconsiderable
portion of the fund had witnessed it, I sincerely believe that
conscience would have twinged them right sharply."

William Baker

DURING THE SUMMER OF 1864, the Indians at the Bosque Redondo worked
diligently in the fields and on the irrigation ditches anticipating a bountiful
harvest in the weeks ahead. H. B. Denman, who had delivered cattle to the
reservation, reported in Santa Fe that the crops were flourishing and that the
Indians appeared to be content. The apparent contentment, however, soon
turned to great disappointment. In the early fall swarms of insects devastated
the ripening crops and created great concern over food supplies. This concern
turned to disgust when it became known that swindlers had made off with
one-half of the Congressional appropriation for the Navajos.[1] These develop-
ments marked the first major setbacks Carleton experienced in running the
giant reservation on the Pecos.

The post commander at Fort Sumner routinely reported in July that
there were 5,916 Navajos and 394 Apaches at the Bosque Redondo. During
the preceding month the Apaches had suffered five deaths, the result of "diseases unknown"; four Navajos also succumbed to the mysterious ailments.
Nine Navajo adults and two children drowned while trying to cross the Pecos
River, presumably in a flash flood. The birth rate on the reserve continued to
be extremely low; only five Indian births had been noted.[2]

Problems with renegade Indians continued. The Santa Fe *Weekly New
Mexican* in August commented on stock losses. On the first of the month, a
Navajo band had stolen twenty-three animals from Ramon Virgil of Santa

Navajos at work on the Indian farm.

Clara, a community on the Rio Grande about twenty miles northwest of Santa Fe. Several days later renegades took stock near Abiquiu, some forty miles north of Santa Fe. Near Las Vegas, Thomas Baca lost his entire flock of sheep to Mescalero raiders. On the same day, Apaches also struck a wagon train in the Gallinas Mountains north of Fort Stanton. Carleton's statements that both the Navajos and Apaches were totally prostrate was obviously premature, the *Weekly New Mexican* said.[3]

When renegade Apaches conducted raids near the Bosque, Navajos joined the military in retaliation. For example, in mid-August, stock thefts at a neighboring ranch prompted a vigorous response. Captain Calloway, in charge of the Navajo farms, collected Delgadito and some Navajos, plus a detachment of thirty-three regulars, and went in pursuit. The Navajos overtook and attacked the raiders before the soldiers arrived and captured the 4,000 sheep they were herding. However, on returning to the Bosque, the Navajos suddenly were attacked by the same Apache band, who retook the sheep and rode away. The Apaches killed four Navajos and seriously wounded Delgadito in the affair.[4]

In early August Carleton authorized the quartermaster to spend $18,000 on the construction of storerooms and an Indian hospital at the Bosque. The health of the Navajos was appalling. The post surgeon, George Gwyther,

Navajo hogans at the Bosque Redondo

stated that the Indians suffered from many diseases due to filthy living habits. Navajo camps emitted unbearable odors from the offal and dead animals that littered the ground. The Indians complained about drinking the water of the Pecos, saying it made them intensely sick. Cases of pneumonia also had occurred during the previous winter. In short, the Indians urgently needed a hospital.

The most serious health problem at the reservation for Indians and soldiers alike probably was venereal disease. Unlike the Mescaleros, who prized chastity and fidelity, the Navajos had long been infected with syphilis and gonorrhea. At the Bosque a majority of the male and female Navajos had venereal diseases, and, according to Captain Bristol, even the children were afflicted with syphilis. Prostitution was rampant, the soldiers generally paying the Indian women a pint of cornmeal for intimate favors. According to Epifano Vigil, a Navajo interpreter, the women came to the soldiers' tents outside the fort and spent the night in return for food or money. In several instances, Indian parents forced their young daughters of only twelve or thirteen to work as prostitutes in order to obtain enough food to survive. Because of these conditions, a majority of the soldiers became infected with the disease at one time or other. Very early, venereal disease surpassed malnutrition as the biggest health problem at the Pecos reservation.

Many buildings at Fort Sumner still remained unfinished. On August 5, Bristol wrote Carleton that projected construction was falling short of expectations, particularly the schoolhouse. Only the officers' quarters, bakehouses, and privies would be completed before fall. Dissatisfaction among the workers hindered the laying of adobe, and the obtaining of building materials posed a constant chore. Bristol stated that those few Indians who were inclined to work spent their time watching their corn fields.

In general, the crops looked good. Worms had been found in some of the ears of corn, but there was no fear of damage. Dry rot had been discovered in some of the turnips. Efforts were being made to teach the Indians how to cook and prepare various kinds of vegetables, because in the past they had not eaten them.

In a letter to Interior Secretary Usher on August 14, Carleton urged that $12,000 of the recent congressional appropriation for the Navajos be used to construct a school. The military and the Indians could erect the building for that price, whereas if constructed by contractors it would cost twice that amount. Several days later Carleton ordered Bristol to begin the construction of a large blacksmith's shop at the Bosque. Tools and iron were en route from Santa Fe. The building should be a long adobe structure, spacious enough to house a forge at both ends. Here, the army would instruct the Navajos in smithing.[5]

In late August supplies for the winter began arriving at the Bosque. Lucien B. Maxwell delivered one hundred eighty-one head of cattle, 125,101 pounds of wheat, and 111,813 pounds of corn on contract — all for $27,271. Andres Dold delivered 212,561 pounds of corn for $23,379, or approximately eleven dollars per hundred pound sack. James Hunter shipped 136,361 pounds of corn for $14,546. Ceran St. Vrain continued to send the products of his farm and mill, delivering 227,273 pounds of wheat meal for $19,351. Herds of sheep and cattle came from Mariana Urissario, and John Dold, the brother of Andres Dold. For the second year C. S. Hinkley won the beef contract for Fort Sumner. In all, approximately $111,000 was spent on supplies during August for the Bosque.[6]

Informed of Steck's criticism of his expenditures for the Bosque, Carleton assured Secretary Usher on August 27 that the Navajos could be fed for one year for $414,856 (Carleton was always precise) and not for the sum of $700,000 for four months as Steck had stated. Steck's estimates were an attempt to discredit the military administration in New Mexico. Carleton believed that his plan was "the only measure that can ever secure peace and prosperity to this impoverished country."[7]

Carleton's experiment suffered a disastrous blow in late summer. When the Indians entered the fields to harvest corn, they found the 3,000 acres, on which they had labored so diligently, covered with rotting corn. Bristol had known that the corn worm had attacked the crop, but he had no idea of the

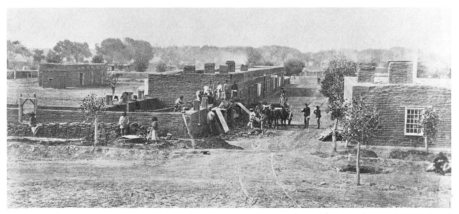

Indians helping construct the post buildings

extent of the destruction. Moths had swarmed through the fields and deposited eggs at the top of the ripening ears. In the silk of the ear, under the husk and out of sight, worms about an inch in length had eaten the growing kernels. Once the worms had bored their way through the husks, a hole was left through which other insects attacked the ears and finished the destruction of the crop. Agent Labadie also had known of the worms but had not realized that the husks covered the damage. The "army worm" completely wrecked the Indian crops.[8]

On August 30 Carleton ordered a military board to inspect the damage and report upon the loss. On the board were Captain Emil Fritz, First California Cavalry, Captain Samuel A. Gorham, First Cavalry, and Surgeon George Gwyther. The officers spent the entire day riding through the fields examining several thousand rotten corn ears. Not a single husk of corn had escaped the attack, and in most instances two-thirds of the individual ear was destroyed. The bottomland near the river which had produced the most abundant crops was the scene of the greatest devastation. The planting time made no difference. The Apache farm, although sown much earlier, experienced the same losses as the Navajo fields.

Fritz's board estimated that under ideal conditions the farms should produce sixty bushels per acre, or a total harvest of approximately 180,000 bushels of corn. The fall harvest of 1864 would be less than one-tenth of that amount. The officers also predicted that the hungry Indians probably would eat the corn right off of the stalks rather than harvest and store it.[9]

The crop losses were not the only blow that struck the Bosque Redondo that fall. Unprecedented rains swept New Mexico, flooding the wheat fields and pounding that crop into ruin. More than one-half of the wheat grown in the territory was destroyed. Moreover, the heavy rains caused the Pecos to overflow, and as the water receded stagnant ponds formed, which soon became infested with mosquitos. Many of the Indians fell ill, infected with malaria.[10]

Labadie informed Superintendent Steck on October 22 that the Indian fields at the Bosque had suffered a total loss. Only the agency gardens had escaped the ravages of the army worm. The Mescaleros did manage to produce a small harvest of melons, pumpkins, chili, green beans, and tobacco. Labadie believed that if the insects (and the Navajos who had stolen from the Apache fields) had not destroyed their crop, the Apaches could have produced enough corn and other breadstuffs to last for nine months. They had managed to save 15,625 pounds of wheat from the rain, despite the fact that they had to use butcher knives to cut the grain. After threshing, the Mescaleros sold 15,333 pounds of straw to the military for twenty-five cents per pound. They also sold some corn to the army quartermaster, in addition to the food they had raised in their gardens. With credit at the sutler's store, the majority of the Mescaleros bought blankets to protect themselves from the cold weather.[11]

Captain Calloway, Superintendent of Indian Farms, felt Carleton's celebrated wrath concerning the corn-worm disaster. Although he did not remove the officer, the General demanded a complete report covering his tenure as superintendent. In February, when he received the Navajos, Calloway stated, the first thing he did was start the enlargement of the irrigation canal supplying the Apache farms. He selected 1,500 acres between the Apaches and the post for Navajo farms. The tract proved too small, however, and as additional

Navajos arrived, he tried to find more land to the north of the Apaches. In March, Calloway assigned Indian laborers to building a main irrigation ditch, branching off of the Pecos River five miles north of the post. In less than a month, the Indians, with only fifty spades, had opened a ditch twelve feet wide and over six miles long, an amazing feat. Many of the Navajos dug until they dropped from exhaustion. Upon completion of the ditch, Calloway divided the adjoining land into fields of ten to twenty-five acres, according to the size of the Navajo group that was to work them.

Calloway estimated that crop losses to the insects amounted to more than $150,000. The Indians were greatly disappointed by the loss, but they endured it with calmness and fortitude, speaking of better luck next year. The Navajos always showed a cheerful contented nature and a willingness to work, he said. With a favorable season, the Navajos possibly would raise all the breadstuffs and vegetables needed for the following year. The conduct of the Navajos indicated by word and deed that they were determined to lead a quiet and useful life. They worked hard when they received adequate rations, but when their food was curtailed, the farm work suffered.[12]

The problem of stolen livestock continued. The Santa Fe *New Mexican* in September criticized the military for allowing the Navajos to keep stolen livestock. Any person claiming an animal could go to the Bosque, but he had to pay ten dollars to get it back. Most ranchers and farmers who had lost livestock refused to make the trip and then pay for their own animals. The policy was legalized-theft, said the *New Mexican,* and "the thief goes rejoiceing [sic] on his way to 'Carletonia's rich and verdant lands' there to be feasted, till he recruits for another raid."[13] Navajo depredations continued. Bonifacio Chaves reported that Navajos killed four herders and stole a flock of nearly 8,000 sheep from a pasture near Sumner. The implication was that Navajos from the Bosque had raided the Chaves pasture and returned to the reservation. In Rio Arriba County, near the homeland of the Navajos, renegades stole fifty-nine cattle, seventeen horses, a mule, and a burro. Clearly, the entire Navajo tribe was not quartered at the Bosque.[14]

On September 12, Carleton penned a bitter note to Captain Bristol, military superintendent of the Navajos, about Mescalero agent Labadie. The agent had purchased sheep from the Indians and kept a personal flock on the reservation. He instructed Bristol to warn Labadie not to use reservation pasturage for his own flock, nor in the future to purchase a "single ounce of food" including sheep from the Indians. Only the quartermaster could make such purchases. Bristol was to require that the corn raised by the Apaches be stored and issued to them later. As Labadie was the only Indian Department representative on the Bosque, Carleton also questioned the need for his being there when the military was in charge. Because of the difficulty in procuring beef for the Bosque, the individual daily ration must be cut to half a pound each of meat and breadstuffs. The Navajos must exhaust their own harvest before they were given military stores.

Worried about the effect of the coming winter, Carleton wrote Commissioner Dole urging that the supplies purchased with the Congressional appropriation be rushed to the Bosque. Nearly 8,000 Indians were on the reservation, "almost destitute of Clothing and Blankets." Unless supplies arrived soon, hundreds of "naked women and children will be likely to perish."[15]

Brigadier General Marcellus Crocker, United States Volunteers, commanded Fort Sumner from September 1864 to February 1865.

A new commander arrived at Fort Sumner in early September. He was Brigadier General Marcellus M. Crocker who previously had commanded the Thirteenth Iowa Infantry. Crocker allowed Bristol to remain in command of the post for several weeks, while he learned the problems of governing the unique garrison and reservation. In his first report, Crocker stated that Bristol, Captain Morton, and all of the other officers at the post had done a splendid job. Noting the difficulty in obtaining materials, he felt that remarkable progress had been made in constructing the fort. The officers' quarters now stood nearly complete, the soldiers' hospital and large spacious storerooms had been finished, and only finishing touches remained to be done at the Indian hospital. On September 19 Crocker officially assumed command of Fort Sumner. His first orders called for the enlargement of the irrigation ditches, the allotment of farming lands to individual families, and the construction of villages on elevated nonirrigable lands. The last was probably a health measure to prevent further outbreaks of disease.[16] By the end of the month most of the enlisted men were quartered in one immense adobe building containing several barrack bays, while the officers had moved to more spacious quarters. It had taken a year and a half to build the post — by far the largest in the Southwest.

The condition of the fields and the friendly disposition of the Indians at the Bosque pleased Crocker. Although insects had destroyed most of the crops, he described the farmland in the valley as "the richest in the territory." But to have 9,000 acres ready to plant in the spring, it would be necessary to drive the Indians hard. The next harvest, he hoped, would provide sufficient food for both the Indians and the garrison. The Indians were working cheerfully on the ditches and appeared "docile, polite, and well-disposed." Crocker had rarely witnessed such universal content.

One of Carleton's long-range plans was the planting of trees at the Bosque for subsequent use as firewood. In the fall of 1864, the Indians could still find abundant mesquite roots, but they had to go farther and farther away to obtain them. The proper solution for fuel, Carleton believed, was to plant trees which could be cut down in several years. The 1,400 seedlings he had sent the previous year either had died or were destroyed by horses. On October 9 Crocker ordered that 5,000 trees be planted, particularly along the banks of the ditches. The cut soil was unstable and often caved in, and the trees could strengthen the sides of the ditches. Under the direction of Captain S. A. Gorham, First California Cavalry, the Indians set out 12,068 trees of different varieties between December 7 and the following April 30.*[17]

While farming continued at the Bosque, Carleton launched a campaign against the Comanche and Kiowa bands who had been terrorizing the neighboring plains to the east. Hoping to enlist the aid of the Navajos, Carson and Crocker counciled with the chiefs, urging them to join the expedition. The Indians refused, vigorously proclaiming that they had had enough of war and declined to have anything to do with the military operations. If attacked by Comanches, they would fight, but for the present they wanted peace. The Apaches, on the other hand, always eager to fight their ancient enemies, volunteered every able-bodied Mescalero for the expedition, a number in excess of sixty. Some Apaches later took part in the campaign, but far fewer than Carson had hoped, and not nearly the entire male population.

During Carson's expedition after the Kiowas and Comanches, Carleton instructed Crocker to permit parties of Navajos to go hunting. Crocker gave each party a passport and placed it under a responsible chief. A reliable noncommissioned officer also went with each group to insure that the Indians did not depredate. The hunting venture appeased the Navajos, who had been irritated by the Apaches' absence from the reserve.[18]

In early October Crocker requested Carleton to define his position at Fort Sumner. Crocker stated that he preferred to leave Bristol in command of the fort, while he himself assumed command of the troops and the superintendence of the Indians. In this manner Bristol could handle the routine work of the post, leaving Crocker for more important duties. Progress was being made, Crocker reported, in alloting land to the bands and families. New sites for villages had also been selected. By the most recent count the Indians

*Photographs of the post indicate the success of the tree-planting project. In December 1864 they planted an average of seventy trees per day. In March and April of 1865 the figure soared to more than 160 per day.

totaled 427 Apaches, and 7,634 Navajos. The Indians were clearing additional farmland and had nearly completed the enlargement of the main ditch. The matter of irrigating the farms, however, required the supervision of an experienced farmer; the soldiers displayed an amateur's knowledge. He asked Carleton to send a farmer very soon.[19]

The beef herds reaching the Bosque in the fall of 1864 were larger than in previous months. Hinckley delivered 1,500 head for $170,852, or over twenty cents per pound. Prices were rising. John Dold shipped 175 head of cattle, weighing 83,156 pounds, on a contract for $7,691; his herders also delivered 541 sheep for $1,376, averaging less than ten cents per pound. With the price of mutton much lower than that of beef, economy suggested that the Indians be fed mutton. However, Carleton's friends and backers raised cattle; consequently the Indians received beef.[20]

Superintendent Steck wrote Commissioner Dole on October 10 that the Bosque was doomed to failure. In the first place, the tribes were unable to cast aside ancient customs and superstitions. For example, the attempt by the military to house the Navajos in adobe buildings had failed. When a death occurred in a dwelling, the Indians, true to their traditions, refused to enter the building in which a person had died. Moreover, Steck thought it would take at least twenty years for the Navajos to become self-sufficient at the Bosque. On the other hand, in their own country, acorns, berries, cactus, wild potatoes, mescal, and mesquite beans grew in abundance, and constituted a large part of the Navajo diet. Only a small expenditure would be needed to maintain them if they were taken back to their own land.[21]

Calloway's successor as Indian Farms Superintendent at the Bosque was Captain Lawrence G. Murphy, First New Mexico Volunteers. Calloway became Superintendent of Indian Labor, a new position. Murphy's company was detailed to work on the farm in various capacities as laborers and supervisors. Lieutenant Thomas Holmes held the new post of Rationing Officer and was charged with supervising the actual issuance of rations, an extremely important position. Crocker held Murphy and Holmes personally responsible for precise information concerning the number of Indians employed, their work progress, and the quantity and kind of agricultural equipment they used. Each day either Murphy or Holmes organized Indian work forces and visited them in the field. They also filed daily progress reports on the work completed by the Indians and soldiers. Special attention was directed toward completing and clearing the main canal. The ditch repeatedly collapsed and had to be dug out again, a never-ending chore. Other ditches constantly were repaired and cleaned. Crocker noted that rapid progress was demanded in clearing ground in order that enough land might be sown in the spring to insure that the Indians became self-sufficient after the next harvest.[22]

Several months earlier Labadie had told the Mescaleros that they would be paid for the fodder they raised for the Quartermaster. The manner of payment now became an issue. Labadie apparently had indicated to the Apaches that they would be paid in cash. Crocker, however, believed that an Indian fund should be established with credits given for their deliveries. The military then could expend the money for the benefit of the Indians. But as the Indians understood they were to receive cash, Crocker hesitated about what to do. The officers at the post felt the Indians would be sorely disappointed on learning that, instead of the tangible cash, they would receive an ink marking in a ledger. On October 20 he wrote Carleton that the Navajos would agree to the establishment of the Indian Fund if the military spent the money for sheep or goats, the traditional Indian symbol of wealth and power. However, they would object if their money went to purchase food or clothing, things that the government should provide. Carleton endorsed Crocker's suggestion, and the funds were created.

The status of the Navajo leaders was reflected by the amount of fodder they delivered to the quartermaster. Ché turned in the largest amount, 32,860 pounds, the work of many families. He received a credit of two hundred twenty dollars. Delgadito, now also an important leader, received one hundred fifteen dollars. Sandoval and Ganado Blanco each delivered fodder to the amount of one hundred three dollars. El Hijo was given one hundred nine dollars, while fifty-two other Navajo leaders and family heads each received credit for sixty dollars or less. Several Navajos, such as Delgadito, moved up in importance with the journey to the Pecos; while others, particularly those who had counseled war, lost standing in the tribe. A number of prominent Navajos, including Manuelito, still roamed at large.

Crocker approved the designation of Delgadito to represent the Navajos in financial matters. The military selected Delgadito to represent the Navajos, in recognition of his role in encouraging them to come to the Bosque and because he had some education (he could write his name). He also forced his band to work diligently, and he had made two large deliveries of fodder for $2,000 approximately, at a rate of seventeen dollars per ton. Also, a sum of $2,589 was turned over to Lorenzo Labadie. He received $2,000 drawn from the Navajo Fund in payment for sheep from his personal flock. The remaining $589 was credited to the Apache fund for deliveries of fodder to the quartermaster.[23]

Crocker worried about the arrival of the Indian goods from the East. The weather had turned cold, and many of the Indians, especially the children, were destitute of clothing. Unless the goods arrived soon, there would be "great suffering." The Indians had been informed long ago that these goods were on their way, and the Navajos were making constant and persistent inquiries about their arrival. Many were beginning to think that the promised gifts were another example of the White Man's bad faith. Crocker asked Carleton for word as to when the goods were expected.[24]

On October 22 Labadie reported to Superintendent Steck on the Mescaleros. During the previous year their conduct had been admirable. They had requested a school for their children and would have sent them to the sessions, except that they flatly refused to associate with the Navajos. Furthermore, two of the Apache chiefs had been baptized, an indication of their desire to be civilized. So far as Labadie knew, the Mescaleros had obeyed all of the orders given them by the military and had gained the respect of everyone at the Bosque.[25]

Unfortunately, the Mescaleros had a poor harvest. They produced 125 fanegas of wheat, 12 fanegas of corn, and 3 of beans. Wheat straw exceeded 15,555 pounds, and corn forage totaled 39,200 pounds. Individually, the

Mescaleros had gathered over 60 costals (sacks) of corn, and 8 to 10 costals of beans. Additionally 12 tons of pumpkins and watermelons were gathered. This was only enough to feed them during the summer months. Previously, Labadie stated that the Apaches had raised over 7 tons of pumpkins, but they either had eaten them or had sold them illegally to the post sutler, J. A. La Rue. The majority of the Apaches depended exclusively on government rations.[26]

Crocker announced another cut in Indian rations at the Bosque; beginning in late October, each Indian would begin receiving twelve ounces of breadstuffs and eight ounces of meat per day. He explained to the Navajos and Apaches the reasons for the reduction. First, the worms had destroyed most of the local crops. Second, the Kiowas and Comanches had attacked the wagon trains bringing supplies from the states. Carson would punish those Indians, but it would take time. Third, hail and frost had ruined the cornfields in Taos and Mora counties, where the contractors, St. Vrain and Maxwell, had large farms. Finally, there now were simply more Indians at the Bosque than the military had anticipated. Crocker also announced he was introducing a new rationing procedure to curb excessive food distribution. Shortly thereafter, he tried issuing cardboard ration tickets to the Indians. Rations, however, dwindled faster than expected, as the Navajos managed to duplicate the tickets. Consequently, he issued metal tickets with stamped serial numbers.[27]

Carleton cast about for methods to improve the quality of food. He suggested that Crocker turn one of the two storehouses at the Bosque into a bakery. Here, the military would construct a set of ovens, and the Indians would be given rations of bread instead of flour. Bread would be more economical than the tortilla-like substances the Navajos cooked and consumed. Carleton reemphasized the need to restrict the Indians to twenty ounces of food per day and to insist that they make soup. When the next planting time came, the Indians must sow a great quantity of wheat. During the summer past, hungry Indians had eaten a large quantity of corn before it ripened, but they would not be able to do the same thing with wheat. Finally, the Indians must understand that the government was doing the best it could for them, but they would starve if proper steps were not taken.[28]

Crocker held a council with the various Navajo chiefs. He explained Carleton's instructions regarding rationing. The Indians expressed no dissatisfaction but were far from cordial to the idea of less food. As Carleton also had directed, Crocker stated that money from the Indian Fund would be used to purchase sheep to be consumed as part of their ration. The Indians were happy with the idea of buying sheep to increase their property, but they balked at buying their own rations. Crocker also tried to get the Navajos to sell some of their horses, but he found it was impossible to do so.

Crocker also endeavored to discover how the sutler La Rue had obtained the pumpkins he had up for sale. An investigation convinced him that La Rue had not made purchases from the Indians; instead he had obtained them from a private garden cultivated by Captain Calloway, when he had been Superintendent of Farms. At any rate, because the price La Rue demanded for the pumpkins was far too high, Crocker refused to purchase any.[29]

Carleton went to great lengths to secure food for the Navajos. He wrote to Captain Herbert M. Enos, Quartermaster at Fort Union, the main supply point for the southwestern posts, instructing him to issue only oats, grain, and bran, instead of corn fodder, to the government animals. The corn was to go to the Indians at the Bosque. The General also ordered Enos to purchase all the corn and oats that William Kronig (a Carleton supporter) and others living on the Rio Mora had for sale, paying nine dollars per fanega. Kronig had 2,000 fanegas for sale. The high price, three dollars above the average rate, induced everyone who possessed corn to bring it in. Carleton believed that it might be necessary to offer an even higher price. Enos could use every inducement to get individuals to deliver directly to Fort Sumner, tacking on an additional amount for transportation expenses. The emergency was great, Carleton said, and the army had to get enough grain to last until the next summer. He would not hesitate "between feeding the Indians on the Reservation and public animals. Humanity and the obligations of our treaties demand that we shall feed them first," even if he had to slaughter and issue every public animal in the Department of New Mexico.[30]

With difficulty, Carleton obtained 4,000 sheep from Rio Moro and sent them to the Bosque. He hoped that the Indians would use the wool for weaving blankets for the small children and that they would prepare the skins as clothing. He ordered the Navajos to dig circular pits four feet deep — as protection from the winter cold — with steps cut on the south side for an entrance. On the floor of the pits they were to place coarse reed grass or wild hay. Such an arrangement would be warmer than the huts which the Indians occupied. Furthermore, timber was scarce, and the pits required no lumber. In this way the Indian children, whose welfare apparently concerned Carleton, would be protected from the chilling winds.[31]

On October 30 Carleton forwarded a report to the Adjutant General in Washington concerning the problem of subsisting the Navajos and the Apaches at the Bosque Redondo. He repeated his usual refrains about the Navajos growing enough food on the reservation to subsist themselves, and he blamed the unfortunate strife of recent months solely on "a visitation of God" which no human forecast could have prevented. Regarding Superintendent Steck's arguments, Carleton declared that the Navajos could not be returned to their homeland, for such a move would mean another costly war. The future of New Mexico and Arizona depended upon "the determination and ability of the General Government to hold this formidable tribe," he declared. The system that proved cheapest was best for the government, but he emphasized that the success of the Bosque would be a question of "the long run."

Carleton inquired about the long-expected supplies from the Indian Bureau, the fruit of the Congressional appropriation. Thousands of women and children needed blankets. The Indians, having been told so long ago of the purchases, were growing discontented. Help was needed immediately, and twenty-five hundred head of good cattle must be sent out at once. If necessary they must be purchased in the open market. The situation was desperate.[32]

Carleton made a concerted effort to increase the acreage in cultivation. At Crocker's suggestion he reassigned Captain Calloway, former superintendent of farms (currently superintending Indian labor) to oversee the Navajo and Apache farming at the Bosque. The farms had to be enlarged. Calloway estimated the proposed enlargement would bring the total acreage to nearly 9,000.

He felt he could requisition from Labadie the Apaches needed for laborers. Calloway also assumed charge of all farming equipment the post quartermaster had loaned the agency. He hoped Labadie would cooperate and give him the use of the agency's farming implements as well. Calloway also was to enlarge the irrigation ditches and have all the fields plowed and planted as quickly as possible.

To expand the farms, Calloway found it was necessary to relocate some of the Indians, particularly the Navajos living north of the post. Acting promptly, he moved the present villages to elevated ground on the east side of the main ditch (acequia madre), which ran along the eastern edge of the farms. He resettled the Indians by clan or band. The Cebolletan Navajos presented a touchy problem. The other Navajos did not want to live near them because of their long-time friendship with the whites. Moreover, the Cebolettans had begun the construction of fairly substantial adobe dwellings on a site selected by Kit Carson. Although they did not have to move for the present, Calloway ordered them to stop construction on additional houses.[33]

Carleton's Indian policy became an important issue in the elections of 1864. Opponents of the General and his friends pointed to the growing problems of the Bosque. They sought to discredit his backers and turn them out of office. The fact that the Indians had not been able to raise a crop, that depredations had continued, even coming from the reservation, and that prices had taken a great jump, turned most of New Mexico's voters against the righteous general. Carleton himself clouded the picture by announcing openly that he was a former Democrat and now supported General McClellan for the presidency. William F. M. Arny, Territorial Secretary and Acting Governor in the absence of Governor Connelly, became Carleton's most vociferous critic. When the election was over, local politicians who backed Carleton's efforts suffered resounding defeats. Although the election had little impact upon the reservation, it revealed a distaste for Carleton's policy, and it gained attention in Washington. Carleton would have to make certain the experiment succeeded or risk his military career.[34]

On November 5 Superintendent Steck sent his annual report to Acting Indian Commissioner Charles E. Mix. Several weeks before he had forwarded his estimated needs for the New Mexico Superintendency for the coming year. He projected that the Apache tribe would requite a total of $8,000; and if the Navajos returned to a reservation in their own country, they would only need $200,000. He did not include an estimate of the expenses to maintain the Navajos at the Bosque, believing that the Congress would refuse to consider the amount he thought necessary — a figure he set at $1,250,000. In his annual report he continued his attack on the Bosque. He described the paralyzing crop failures in New Mexico and inquired about the supplies purchased with the special Congressional appropriation. Purchasing of provisions in New Mexico had become impossible due to the crop losses and inflated prices. Steck blamed the inflation on the gigantic Bosque Redondo contracting system, and he hoped that the Indian Department would not support the "ruinous policy."[35]

To avoid continued high costs, Carleton counseled Crocker about planting. The Indians must draw seed from wheat on hand, and he estimated that 300,000 pounds of wheat would sow 3,000 acres. Although the seed requirement reduced the amount of stores, Crocker dutifully set aside the 300,000 pounds. He also had a separate cornfield planted, where the Indians would be allowed to eat unripened ears, thereby preventing the plundering which had destroyed a large part of the fall crop. Trying to conserve every possible ounce of nourishment, Carleton even suggested that the blood from slaughtered animals be saved. The Indians could make blood puddings like the French; these would be particularly nutritious for the orphan Indian children attending the reservation school.[36]

Despite these plans, the Indians at the Bosque grew hungry and restless. In November Crocker tried to seek out several Indians who had butchered a steer belonging to a Mr. Giddings, who lived near the reservation, and announced that future depredations or thefts would be punished by executions. Forcing the Indians to watch, Crocker personally compensated Giddings for the steer, drawing on the Indian Fund, which they had accumulated from the sale of fodder. He hoped it would be an object lesson. Another incident occurred when the water level of the Pecos suddenly dropped during a dry spell. Employees of the Navajo farm, both military and civilian, confronted Carillo, Labadie's majordomo for the Apache farm, and charged that he had diverted too much water to the Mescalero fields. They threatened Carillo with death if it happened again.[37]

A question also arose over Indian land assignment. Informed that the Apaches would be moved to expand the farms, Labadie proposed that they be placed at the north end of the new farmland. Crocker disagreed vehemently with the suggestion. The Navajo *ricos* already occupied that land, having been told that if they settled there they would not be moved. The military did not dare anger these Navajos of wealth and position. Crocker and Labadie then examined a site south of the post for the Apaches and decided the Indians should be placed there. With this arranged, the fort acted as a barrier between the two tribes, with the post canal furnishing water for them. Crocker directed Calloway, as soon as the more pressing work terminated, to dig an acequia for the Apache farms to be opened south of the post.

Rationing remained a thorny problem. Crocker issued rations every third day, rather than every second, as Carleton suggested. If he had followed instructions the Indians would not have worked at all. The Indians watched closely whenever animals were butchered and then returned the next day for their ration. On the third day they went out in the fields to work. Crocker was careful not to press the Indians too hard, as it was difficult for them to labor on the short rations.

Crocker also discarded Carleton's suggestion for a bakery. In the first place there was no wood in the area for the ovens. Also, if baked and issued in loaves, the bread would be consumed by the able-bodied men before they left the issue point, leaving nothing for the sick and young. Instead, Crocker issued flour and recommended that it be cooked as a soup, thereby compelling the Indians to take the flour home to prepare it. This placed the food in the hands of the women and gave them some influence in the distribution.[38]

The Santa Fe *Weekly New Mexican* on November 11 commented on the rising prices in the territory. How could a laboring man, working for a dollar a day, buy flour selling for sixteen dollars per hundred pounds and corn for ten? And the price could go even higher! The advertisements in the Santa Fe *Weekly Gazette* predicted that 4,000,000 pounds of breadstuffs would be required to feed the Navajos and Apaches at the Bosque — breadstuffs that the working man needed to feed his family. Speculators were buying up all available supplies for the explicit purpose of selling to the government at a handsome profit. Already want and misery were being felt among the poorer New Mexicans. The newspaper urged all people to husband their resources and "guard against the dark future" that lay before them.[39]

Indians at the Bosque continued to complain of the miniscule ration. They were hungry and could not live on the amount issued to them. Crocker told Carleton in mid-November that the Navajos probably exaggerated their suffering, but he personally felt that the ration was barely enough to keep them going. Moreover, he had reduced the ration, and it required extraordinary vigilance to prevent the Indians from stealing everything that resembled food. Frequently the post commander had counseled with the Indians and explained the government's position. It was useless to talk with them, as they did not seem to comprehend the necessity requiring their reduced food allowance. Appeals to their pride were fruitless. Crocker's views of the Indians were changing. The only talents the Indians had, he said, were tricks of rascality to satisfy their hunger. They felt no obligation to the government for the favors they had received. The longer Crocker commanded at Sumner, the more discouraged he felt about the policy.

Regarding the farm, Crocker felt that minimal progress was being made. Most of the labor, including all the plowing, was being done by soldiers. Hopefully Calloway could soon place more Indian labor in the fields. If the army forced the Indians to do more work, there could be more unrest. Their labor, however, would prove valuable in preparing the ground for planting. The Indians had worked on the ditches previously when offered increased rations, usually the entrails of slaughtered animals. The Indians were so hungry that an armed guard accompanied these entrails when they were transported along the road.

At the same time, the school had made little progress. Indian children came only because of the issue of daily rations inside the schoolroom. The same children rarely came two days in a row, and most of them were orphans who had no adults to procure their rations. The school was being operated in the Indian Hospital, still under construction. When completed it would be more than adequate to accommodate both the school and the sick.

Previously Carleton had written Commissioner Dole, requesting that the Indian Bureau survey the boundaries of the reservation and make a large contribution to the Indian school. Dole wrote Secretary Usher that no funds existed for a reservation survey, commenting that the idea was another scheme to get the Indian Bureau to acknowledge responsibility for the Navajos. Regarding the school, the only funds available would be from the Congressional appropriation. To take such money would deprive the Indians of clothing and tools. Dole rejoiced in Carleton's zeal to educate the Indians and had confidence in them, but recommended that his request be denied.

Several rooms in the hospital had been completed, and a few patients were admitted. The surgeon experienced great difficulty in getting Indians to apply for treatment. Most of the sick Indians preferred their own doctors. Crocker called these doctors the "worst class of humbugs," who often deprived a whole family of clothing for a few days of attending a sick member.

No friendly feeling existed between the Navajos and the Apaches. Constantly one tribe committed small depredations against the other, killing stock and increasing tension. One cause of trouble stemmed from a Navajo superstition that the toenails and fingernails of a dead enemy, obtained secretly, constituted an effective charm when placed in the knowing hand of a Navajo doctor. At night small Navajo parties hunted out the secret Apache burials of the Apache dead to mutilate the bodies. These nocturnal forays had been "the cause of serious and repeated complaint on the part of the Apaches." *[40]

Colorado State Historical Society

Colonel Jesse Leavenworth, special agent, in charge of purchasing supplies for the Navajos, with a $100,000 congressional appropriation.

In the meantime, Special Agent Jesse Leavenworth had traveled east to New York City to purchase goods for the Bosque Redondo. On July 29, he wrote Indian Commissioner Dole that there was no time to take bids, and it would be necessary to make purchases on the open market. He thereupon spent $17,000 for goods. Some of the money may have been paid to an eastern firm for excessively high-priced merchandise so as to establish a high market price for Indian goods in the St. Louis–Leavenworth area, where Leavenworth hoped to reap large profits with his friends, Thomas Carney and Thomas C. Stevens, local merchants.

---

*Crocker reported that his soldiers had captured three Navajos who had been committing depredations for the past year. They had been identified by Delgadito, who had been in a skirmish with them the previous spring. They were believed to have been responsible for killing Lieutenant Gilbert. Delgadito and other Navajo leaders thought the three had come to the Bosque for the purpose of running off stock.

*Thomas Carney, of the firm Carney and
Stevens, received most of the benefit from
the $100,000 Navajo appropriation.*

Leavenworth purposely delayed his departure from New York so his
fellow agent, William Baker, would also be forced to make purchases in
Kansas and Missouri without bids. At Weston, Missouri, where he had been
waiting for Leavenworth for nearly two weeks, Baker wrote Commissioner
Dole on August 19 that "every day's delay must be made up by quick purchases at the sacrifice of economy." Finally Leavenworth arrived, and the two
men began procuring Indian goods. Because of their late start, it became
obvious that the shipment to the Bosque could not arrive until December 1.

Leavenworth instructed Baker to make purchases in Weston, while he
proceeded to buy supplies in Leavenworth, Kansas. Because the law demanded
that both men sign purchase bills, Baker would return from Weston on
Mondays and examine the forms for a day or two. There was little else for
him to do, as he had been unsuccessful in finding goods in Weston that were
priced at a resonable level. Fortunately Leavenworth had been able to make
large purchases. All of Leavenworth's dealings were with Carney and Stevens,
a large and supposedly reputable establishment. By the time the purchases
had been completed, only the goods secured in New York were from another
firm. Thomas Carney was a former governor of Kansas, and Thomas Stevens
was active in the campaign then being waged for General George B. McClellan
for the presidency.

At the first meeting between Baker and Leavenworth, Leavenworth had
informed Baker that Commissioner Dole desired that they place most of their
orders with Carney and Stevens. Baker was somewhat skeptical, but Leaven-

worth produced a draft from Dole to the firm for $10,000. Baker then endorsed the purchase price. When Leavenworth then presented bills from Carney and Stevens, Baker again grew suspicious. The long itemized lists had the prices for the individual items razored off. Upon questioning, the wily Leavenworth replied that Baker had only to endorse the total purchase price. He had cut off the long listings from the bills, because they merely used up postage when the bills were forwarded to Washington.

For several weeks the two agents continued to make arrangements for supplies. Finally, Baker was convinced that irregularities were occurring. He confronted Leavenworth and accused him of misconduct. Leavenworth promptly explained that he had made all of the purchases because he was the director of purchases and Baker was his assistant. Baker was infuriated and threatened to go to the president, for he had been appointed as an equal to Jesse Leavenworth. The harried Leavenworth then wisely soothed Baker's feelings by paying his salary of one thousand dollars in advance. Baker next decided to accompany the goods purchased in New York and Kansas to Santa Fe. He was suspicious of Leavenworth, but he lacked concrete proof. He had never seen the complete detailed purchase lists.

Fewer shipments than in previous months arrived at the Bosque in November of 1864. Lucien B. Maxwell delivered a herd of two hundred thirty-five cattle and 2,300 pounds of flour, receiving $9,355 for the cattle and $964 for the flour. The flour averaged about forty dollars per hundred pounds, an outrageous price, indicative of the acute shortage. Other small deliveries were made for the quartermaster. Occasionally there were complaints. For example, on November 25 a freighter protested that the government paid him for hauling goods one hundred thirty-one miles from Fort Union, whereas the actual distance measured at least one hundred fifty-eight miles. A canyon on the road had proved impassable for oxen and wagons, causing the extra miles.[41]

With great delight, Carleton in late November received formal approval from the War Department to take complete control of the Indians at the military reserve at the Bosque Redondo. Receiving letters from Carleton complaining about his problems with the Indian Bureau and the poor showing by Labadie's Apache farm, Secretary of War Edwin M. Stanton endorsed the statement that "Indian agents should not be permitted to interfere or exercise any authority on this military reservation." Until the Indian Bureau decided to assume full responsibility for the Bosque, the military would have absolute control. Obviously, Labadie's days at the Bosque were numbered.[42]

In November and December the Santa Fe *Weekly New Mexican* published numerous stories of Indian depredations. In the Pecos country, eight Apaches, half of them women, attacked the ranch of Felix Ulibarri, killing five persons and running off his livestock. Ulibarri pursued the Indians as far as Fort Sumner. Later, the stolen animals were found in the Navajo camps on the reserve. Fourteen persons testified in a sworn affidavit that the Indians were Mescaleros. In western New Mexico, on the Puerco River, Navajo bands drove off five hundred head of sheep. These raiders acted so polite and cordial, the newspaper said, they "seemed like the Navajo gentlemen at the Bosque." In San Miguel County, the citizens became alarmed by the depredations and drew up a long petition demanding the removal of the Indians from the Pecos.[43]

Carleton now decided to organize a permanent police force for the reservation. He directed the Provost Marshal at Fort Sumner, Lieutenant L. O. Faringhy, First New Mexico Cavalry, to begin forming the force. Faringhy may have included some Indians in the force. The police were to keep the Indians from depredating upon each other and from stealing government property. The Indians were to remain in their designated camps, and they were not to loiter around the garrison or company quarters. No Indians could visit the soldiers, and the soldiers were not allowed in the Indian camps unless on official business. Finally, the police had to watch the irrigation ditches. An attempt was being made to destroy parts of the acequias to hamper farming operations. The ditches must be kept in repair and clean. Indians, or possibly soldiers, had thrown garbage or waste in the canals, which also served as a water supply both for the garrison and the Indian camps.[44]

In December Indian complaints at the Bosque reached a new high, and the authorities feared that both Apaches and Navajos might bolt the reservation. Informed of this situation Carleton ordered Crocker to increase the daily Indian ration to twenty-four ounces — twelve of meat and twelve of breadstuffs, thus doubling the ration they had been receiving. Carleton also worried that the Indians would tell Steck that they were starving. He directed Crocker to warn Steck not to create trouble on visiting the Bosque. If the Superintendent made any unsettling statements, the military should bodily remove him from the reserve.[45]

National Archives

Soldiers counting Indians, possibly new arrivals, seated on the ground.

The number of Navajos at the Bosque increased. Another group turned themselves in at Fort Wingate in early October and were started to the Bosque. This group totaled 1,020, with 243 men, 534 women, and 443 children. Lieutenant Charles Hubbell, First New Mexico Cavalry, escorted them to Sumner. With the party rode the notorious Pino Baca, probably a half-breed. Baca had escaped from a guard at the Bosque in April, where he was being held after the Navajo leaders charged him with selling Indian children into peonage. The charges were well documented. Upon his arrival at Sumner in November, Baca quickly found himself placed in irons and locked in the guardhouse to await Carleton's orders.

Cattle stealing still continued at the Bosque. On the night of December 1, a renegade Navajo band stole several head from the government herd. The chiefs tried their best to prevent these depredations and keep order. When a Navajo killed a horse belonging to another Indian, the Indian leaders held a consultation. They concluded that if the culprit was turned over to the soldiers, he would be put in the guardhouse for a time and then returned to the camps, as bad as ever. They decided to execute the man, and promptly killed him with knives. Commenting on the incident, Crocker believed the leaders had erred in executing the fellow, but he felt the act would have a deterrent effect upon other crimes.[46]

On December 6, Governor Connelly, a staunch Carleton supporter, delivered his annual message. As expected, he spoke glowingly of the Bosque experiment. The reservation, he said, was a complete success, far exceeding the expectations of its most enthusiastic proponents. The Indians on the reserve were peaceful and contented, and by spring not one Navajo would remain west of the Rio Grande. He called the reservation the best thing that had ever befallen the Territory of New Mexico. The location of the Navajos on the Bosque would not be a permanent feature, Connelly said in conclusion, but simply "their first day's march to that great Reservation of all Indian tribes," the Indian country to the east. Carleton also hoped that the Navajos might eventually be moved east.

Too many scare stories had been spread about the reservation, Connelly declared. One stated that if disease broke out the Indians would flee and the troops would not be able to hold them. The Navajos had caught diseases in their own country and had not fled that region, he wryly remarked. The critics, of course, wanted a reserve in Navajo country, but even if one could be found, the Indians could not be placed there. They would block the main avenue of trade with Arizona. Moreover, the great Railroad and Telegraph Line from the Mississippi River to the Gulf of California would pass through their old country. The Bosque Reservation, Connelly stated, had been chosen with great care as to soil, climate, and location. The experiment was succeeding, and he felt the critics had no ground for complaint.[47]

In Santa Fe, Steck finally heard from his assistant William Baker in early December. Baker was at Fort Union, and the wagon train carrying the Navajo supplies was due to arrive in the next few days, bound for the Bosque. Steck immediately wrote to Washington for instructions regarding the distribution of the supplies. He foresaw trouble with the military authorities at the Bosque. When no instructions came, he took the matter into his own hands and left

Santa Fe for Fort Union. When the train arrived he planned to take charge of it and accompany it to Sumner. The supplies, particularly blankets, would arrive none too soon, as the weather had already turned freezing cold.[48]

Both Baker and Leavenworth were supposed to accompany the wagons to New Mexico and turn them over to Steck. Leavenworth, however, told Baker that he planned to travel on ahead. When the train reached Council Grove, Baker, who was accompanying the supplies, met Leavenworth by chance. Leavenworth gave an awkward excuse for his presence, claiming that urgent business demanded he return quickly to the East. Baker continued with the wagons down the Santa Fe Trail in New Mexico, buffeted constantly by snow and sleet, which slowed their progress.[49]

At Fort Union, Steck conferred with Baker about the purchases. Leavenworth had sent along unsigned bills, typical of his shady operations, but Baker fortunately carried a set of signed bills concerning some of the purchases. On comparison there were discrepancies between the two sets, with Leavenworth's merchandise seeming to cost more. Furthermore, the wagonmaster failed to deliver a bill of lading with the train, but that may have been a coincidence. Leavenworth "forgot" to arrange for payment of the teamsters, costing the New Mexico Superintendency an additional $5,000. Both Baker and Steck sensed that the shipment was irregular, but Steck realized the supplies must be rushed to the Bosque. Steck put John Ward, a former agent to the Navajos, in charge of the train, and the wagons pulled out for the Pecos.[50]

When the goods reached the Bosque, Crocker ordered a board of officers to inspect and count the supplies. On December 17 Captains Bristol and Murphy reported on the inventory. The supplies included many items not essential for Navajo welfare, such as nails and hunks of steel. Admittedly, the blacksmith's shop could use them. Clothing and agricultural implements were sorely needed.

The supplies were distributed to the Navajos on Christmas Eve of 1864. Steck supervised the distribution, dispensing gifts to nearly 7,800 Navajos who sat quietly on the cold ground in a circle around the superintendent and his assistants, Ward and Labadie. As Steck handed out the supplies it became clear that Leavenworth, Carney, and Stevens, and perhaps others, had engineered a gigantic swindle. Clearly there were too few supplies for the size of the purchase. However, Steck saw that every man, woman, and child received some article. The men were given brightly colored red and blue blankets; bolts of cloth, cut into pieces 2½ yards in length, were handed out to the women. The badly needed blankets and cloth rapidly ran out, and many of the Indians ended up with awls, buttons, or beads. Others received sheep shears, scissors, knives, hoes, shovels, and axes. Clothing, of course, was the real prize. The Indians had anticipated the supplies for several months; they were bitterly disappointed with what they received.

Crocker appointed another board to inspect the quantity and cost of the Indian Department's supplies. In examining the purchase orders, the officers reported that the prices paid, particularly for blankets, were exorbitant. Blankets, for example, cost between $18.50 and $22 per pair, while the military usually paid only $5.85 for a pair of equal or better quality. Other supplies had been over-priced in a like manner. Captain Robert Lusby, who in civilian life had been a merchant, estimated $20,000 for goods and $10,000 for shipment. The post sutler, J. A. LaRue, estimated the value of the supplies at $30,000. Carney and Stevens, the principal firm from which supplies had been procured, had in collusion with Leavenworth apparently defrauded the government of nearly $60,000. Baker was furious when he learned that he had been duped. Leavenworth's "bad reputation smells from the Missouri to the Rio Grande," he wrote. Baker vowed to kill Leavenworth if he ever saw him again.*[51]

Steck was baffled by the complexity of the operation, but he defended the shipment of goods, believing the military was simply trying to attack the Indian Department. On February 15, 1865, he wrote Commissioner Dole that the military estimate of $30,000 would not even cover the cost of blankets at Eastern prices. However, the evidence was undeniable; the Indians had been cheated out of more than $60,000 in supplies. Carleton now had ammunition to continue his battle with the Indian Department.

In the last six months of 1864, the Bosque Redondo experiment had suffered two serious setbacks. The harvest, which would have quieted most of the complaints about the high cost of the reserve, had been almost totally destroyed. The long-awaited supplies, when they arrived, proved seriously inadequate for approximately 8,000 Navajos. Depredations in New Mexico increased, and opposition to the reservation had mushroomed. Finally, the conflict between Steck and Carleton had taken on new dimensions as each arm of the government seemed locked in a death struggle to discredit the other. The year ended on a dismal note. The future of the reservation looked uncertain. It was clear that many Navajos would be buried that winter, in the cold strange Pecos country, for want of food and clothing.

---

*Jesse Leavenworth's career was varied and controversial. Dishonorably discharged from the army, Leavenworth used his friendship with important Washington personages to help reverse the black mark to an honorable discharge. Baker tried unsuccessfully to bring Leavenworth to justice by publicly exposing the affair to Secretary Usher. After the swindle with Carney and Stevens, Leavenworth continued his career as an Indian agent on the Plains, where he was accused of trafficking in stolen cattle. The Kansas Legislature went so far as to adopt a resolution calling for his removal. A clever man, Leavenworth always remained one step ahead of his critics.

5

A Controversial Experiment

"The Democratic Party 'favors the benefit of the lazy thieving Indian at the expense of the honest and industrious white man. We are for the white man. We hold that the people, the farmers and stock growers, should not be crowded off their lands for the benefit of a pack of thieving redskins. An Indian steals a herd of mules or flock of sheep, delivers himself up as a prisoner, and then the Department Commander confirms his title to the plunder, and the unfortunate loser must submit to the wrong. The theft is legalized and the thief goes rejoiceing [sic] on his way to "Carletonia's rich and verdant lands" there to be feasted, till he recruits for another raid. Should the white man be deprived of his rights and property that the Indian may enjoy them? Should the white man hunger that the Indian may rejoice in a full belly?' "

Santa Fe *New Mexican* [Republican]

"Henry B. Bristol [was] promoted to Brevet Lieutenant Colonel on March 13, 1865, 'for his untiring zeal and energy in controlling the Navajo tribe of Indians at the Bosque Redondo, and for his praiseworthy efforts in advancing their condition from that of savages to that of civilized men.' "

DURING THE WINTER OF 1864 the Bosque Redondo suffered further setbacks. Many Indians died because of freezing weather and malnutrition, while others fled the reservation and began committing depredations. Hostility to Carleton's operation of the reserve became so intense that he was forced to make a public defense of his program. Problems of securing supplies for the Indians continued, complicated by the discovery of swindling among the government employees. During these months also, the long smouldering conflict between the military and the Indian departments in New Mexico flared up. Superintendent Steck, feeling defeated at every turn, resigned his position the following spring.

By the fall of 1864, the controversial Bosque Redondo experiment had become a major issue in New Mexican politics, and Carleton felt compelled

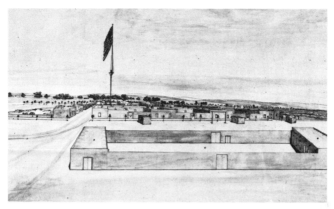

Fort Sumner, New Mexico, viewed from the east.

to answer his critics in a public statement. As early as November he had planned a reply, but the politically astute general waited for the most opportune moment. Finally, in early January, Carleton's defense of the Bosque Redondo, entitled "To the People of New Mexico" was printed as a pamphlet for distribution to the members of the Territorial Legislature, who had been urged by Governor Connelly to take a stand on Indian policy. The well-reasoned statement by Carleton was probably instrumental in the legislature's adoption of a resolution fully supporting and commending the experimental Indian policy.

In his open letter "To the People of New Mexico," Carleton outlined the history of Navajo–New Mexican relations over the years and discussed his hopes for the Bosque reservation. He stated that the public controversy had grown so large that it compelled him to speak. Citing a long list of treaties made with the Navajos, he reminded his audience that they had failed to achieve peace. Shifting to a moralistic tone, the General stated that by removing the Navajos to the Bosque, he felt that he was doing his duty as a servant of the Almighty. He then proceeded to attack Steck, Arny, and other opponents of removal, stigmatizing their opposition as prompted by selfish interests.

Carleton devoted his address primarily to the specific charges which his critics had leveled against the reservation. First, he blasted the charge that the Navajos were Arizona Indians and therefore an Arizona problem. He questioned that a majority of the tribe resided in the Territory of Arizona, and he emphasized that New Mexicans, not Arizonans, suffered primarily from Navajo depredations. Another charge was that the Bosque Redondo had caused sheepmen to lose one of their best grazing areas. Carleton pointed out that this section long had been a dangerous place to run sheep, adding that many sheepmen had lost their flocks there to Plains Indians. Would the Navajos at the Bosque arise and attack the people? He dismissed this charge with a rhetorical question: How could 10,000 destitute Indians attack 100,000 well-armed citizens? He apparently ignored the fact that the commander at Sumner had warned that the garrison could not prevent the Indians from leaving if they chose to do so.

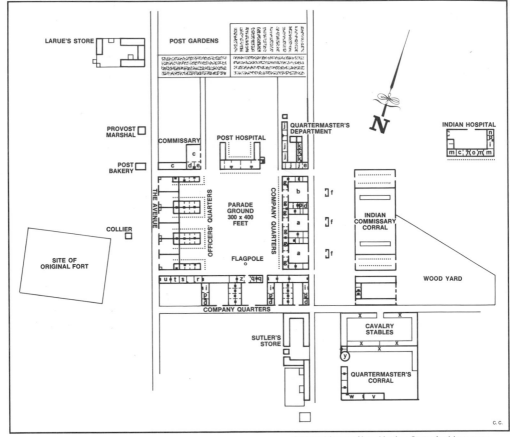

The layout of Fort Sumner.

Adapted from a *New Mexico State Archives* map

a. Cavalry	j. Storeroom	s. Seed stores
b. Infantry	k. Clerks' room	t. Indian Agent's office
c. Stores	l. Corn cribs	u. Council room
d. Sergeants' room	m. Ward	v. Carpenter's shop
e. Office	n. Wood house	w. Blacksmith's shop
f. Sink	o. Dispensary	x. Stables
g. Squad room	p. Kitchen	y. Lookout cupola
h. Hall	q. Prison	z. Guardhouse
i. Dining room	r. Adjutant's office	

Finally, Carleton turned to the most important charge: that the cost of feeding the Navajos had raised food prices in New Mexico. He acknowledged that prices had risen slightly, but he attributed the phenomenon to currency inflation, not to army contracts. At any rate, he believed that New Mexicans profited by the large expenditures for foodstuffs. He failed to mention that prices for such basic commodities as wheat and corn had tripled, nor did he comment on the fact that contractors were profitting most. Carleton concluded his statement with the old refrain that if the worms had not eaten the crops the Navajos would have raised enough food to carry them for a year. His statement quickly gave his critics more ammunition to continue their assault upon his Indian program.[1]

In the meantime, life at the Bosque Redondo continued to be hectic. Carleton's officers reported some success in getting the Indians to work the fields. Under Calloway's supervision, Indian crews, led by soldier overseers, had started plowing and harrowing, despite the great shortage of tools. Captain Gorham directed one party in planting trees, hopefully to provide firewood. After a work stoppage for two months, the Cebolletan Navajos resumed construction of their village. The unpopular Cebolletans resided in the middle of a farming area. The military thought it was wise to keep them there and away from the other Indians.

Following Carleton's instructions Crocker ordered that a model Indian hut be built to show the Navajos the best way to combat the winter's chill. However, after examining a number of Indian homes or hogans, he found them the best that could be constructed with available materials. It would be a mistake, Crocker wrote Carleton, to make warmer huts, for the Indian homes were too warm already. The hogans were conical, crowned with a thick layer of earth, and built over an excavation. A small door faced north, away from the wind. Carleton concurred.

Rations posed a never-ending problem. Crocker increased the meat ration by a quarter of a pound, but he still believed that the Indians should have an additional quarter pound. "If this could be done," he wrote Carleton, he would be able to "manage this delicate matter without further trouble to you." Also, he noted that a problem had developed in keeping records of the weight of meat rations issued. Captain Prince G. D. Morton, the commissary officer, made deductions on his books for shrinkage, the head, pluck, and other parts that were not included in the regular issue. However, he had been showing the entire weight as having been issued, making a considerable difference in his favor every month. Crocker directed Morton to go back over his books and take up the difference. When Morton questioned Crocker's orders and appealed to Carleton to intervene, saying the task would be sizeable, and perhaps unnecessary, Carleton grew wary of the young officer and ordered the books corrected.[2]

In December, the military made a count of the Navajos at the Bosque. This census revealed a total population of 8,354, or 1,782 families, living in 1,276 lodges.* The Indians owned 3,038 horses, 6,962 sheep, 2,757 goats,

---

*A month later the count was 8,577 Navajos, 465 Mescaleros, and 20 Gila Apaches. In the Navajo camps there were 2,361 men, 2,742 women, 3,180 children, and 274 infants. The Mescaleros numbered 113 men, 153 women, 138 children, and one infant. Ten Navajos died during January, but no causes of death were cited.

and 143 mules. Each family averaged five persons and possessed two horses and four sheep. Wealth was not evenly distributed; many families owned no livestock. Food was scarce. The Indians refused to eat their goats for they provided milk, nor could they sacrifice their sheep because of their wool. At times, however, they did kill sheep, especially when they thought the military had issued spoiled meat. Although several families on the Bosque owned as many as forty head of sheep, the flocks were relatively small in comparison with the size of the flocks which many of them had possessed in the past. The survey also noted that the Navajo women labored daily at 630 looms in an effort to weave blankets to combat the bitter cold.[3]

Judge T. W. Woolson, a Special Indian Commissioner, arrived at the Bosque in early January of 1865 to collect material for a report to a Senate committee. At the Commissioner's request, Steck drew up a lengthy statement for him. Steck predicted that the reservation experiment must fail. In the first place, the Navajo people were divided. Many Navajos, perhaps 5,000, still lived in the old homeland. They were principally *ricos,* who possessed substantial flocks. To conquer them and bring them to the Bosque required enormous expense. Steck also estimated that five to six Navajos fled the reserve every day. Furthermore, the reservation lacked firewood. The large cottonwood groves along the river which had given the area its name had virtually been exhausted in the construction of Fort Sumner. Only a few of the towering, majestic trees remained. To complete the fort, lumber had been hauled over one hundred miles, at a cost of $115 per 1,000 board feet. The Indians had dug up most of the local mesquite trees for fuel, and they now walked up to twelve miles for firewood. Many complained that the strain of carrying heavy loads of wood for such a long distance made them ill. Although trees had been planted for firewood, Steck felt they merely reduced the limited irrigable acres necessary for farming.

Steck concluded his statement to Judge Woolson with a comment on the cost of feeding the Indians. To subsist all the Indians at the Bosque required $3,280 per day, or about $1,250,000 per year. Whereas in their own country, the Navajos could be supported for $250,000, with only a small military force needed to control them. The Navajo country was fertile; in 1863 it had taken Colonel Carson a week to destroy the Indian fields in one area. Steck felt certain that the Navajos would be content in their own country, where shelter existed for their stock from the winter storms which swept across the plains.[4]

After a week's stay at the Bosque, Woolson left for Washington. Crocker asked him to deliver a letter addressed to his friend James Harlan, a senator of Iowa. Crocker wrote Harlan that Woolson would doubtless tell of the enormous progress being made in the "magnificent valley." Certainly the Indians had been a sizeable expense to the military, but never before had "the same number of people subsisted with the same economy." Crocker castigated the Indian Department. Knowing of the opposition of Superintendent Steck and Secretary Arny to the role of the military, Crocker stated that the Indian agents opposed the system because "they have come to regard the annuities approved by Congress as their rightful prerequisite" with which to line their pockets. He referred to the corruption and fraud involved in the $100,000 appropriation. Although Crocker made a strong case against the Indian Department, he did admit that the Leavenworth-Carney-Stevens affair had been an extreme example, even for that department.[5]

Military authorities knew that the Navajos were leaving the Bosque at every opportunity. In mid-January Crocker learned that many Navajo women escaped in the wagons of Mexicans who came to the reservation with supplies. He immediately tightened the security at the Bosque with additional pickets, and he instituted a system of passes. Indians without proper papers were not allowed to leave. When short rations were issued, he also allowed passports for hunting.[6] Crocker placed some of the blame for the Indian exodus on his troops, who had become too lax in their duties. He changed the daily schedule for the garrison, ordering two daily drills, one in the morning and the other in the afternoon. Daily he reviewed a dress parade. All commissioned and noncommissioned officers attended at least three recitations a week in tactics. Even the buglers were not exempt. Crocker ordered them to practice for two hours every day, which probably annoyed fellow soldiers greatly.[7]

Navajo stock raids continued. In one instance, a renegade band drove off all the livestock at Casa Colorado, a settlement on the east bank of the Rio Grande about thirty-three miles south of Albuquerque. Another party stole 2,000 head of sheep from Antonio Jose Otero, who had been judge of the Third Judicial District, and now resided in Peralta, on the west bank of the Rio Grande halfway between Albuquerque and Casa Colorado. Witnesses stated that the Indians came from the Bosque, as they dressed in partial army uniforms which had been issued at the reservation. Stockmen in New Mexico stated that depredations that spring were worse than ever before. In the past the stockmen had guarded against attacks from the west, but now they faced the threat of Navajo raids from both directions. On January 27 the *Weekly New Mexican* published a petition signed by 1,974 citizens requesting the removal of the Bosque reservation.[8]

Expenditures for December and January for the Bosque totaled nearly $210,000, with $36,000 spent on extra supplies. In December, C. S. Hinckley delivered 1,020 head of cattle for $92,783, or roughly 12.5¢ per pound. H. B. Denman turned over six hundred forty-two head for $41,890. C. E. Cooley, a rancher and army scout, received vouchers for 4,331 head of sheep for $15,158, or approximately $3.50 per head, up a dollar over a few months before. Andres Dold and William H. Moore delivered $21,000 worth of corn and wheat. Smaller shipments were received from Maxwell, C. W. Kitchen, and Julius Freudenthal, a recent settler in Las Cruces.[9] In January, Andres Dold contracted to deliver one million pounds of corn (at approximately 25¢ per pound) in shipments of 500,000 pounds in May, 250,000 pounds in June, and 250,000 pounds in July. To relieve the strain on the New Mexican economy, the contract required that he make the purchases in the States.[10]

Throughout the winter Captain Calloway kept the Navajos at work in the fields. Beginning on January 16, the Indians plowed sixty-six acres a week on an average, with twenty-one plows running every morning. Then Calloway started keeping the Indians in the fields all day, and the number of tilled acres soon doubled. The continual breaking of equipment posed a major problem. Everyone blamed the blacksmiths for making poor implements. Miserable weather also interfered. From February 6 to 11, temperatures dipped low, the ground froze completely, and no sod was broken. Nevertheless, by the end of the following week, the Indians had plowed a total of eight hundred fifty-five acres.[11]

Jose Gallegos, an experienced farmer hired at Crocker's request, reported to Fort Sumner in late January. According to his contract, he would give instruction on the Navajo and Apache farms, with particular attention to irrigation, supposedly his specialty. When he first saw the extent of the Bosque farms, he wondered if his experience equaled the task. Never in his entire life had he seen such an extensive farming and irrigation system.[12] Gallegos remained at Fort Sumner for two months, drawing one hundred fifty dollars per month for his efforts, plus one ration per day, quarters, and fuel.

While more Indians arrived at the Bosque Redondo, others took the opportunity to flee the reserve. On January 30 two Apache chiefs turned themselves in at Fort Sumner along with seventeen of their people. "Carcasse de Collote" and "Cavalere" told Crocker that they would have come in sooner if they had not been detained by the recent snowstorms. The remainder of their people, over two hundred in number, would arrive in a day or two. To Crocker this was a good sign. To check reports that Navajos were leaving the reservation, he sent out scouting parties toward the western passes, Puerto Carrizo and Abo Pass, believing that Indians heading west would take these routes. He also wrote the commander at Fort Stanton for news on any strange Indians in that part of the country.[13]

Learning that allegations had been made concerning his distribution of the Indian goods at the Bosque Redondo in December, Steck sought to defend himself. On February 4 he wrote Commissioner Dole that the charges and slanders were unfounded. He admitted that not all of the Indian supplies had been distributed; some were put in storage in Santa Fe and some at the Bosque. Steck declared that the cost of the supplies confused him and was perhaps too high. So far as the slander was concerned, he blamed it on Carleton, saying that such a charge could be expected from an officer who possessed such "a mean, low, and malicious spirit."[14]

Judge Joseph G. Knapp of Mesilla joined Steck in denouncing Carleton's policy. "Indians in scattered bands," he wrote Dole, were "roving everywhere" and destroying property. Moreover, other tribes, probably Comanches and Kiowas, were complaining about the Navajos and Mescaleros being located near their homeland. Knapp regarded the Bosque as a "complete barrier" between Mesilla and the States. He strongly disapproved of Carleton's policy of exterminating the Mimbres Apaches in the Pinos Altos district because it had stirred them to raid the settlements without restraint. The military had singularly failed to stabilize the Indian problem, Knapp said, and he recommended that the Department of Interior reassume the direction of Indian policy in New Mexico.[15]

Carleton was sensitive to the fact that a number of Navajos still remained in their homeland. Aware that Steck had estimated that more than 5,000 still roamed at large, Carleton took the opportunity to mail to government officials in Washington copies of a letter that presented a more realistic figure. The letter he sent reported on a contact with Manuelito's Navajo band; it stated that the Indian leader said there were only three hundred remaining in Arizona.

Directing this information to Commissioner Dole and Secretary Usher, Carleton stated in a cover letter that "the cock and bull stories that half of the Navajo tribe was still back in the Old Navajo Country have no foundation in fact."[16] A more accurate figure would probably have fallen somewhere between the estimates of Steck and Carleton.

At the Bosque Redondo, the military finally removed Agent Labadie from the reservation. Crocker had been suspicious of him for some time. In January, Labadie and Captain Morton, the commissary officer, were accused of conspiracy to steal cattle from the government. Morton was placed under arrest, and Major William McCleave, First California Cavalry, succeeded him as Acting Commissary of Subsistence.

A general court-martial assembled at Fort Sumner heard testimony concerning the conspiracy. P. J. Goodfellow, Morton's chief herder, testified that his superior had directed him to deliver seventy-five head of cattle to Labadie, who was charged forty dollars per head for the animals. When Goodfellow wisely questioned the transaction, Morton calmly told him that the cattle represented an agreement that had been made before the herder had been hired. Goodfellow then directed his helper, Guadaloupe, to drive the cattle to Labadie. He knew that the exchange of cattle or any other form of supplies was positively forbidden, and Labadie knew it, too, having been warned several times in the past. According to Goodfellow, this was not the first time that Morton had engaged in the activity. Upon receiving a beef delivery, the officer customarily divided all the cattle he received into two herds. He branded the lower herd, kept close to the post, with the government "U. S.," but the upper herd was never branded.

Testimony also revealed that on January 1 Morton ignored orders to slaughter a large number of cattle for Indian rations. When the Indians complained, Crocker sent Lieutenant Ben Fox to examine Labadie's herd, which recognized seventy head as belonging to the government, because they had grazed approximately forty miles north on the Pecos at Alamo Judo. Fox been delivered only a short time before and bore the distinctive Maxwell brand, a heart on the left hip. When Fox questioned Labadie, he pleaded ignorance about the government cattle. He denied having purchased them from Morton, and stated that someone had put them in his herd without his knowledge.

Other witnesses testified against Morton. Lieutenant Edwin J. Edgar, commanding the picket guard, reported that on one occasion he had inspected Labadie's wagon and found it loaded with sacks of corn, plows, shovels, and pickaxes belonging to the Navajo farm. The agent stated that he had purchased the articles from Captain Calloway. He also told him that he had purchased cattle from Captain Morton. A civilian employee of the quartermaster department, George W. Robinette, testified that in May of 1864 he saw Goodfellow drive off a small herd; he asked Goodfellow what he was doing. Goodfellow sarcastically retorted that back in the States the abolitionists had ruined him and he was in the process of getting even. Robinette, doing his duty, reported the affair to his superior, Captain Morton, but nothing happened.

Crocker now began to comprehend the irregularities he had spotted earlier in Morton's accounting procedures. By deducting for shrinkage and loss of weight on his books, the commissary officer had been able to build up a sizeable herd. At a later date he could sell the animals to the contractors who were always searching for beef to satisfy their contracts. The court found Morton guilty of embezzlement, and several weeks later he was dismissed from the service. Major McCleave replaced him. Although Labadie fell outside the jurisdiction of a military court, it was obvious that he would be requested to leave the reservation. Captain Calloway, who had always given Crocker an uneasy feeling, also was dismissed from the army.[17]

Despite the cold weather, Captain Calloway kept the Navajos busy in the fields during his last days as Superintendent of Indian Labor. The plowing progressed fairly well, but in February heavy snowstorms stalled the work. Labadie reported that over one hundred Indians died from exposure and other effects of the cold. On February 23 another violent blizzard struck. While Navajo families struggled vainly to keep warm in their hogans, the military forced others to continue plowing. Snow fell for three days, leaving nearly a foot on the ground; another three days passed before warmer weather came. When the fields had cleared, the Indians stoically returned to their work.[18]

During the freezing weather, two military boards reported on the supplies received during the previous two months. The wheat meal delivered by William H. Moore was poor in quality, being two-thirds ground husks, or skins of the wheat grain. As Moore repeatedly had shipped inferior grain, one board directed that the wheat problem be reported to General Carleton, the inference being that Moore should not be allowed to supply foodstuffs on government contracts. Carleton could not risk losing the support of Moore and his powerful friends, so the suggestion went unnoticed. Another board, examining cattle delivered by H. B. Denman in December, declared the animals unfit for issuance to the Indians. They had suffered a noticeable decline in weight, due to the severe frigid weather.[19]

Other evidences of fraud soon came to light. Lieutenant George W. Arnold, First New Mexico Cavalry, who had been commended in December for working out a rationing system for the Navajos, had also perfected a system for stealing some of those rations. Over a period of several weeks he held back a sizeable amount of coffee and sugar, given only to the Indian head men, and in turn sold it to fellow soldiers for a total of forty dollars. Furious at the conduct of the officer, Carleton in early March permitted Arnold to resign rather than have the spectacle of another trial. The righteous general, despite recent disclosures, vowed repeatedly that his command would not develop a reputation for corruption.

Almost simultaneously with the Arnold affair, Carleton sent orders for Labadie to leave the reservation. Eight persons involved in the sale of government cattle had already been dismissed. Labadie received notice in mid-March that "his services upon the Reservation which remains under the sole charge of the military, will not be required any longer." Carleton gave the Mescalero agent ten days to prepare his departure, and warned that if he had not left by that time, the military would escort him bodily from the reserve.[20]

With the New Mexican newspapers running stories of depredations supposedly committed by Navajos from the Bosque Redondo, Carleton decided to take stringent measures against any Indian found off the reservation without a passport. When a Navajo was apprehended in the neighborhood of Chaperito, twenty-five miles southeast of Las Vegas, and returned to Fort Sumner, Carleton ordered McCleave, unofficially in command, to have him wear a heavy ball and chain for the next two months and to be kept at hard labor. The officer also must explain to the Indians the reason for their brother's punishment. If this example did not deter further outbreaks, there would be more severe treatment for offenders.[21] These incidents must stop.

Always a large post, the garrison at Sumner in early March included five companies of troops, or two hundred and nineteen enlisted men and ten officers. The companies, however, were understrength. Many men of the post served on picket duty at strategic locations circling the reservation to prevent Indians from sneaking away to terrorize the countryside. On March 11, Crocker was relieved of command of Fort Sumner and assigned to the Army of the Cumberland. Carleton lauded the officer for his judgment and dedication. Crocker had never disagreed with his commander and occasionally had shielded him from unpleasant facts about the reservation.

Lieutenant Colonel William McCleave, dedicated to "civilizing" the Navajos and Apaches, was one of the most effective commanders of Fort Sumner.

Museum of New Mexico

Major William McCleave, the commissary officer, succeeded Crocker. Captain William L. Rynerson, First California Infantry, succeeded him as Commissary of Subsistence.* In this important position, Rynerson supervised the receipt of shipments and was closely involved in issuing rations. A native of Ireland, McCleave bore a striking physical resemblance to Carleton. Whereas the General usually wore mutton chop whiskers, with a clean shaven chin, McCleave sported a full beard. Entering the army in 1850, the new post commander had worked his way up through the ranks, and by May of 1863 he was a captain in the regular army. In that month he was commissioned a major in the First California Volunteer Cavalry. He was popular with the men and was regarded as a fine officer. By laboring conscientiously at the Bosque, McCleave had proved his dedication to the great task of civilizing the Navajos. He therefore was a logical choice for the command.[22]

---

*Twenty-nine years old and Kentucky-born, Rynerson had served under Carleton for several years and held the confidence of the superior officer.

Two days after McCleave assumed command, he presided over a ceremony that seemed to embody Carleton's efforts in New Mexico. On March 13, Captain Henry Bristol received promotions to Brevet Major and Brevet Lieutenant Colonel. Bristol, Carleton's personal representative at the Bosque, had demonstrated untiring zeal and energy in his job of controlling the Navajos. His promotion stated that he had made "praiseworthy efforts toward advancing the Navajos' condition from that of savages to that of civilized men." Carleton and high-ranking officers of the War Department believed the Bosque was accomplishing the intended goals.

Carleton informed McCleave that conditions at the Bosque Redondo must improve. If the reservation proved as unsuccessful in 1865 as it had in 1864, he felt that the government might heed the arguments of his critics. On March 10 he sent a small sack of apricot seeds for experimental planting. The next day, he stated that the ditches must be extended to irrigate the required number of acres. Also, McCleave should allocate land to individual families and have the Indian villages relocated along the ditches, a recommendation made several months before. The garrison at Sumner must realize the value of the overall program both to the Indians and to civilization, and give a hand in plowing, planting, and enlarging the ditches. While further changes were being made at the Bosque, Carleton instructed Carson that any additional Navajos who came in should be held at Forts Wingate and Canby. The military could only feed 6,000 Indians at the Bosque, and there already was an excess of 3,000. For the first time the General apparently sensed that a limit existed as to the resources of that rich and fertile spot on the Pecos.[23]

Scouting for renegades was stepped up. On March 14 Lieutenant James C. Edgar led a detachment of six troopers of First New Mexico Cavalry out of Sumner to search the countryside and capture all the Indians they encountered. Edgar had orders to proceed to La Turpentina Ranch near Las Conchas, seventy miles north of the post. Miguel Desmarias had written from Las Vegas that twenty Navajos visited his ranch at La Turpentina and killed some sixty head of sheep. After investigating this claim without results, Edgar proceeded to Hamilton's Ranch and to Anton Chico. McCleave also established a picket post four miles below Point of the Rocks, about twenty-five miles below Sumner, to protect the government herds. Here, a noncommissioned officer and six privates would take permanent station.[24]

In southern New Mexico, the Mimbres Apaches west of the Rio Grande continued to commit depredations on a large scale. Michael Steck, who had served as their agent for six years, believed that he could end the hostilities by having a council with the Mimbres. He wrote to Charles E. Mix, Acting Commissioner of Indian Affairs, that the military's treachery, especially in the killing of the Warm Springs' chieftan, Mangas Coloradas, had brought on the trouble in the region. He had received a petition signed by the settlers around Mesilla, stating that the Mimbres desired peace and requesting him to meet with the tribe. Steck also informed Carleton of his intention to meet with the Mimbres.[25]

Carleton disapproved of Steck's move. On March 16 he warned "Mathew" Steck (deliberately using the wrong given name) that as long as Indian hostilities continued, the military would deal with the Mimbres. The army, not the Indian Bureau, had the responsibility to make the peace. He could not permit Steck to hold negotiations with the Mimbres. Carleton had given the

Apaches an ultimatum: go to the Bosque Redondo or be exterminated. As soon as the Department of Interior would agree to feed the Mimbres, as well as the Navajos and the Mescaleros, he would gladly turn them over to the New Mexico Superintendency.[26]

On March 20 Steck complained to Dole that Carleton continually interfered with his plans. Between 1854 and 1859, the Mimbres Apaches had lived at peace on a reservation in their own country. By forbidding Steck from visiting the tribe, Carleton had usurped the right to make treaties, a right belonging to the Indian Department. Steck declared that the government already had endured "too much of Military management of Indians." Dole, in contrast to the fiery Steck, preferred to let nature take its course. Carleton's plan would fail of its own accord and did not require any efforts on the part of the Bureau to kill it.[27]

A problem arose at the Bosque Redondo concerning corn delivered by Andres Dold. As his contract called for corn from the States, Dold's shipments had not been expected until May at the earliest. But Dold now claimed that when the contracts had been made the corn was already in wagons on their way to New Mexico. Carleton, however, suspected that Dold purchased New Mexican corn and was trying to turn it in for the price of States' corn. He informed William Bell, Commissary Officer for the Department of New Mexico, that if Dold were allowed to turn in New Mexican corn there would not be enough corn in the territory to last the Indians at the Bosque until the next harvest. However, Dold apparently had been honest in the matter, and indeed the shipment had been from the States. Carleton seemed to have reached the point where he would not trust anyone, including the members of what his critics now called a contractor's ring.[28]

The desire to educate the Navajos constantly preyed on Carleton's mind. In late March he wrote Secretary of the Interior Usher, again asking for help in educating the Indian children at the Bosque. Previous requests to Commissioner Dole had gone unheeded. The reservation sorely needed funds to construct a schoolhouse. Education, Carleton said, constituted the fundamental ingredient in "making the Navajos a civilized and Christian people." There were 3,000 intelligent children at the Bosque who should receive the attention of the Indian Department. To Carleton, the education of these children probably was the most important reason for the reservation. If his program received adequate financial support, the Indians would be completely civilized within ten or fifteen years. Carleton again indicated the need to survey the reservation. As the exterior boundaries had not been marked, no one could determine its exact limits. The irrigable land at the Bosque also needed surveying, so the acreage could be allotted in lots of ten acres or smaller to the Indian families. Land division, Carleton believed, served to organize the bands on the reservation and identify them with particular fields. This would be the first step in giving the Indians an understanding of the white man's concept of real estate, a basic foundation of civilization. Usher, however, refused to spend Indian Bureau money on the Indians at the Bosque. To do so would acknowledge responsibility by the Department for those Indians.[29]

The cost of supplies for the Bosque continued to soar. C. S. Hinckley delivered five hundred forty-three head of cattle for $38,485, or 18¢ per pound. Sidney A. Hubbell, formerly a judge in the Mesilla District, sent 4,376 sheep for $19,939, or 15¢ per pound. Thomas C. Bull delivered 95,000 pounds of corn on contract for $11,400. Andres Dold supplied the reservation with 63,327 pounds of corn for $15,515, while W. H. Moore shipped 125,680 pounds of wheat meal for $20,645. Corn prices reflected the effect of reservation needs on the economy of New Mexico. In less than two years, the price of corn had tripled.[30]

W. H. Moore, whose grain shipments were notorious, also received an important contract for the transportation of supplies to Fort Sumner. Moore, a mining speculator in addition to a contractor, agreed to haul any supplies that the Quartermaster at Fort Union might turn over to him to any depots in the Department of New Mexico. The contract ran from June 1 to November 30, 1865, the peak period for shipments.* Moore received two dollars per hundred pounds for goods hauled from Union to Sumner, and more for shipments to posts further west. The rate compared favorably with other freighting contracts that had been let in New Mexico, although it probably was higher than the rates in less demanding and less dangerous regions of the country.[31]

By early April of 1865 there were 9,026 Indians on the Bosque, of whom 8,509 were Navajos. During the previous month forty-three Indians reportedly had died in the Navajo villages, although the true figure may have been much higher. The military stated that the Indians died from unknown diseases, but the deaths probably resulted from pneumonia contracted during the cold weather. Post Surgeon Gwyther urged that a system to filter water for cooking and drinking purposes be immediately constructed. The water at Sumner was "saturated with animal and vegetable impurities," and measures were needed to purify it. In late April many Navajos fell extremely ill, and the Assistant Surgeon made daily visits to their camps. Considering their lack of food and clothing, the freezing weather, and the filthy water, it surprised the surgeon that more deaths had not occurred.

Sometime in March, Carleton allowed eight Mescaleros to leave the reservation to bring in their families. Supposedly their relatives lived with a large segment of the tribe in the Guadalupe Mountains, approximately one hundred fifty miles down the Pecos and near the Texas line. Carleton hoped the entire Mescalero tribe would eventually settle on the reserve. In the past he had been far more successful with Indian emissaries persuading their own people to come in than in forcing the Indians to the reservation at gunpoint.[32]

Finally the Indian hospital at the Bosque was completed. Situated seventy yards east of the barracks of the enlisted men, the U-shaped adobe building, fronted with a long veranda, consisted of nine small rooms, several of which were used by the Indian school and its Catholic instructors. Seven of the rooms were eighteen by twenty feet, while the two large rooms were twenty by thirty feet. Two rooms were allocated for surgery and a kitchen. On several occasions the doctors crowded as many as fifty Navajos into one of the small rooms, an amazing feat. The surgeon described the place as "only fit to keep pigs in."

---

*Few supplies reached the Bosque in April. W. H. Moore shipped roughly 80,000 pounds of wheat meal on contract for approximately $13,700. Vicente Romero, prominent in politics and business circles, delivered 47,072 pounds of cornmeal for $7,062, or fifteen dollars per hundred pounds, still a high premium for New Mexican corn. A small shipment of cattle was received from H. B. Denman, on contract for $2,375, or sixteen cents per pound. In total, $31,000 during the month was expended on Indian subsistence.

Many of the Navajos harbored suspicions about the hospital. When several deaths occurred in rapid succession in the building, the majority of the tribe refused to enter the structure, saying it was permeated with the spirits of death and therefore taboo. Sadly, the Navajo medicine men were unable to treat the diseases of their people, for the magical roots and herbs used in making medicine did not grow at the reservation. The Navajos did not totally oppose the idea of a hospital, and the chiefs stated that tents located near their camps might serve just as well.

During a seven-month period, of three hundred twenty-one Indians treated by post surgeon George Gwyther and Michael Hillary, two hundred thirty-five had syphilis. Furthermore, many Indian women had lost their lives in crude attempts at abortion. Many did not want children whose fathers were soldiers; others did not want to bring more children into a place where there was already too little food. Aghast at the widespread venereal disease among the troops and Navajos, Hillary stated that it would "always be the case" so long as the soldiers were around. As the Indian women lacked "the slightest idea of virtue," the only solution to the problem was to keep the women "as far from the fort as possible."[33]

One problem that might have assumed larger proportions concerned the charge that the Bosque was located on private land. John S. Watts, former judge and delegate to Congress, had been involved in the passage of several Congressional acts relocating the large land grant known as the Baca Float, which previously had covered the site of the reservation. Judge Knapp, a fiery opponent of Carleton's policies and politics, wrote on March 30 to the General Land Office, insisting that Watts, who had been designated the attorney for the Baca heirs, lacked the power to act for them. Knapp apparently wanted the reservation declared to be on private property, so it would be necessary to relocate it, preferably in the Navajo homeland. The only reason that the heirs had allowed Watts to move the float, Knapp said, was to make money by defrauding the government. Watts had been working for Carleton, and the two men had a lengthy history of partnerships in business ventures.[34]

Nearly two months later, on May 22, the General Land Office replied to Knapp's letter. The government stated that Watts was the legal representative of the heirs, and Knapp's complaint was invalid. Commissioner J. M. Edmunds, writing to Commissioner Dole, stated that the reallocation of float land had taken place in February of 1863. By giving the date, Edmunds implied that the transfer was unrelated to the large contracts let to supply the reservation in 1864. The subject was closed, and Knapp cast about for another means to break Carleton's control over New Mexican affairs.[35]

Theodore H. Dodd in January of 1865 had been designated the Navajo agent by the Interior Department. Dodd had little actual responsibility. He readily endorsed the acts of the military, as they controlled the reserve, and he apparently was popular with the military and the Indian Department. He had served under Carleton and retired as a colonel in 1864. In early April, Judge Watts, who recently returned from Washington, informed Dodd that Commissioner Dole expected him to come east to purchase supplies for the Navajos with the Congressional appropriation. In mid-April, although he had no written instruction to do so, Dodd left the reserve for Washington.[36]

In Washington, Commissioner Dole was to appropriate $150,000 for the

Navajos for the fiscal year beginning July 1, 1865. The appropriation of $100,000 the previous year had been received only after a prolonged fight. Now rumors circulated in the Capitol regarding the jobbery which had riddled that appropriation. Furthermore, some congressmen felt that the Navajos were being used as an excuse for a large annual grant to the Indian Bureau. Many did not want this sum to become an annuity. Dole urged Usher to support the appropriations. However, Congress continued to delay.[37]

On April 14, Judge Knapp, in a letter to the Santa Fe *Weekly New Mexican*, charged that Carleton had driven Reverend Fialon from the Bosque. The military had constantly harrassed the priest and finally forced him to leave. While Knapp may have exaggerated, it was true that Fialon had been a close friend of Agent Labadie. Carleton apparently believed that Fialon was involved in the cattle fraud which had occurred in January, although little evidence implicated the priest. Carleton previously had tried to retain the backing of Bishop Lamy, one of the most powerful men in the territory. Nevertheless, it was true that he expelled Lamy's friend and fellow countryman, Fialon, from the reservation.[38]

Lamy named a new priest for the Bosque. At his arrival, McCleave gave him three rooms in the Indian hospital, two of the smaller eighteen by twenty foot rooms, and a large, twenty by thirty, classroom. There the priest began instructing, caring for, and feeding the orphans. Using the three rooms in the hospital would not affect the hospital operations. As several Navajos had died in the building, most of the Indians avoided the place anyway.[39]

Carleton searched for the successful reservation formula. In his quest he created a board of officers, directing them to make recommendations for reorganizing the Navajo tribe. The board reported on April 26. The board was composed of four officers: Major McCleave, Captain Murphy, Captain Bristol, and Captain Fritz, who commanded the cavalry detachment at Sumner. They, recommended first that each Navajo band have a separate village, located about a half-mile apart. The chief of the band should be responsible for the village and keep a record of absent Indians. No Indian could leave his village at night. A system of village courts also was needed, with appeal to a general garrison court. The post commander would appoint chiefs and could dismiss them at any time. The Indians needed rule by law, regardless of whether or not they comprehended it. Law was a step toward civilization. The board recommended that punishment for murder be death by hanging, or lashes or imprisonment if there were mitigating circumstances. Lashing or imprisonment at hard labor for a period of at least a week could be punishment for theft. Destroying trees or produce was punishable by imprisonment. As a gesture of humanity, the officers recommended that Indian females guilty of a serious crime not be whipped.

Under the proposed plan, each village would have a "factor" or manager with six assistants to direct farming operations. The manager had the responsibility for the tools, implements, and seeds at each village, and the keeping of detailed records on the produce raised on the farms. He also oversaw the distribution of the crops to the Indians under the post commander's instructions. In each village the factor and his assistants would live in a sturdy house, which also might be used for the storage of tools and seeds.

A church and school were also necessary. The Indians were supposedly Catholics, and it was hoped that the Roman Catholic Church might finance the construction of the buildings. The officers felt that traders should be refused entrance to the reservation unless they had permission from the commanding officer. The sale of liquor, arms, and ammunition to the Indians should be prohibited. The ownership of horses should be discouraged, for the Navajos generally used them to flee the reserve. The village chiefs should be given presents enhancing their position and encouraging them to make the tribe self-sufficient. Finally, the board suggested that an annual award be given to the most productive Indian farmer.

Carleton was pleased with the suggestions and granted McCleave full authority to implement them. He realized the fundamental reorganization of the tribe would be a slow process. However, he believed the officers at the reservation were making a sincere effort to alter the culture and life-style of the Indians.[40]

In Santa Fe, in March or April, Michael Steck decided he could no longer bear the restraints on the New Mexico Superintendency. Unlike his superiors, he lacked the patience to wait for the grand experiment to fall under its own weight. He had been at odds with the military for two years. The Indian Department had been expelled from the Bosque Redondo Reservation: the regular Navajo agent Dodd was really Carleton's representative and had no power whatsoever. Carleton had prevented Steck from making a treaty with the Mimbres Apaches, and charges circulated in the Indian Bureau that Steck had been involved in the fraud growing out of the $100,000 appropriation of 1864. By April 30, perhaps at the request of Commissioner Dole, Steck submitted his resignation. Felipe Delgado, a prosperous Santa Fe merchant, was promptly appointed as his successor.[41]

6

The Foundations Crack

"We have lost a good many of my people, and many are now sick. All but one of my horses have died from starvation. We could live better in our old country than in this. The water and grass are better there. Tell the Great White Father that we would like to go back to our old country."

Cadette, Chief of the Mescalero Apaches

FROM MAY TO DECEMBER OF 1865, dramatic changes took place in the conduct of Indian affairs in New Mexico. Following the resignation of Superintendent Steck, Carleton earnestly believed that his major problem had been removed, but his difficulties seemed only to increase. Depredations by renegade bands caused the citizens to hurl epithets at Carleton, and a Congressional committee arrived in the territory to examine conditions at the Bosque Redondo. To make matters worse, the Indians saw their harvest again ruined by insects. In the fall, when a measles epidemic struck the reservation, the patient Mescaleros could endure no more and fled. The foundations of Carleton's grand experiment began to crack.

From the first, Felipe Delgado, Steck's successor as Territorial Indian Superintendent, expressed no opposition to the Bosque Redondo Reservation, or to Carleton's ideas. The Delgado family had been among the first families to welcome the Americans in 1846; their store in Santa Fe catered to the soldiers and was always well-stocked with dry goods, groceries, and liquors. In time the Delgados became influential in New Mexico affairs. In 1860 Felipe Delgado had joined others who clamored for a campaign against the Navajos, and from 1862 to 1865, he was a member of the territorial legislature. Like many New Mexicans, he could neither read nor write English, although literate in Spanish. As Indian superintendent, Delgado blamed the Indian troubles in New Mexico on a lack of funds, but he was vague in his reasoning on the matter. Because the government failed to supply the Indians adequately, they periodically left the reservation in search of food. Delgado's views on peonage and Indian slavery seemed equally vague. He was aware that a number of New Mexican families had Navajo servants, but he did not consider them slaves. Due to his

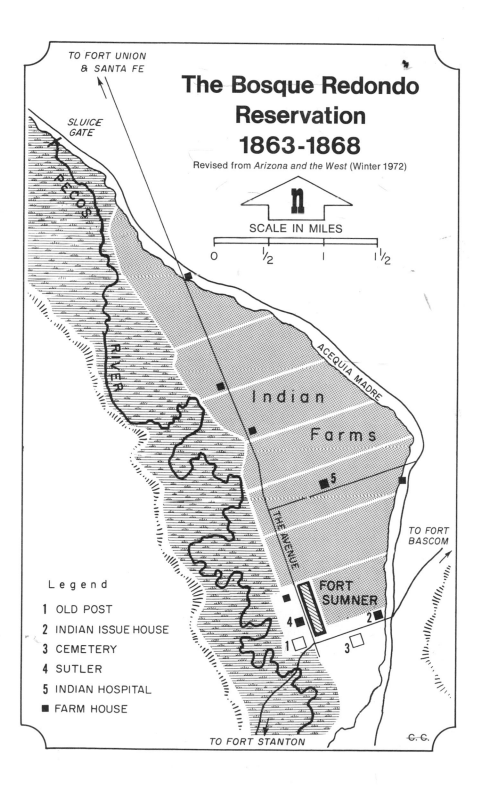

The Bosque Redondo Reservation 1863-1868

Revised from *Arizona and the West* (Winter 1972)

TO FORT UNION & SANTA FE

SLUICE GATE

PECOS

RIVER

ACEQUIA MADRE

Indian

Farms

THE AVENUE

SCALE IN MILES

0   1/2   1   1 1/2

TO FORT BASCOM

FORT SUMNER

Legend

1 OLD POST
2 INDIAN ISSUE HOUSE
3 CEMETERY
4 SUTLER
5 INDIAN HOSPITAL
■ FARM HOUSE

TO FORT STANTON

C.C.

*Felipe Delgado, who replaced
Michael Steck as Territorial
Indian Superintendent.*

From Benjamin Read,
Illustrated History of New Mexico

stand on these matters, he soon alienated a number of important New Mexican politicians.[1]

A serious incident took place at the Bosque on May 2. Jose Sena, a young Mexican, had been confined in the guardhouse for "tampering with the Indians." An Indian woman reported that Sena, a Quartermaster employee, had entered into conversation with her, inquiring as to her family. She replied that her husband had died and several members of her family were quite sick. Sena retorted that he knew the cause of their sickness: the government had poisoned them. The soldiers desired to kill them all, "for which purpose a white powder (poison), resembling flour was sprinkled over the beef." When he was arrested, Sena denied ever making such a charge. McCleave later considered the case and released the youth, who seemed to be ignorant of the criminality of the act. Moreover, it was impossible to substantiate the charge, the only witness being a Navajo woman.

Hoping to gain a powerful supporter, on May 8 Carleton wrote to Adjutant General Thomas for permission to send a delegation of Indians to Washington to meet President Andrew Johnson. He recommended that the party include Captain Henry Bristol and six Navajos and five Mescaleros. He suggested Bristol because he had managed to settle most of the differences between the two tribes. Carleton also wanted the delegation to meet Interior Secretary Usher. If Usher saw the Navajos in person, he would be impressed by their appearance and intelligence and might show more interest in assuming the enormous fiscal burden of the Bosque. Apparently the General had forgotten Usher's statements that the Department of the Interior would take charge of the reservation only when the Indians had become self-supporting. Needless to say, Carleton's Indian delegation idea was stillborn.[2]

The Mescaleros on the Bosque grew increasingly restless. Much of this dissatisfaction stemmed from Labadie being forced to leave the reservation. The agent had located his new headquarters on the Agua Negra, some twenty miles north of the fort, just outside the reservation boundary. Military authorities, however, refused to permit the Mescaleros to visit their agency. Occasionally some Apaches managed to sneak off to see Labadie, but he was their agent only in name. The Mescaleros had long regarded Lorenzo Labadie as a true and trusted friend. They believed that he had incurred the displeasure of the military while trying to protect their rights, which was largely true. Livestock which the agent had purchased from Morton had been for the Mescaleros. The Apaches bided their time, waiting for the right opportunity to flee the Bosque.[3]

Depredations in the upper Pecos country continued. As a number of Navajos were absent from the reserve, McCleave immediately sent Captain Fritz and a detachment of seven troopers to scout north toward the settlements. Riding through the Navajo villages on May 10, Fritz halted at the Indian camp near Alamo Gordo Creek at the northern end of the reservation and delivered a warning. The military knew these Navajos had performed no labor on the reserve whatsoever that season, and he ordered them either to report for work on the farm or to start cutting wood. The detachment then rode off toward Fort Bascom to the northeast. Eventually Fritz swung west around to Hamilton's Ranch and Anton Chico.[4] He returned to Sumner later in the month without sighting any Navajo renegades.

In April some Navajos attacked Miguel Arguello and Juan Ignacio Maestas and drove off their cattle. The two men collected a party and took up the trail of the Indians and found the stock in the Canyon del Toro in the vicinity of Las Vegas. In attempting to secure the stock, Maestas was killed. Arguello, in a sworn affidavit, stated that the Indians came from the Bosque. In fact he recognized one Indian as a former co-worker on the newly constructed dam on the Pecos. A Navajo woman with the band was identified by her clothing as residing at the reservation.[5]

Attacks also occurred in other places. In mid-May Indians killed twelve men in the upper Rio Grande valley. The Mexicans who found the bodies stated that they believed the Indians were Navajos who had acquired breechloading rifles at the Bosque Redondo. The *Weekly New Mexican* charged that Indian parties, given permission to leave the reservation to hunt, had committed most of the depredations. These Indians usually attacked small groups of non-Indians; if they encountered a large party, they simply showed their passes and went their way.[6]

Major McCleave tightened his picket line around the reservation. For some time pickets had been maintained close to the fort, but McCleave now decided to locate small units far from the post. If the Indians eluded the first ring, the second line might stop them. In mid-March Lieutenant Ben Fox and ten enlisted men rode out of Sumner to establish a temporary outpost on the east bank of the Pecos in the vicinity of Bosque Grande and Navajo Crossing, some forty to sixty miles to the south. In that area Fox selected a point that gave an extensive view of the surrounding countryside.[7]

During May it was estimated that over 1,300 Navajos were absent from the reservation, despite the fact that additional bands continued to arrive from the Navajo country. Although traveling with escorts, several of these parties had been attacked by Hopis, Utahs, Zunis, as well as New Mexicans. Other Indians, as well as local citizens, saw the Navajos' weakness and sought to take revenge for past offenses. The travelers seemed glad to reach the sanctuary at Sumner. Deaths and departures, however, exceeded arrivals. During May, twenty-seven Navajos died from unknown diseases, two drowned in the Pecos, and three were killed by Comanches. There were 7,169 Navajos on the reservation, a significant drop since the previous return.[8]

The delivery of supplies at the Bosque in May represented an increase in number and value. W. H. Moore furnished 66,919 pounds of wheat meal on contract for $9,770. Vicente Romero delivered 24,060 pounds of cornmeal for $3,609, and St. Vrain sent 49,033 pounds of flour for $7,354. There were also small shipments of tomato seeds, watermelon seeds, pumpkin seeds, chili seeds, and general garden seeds. Most of these seed shipments originated with George T. Beall, an employee at the military post in Santa Fe, who raised them.*[9]

During the month, Vicente Romero, a major contractor for the Bosque, completed a flour mill on his farm below the town of Mora, sixty miles northeast of Santa Fe. Water from the Mora River, which flowed through his property, powered the mill. Romero was rapidly becoming an important personage in New Mexico, having expanded his interests from mercantile to agricultural endeavors. He was living proof that army contracts had benefitted some New Mexicans.[10]

Upon hearing that Comanches had attacked a Navajo group near Anton Chico, Captain Bristol sent Ganado Blanco, Barboncito, and another Indian leader to investigate. At the battle site, they found that three of their people had been scalped and mutilated. From the signs in the area, the Navajo leaders estimated the Comanche-Kiowa party numbered fifty or sixty warriors who were mounted on mules and horses. Riding into the Anton Chico county on the old Fort Smith road, the war party struck the Navajos about sixty miles northeast of Sumner. After making the attack, they had headed back to the Texas Plains.[11]

On May 26 McCleave ordered Lieutenant Fox and twelve men and five Apaches to reconnoiter down the Pecos for a short distance, then strike out onto the Plains to look for signs of hostile Indians. The scarcity of water, however, prevented Fox from leaving the Pecos. He again established a picket at Bosque Grande to watch for hostiles coming upriver. McCleave sent out other scouts. Sergeant Andrews with five privates of the First California Cavalry headed northeast on the Fort Bascom road looking for signs.[12] On June 8, shortly after Fox returned from Bosque Grande, he was ordered into the countryside with ten men and two Indian guides to scout for Navajos who had jumped the reservation. McCleave sent Captain Samuel A. Gorham west to intercept reservation Indians. He drew eight days rations and before leaving was instructed to follow the Indians as far as the Rio Grande.[13]

On the night of June 14 Ganado Blanco and Barboncito, former war

---

*Meanwhile, Andres Dold, the Las Vegas contractor, requested a military escort for his wagon trains, loaded with corn, and ready to leave Council Grove for New Mexico. The Plains Indians had taken to the warpath, and travel over the Santa Fe Trail was hazardous and nearly impossible.

leaders, and an estimated five hundred Navajos left the reserve. McCleave ordered Captain Fritz and Captain Fox to take all the available cavalry, about forty-four men, and intercept the Navajos before they reached the Rio Grande and bring them back. In notifying Carleton, McCleave stated that Delgadito had given the first information on the matter, and that he and the other chiefs intended to stand by the government.

Carleton was shocked by the large outbreak. He called upon the citizens of southern New Mexico to join the militia units being organized under General Jesus Montoya to locate the renegades. In a short time hundreds of troops, militia, and regulars guarded the major passes and trails and tried desperately to catch the elusive Navajos. Virtually the entire command of Fort Craig took the field. Carleton was particularly agitated at the number of Indians involved in the "break out" and in the timing of the event. The Congressional Committee on the Conduct of Indian Affairs, headed by Senator James R. Doolittle of Wisconsin, was then en route west to investigate Indian affairs in New Mexico.[14]

Increasing Indian warfare in the West had created a feeling in Congress that the Indian policy must be changed. In almost every area in the West, Indians were terrorizing settlements and challenging the army. The Doolittle Committee hoped to find a new workable solution to the vexing problem. Carleton's experimental reservation for the Navajos was well known in Washington, and the members of the committee desired a first-hand study of its operations.

The Doolittle Committee reached New Mexico in late June of 1865. Senator Lafayette S. Foster of Connecticut, Congressman Lewis W. Ross of Illinois, and Navajo Agent Theodore Dodd, accompanied Doolittle. On June 25 they visited the Bosque Redondo Reservation briefly; then they proceeded to Santa Fe to hold hearings. Persons called to testify included General Carleton, Chief Justice Kirby Benedict, Surveyor General John A. Clark, former Superintendent Collins, Captain Bristol, Dr. Charles L. Warner, physician for the Indian Hospital, Dr. Gwyther, and various minor personnel, as well as Indian leaders. The testimony conflicted on every point. Although most of the witnesses favored Carleton's policy, Doolittle soon realized the situation at the reservation was nearing a critical point.

The Indian leaders gave interesting testimony. Cadette, the head chief of the Mescaleros, complained that his people had to go more than fifteen miles distant to graze their livestock. To get mesquite for firewood, they spent an entire day going out to it, cutting it, tying it into bundles, and carrying these heavy loads on their backs to their camps and the post. The government had not provided them with teams or even mules to carry the loads. Cadette then discussed the rations, stating that the Mescaleros drew rations for five days but the food lasted only two days. Many of his people had fallen sick and died; consequently they quit going to the hospital, as the doctor had been unable to help. Cadette proudly indicated that venereal disease was unknown among his people, and if they discovered any "bad women" they were punished severely. Apparently the Mescaleros needed clothing, because Cadette requested looms and instruction on how to weave blankets like the Navajos.

Congressman Ross questioned Cadette closely through an interpreter.

Was there a better place for the Mescaleros? Cadette replied that in their old country, near Fort Stanton, grass and water abounded. All of the Apache leaders wanted to return there. The water at the Bosque was unhealthful, as it contained too much alkali. He sorrowfully added that all but one of his treasured horses had died at the Bosque from starvation. In conclusion, Cadette said that four of his people had died within the last few days from the measles which had just made its appearance among them.

The Navajo leaders made similar statements. Herrero declared that although they received practically everything they wanted at the Bosque, his people preferred to return to their old homeland. Congressman Ross, recalling Carleton's statements that the tribe could not support itself there without raiding, asked Herrero if the Navajos could make a living there? The Navajo leader replied quickly that they could. Then Ross questioned Herrero about how the soldiers treated them. The Indian bitterly replied that "the soldiers about here treat us very bad — whipping and kicking us." Undoubtedly abuses had occurred. Many enlisted men in charge of Indian labor details at the Bosque lacked their officers' zeal to civilize and educate the Navajos. Most of them had enlisted to fight Indians, but they found themselves at Fort Sumner working side by side with them.

The Doolittle Committee gathered other valuable data. It collected all the military records connected with the reservation in order to make a detailed study of its operations. The committee then returned to Washintgon. Once back in the capital, the committee recommended that the Interior Deparment now conduct its own investigation of the Bosque. The visit of the Doolittle Committee had no immediate effect on Indian affairs in New Mexico, and several years passed before the government decided on a new policy for Indians.[15]

Senator Doolittle had been impressed with Carleton's ideas and efforts; he sent the General a list of questions about American Indians in general. Carleton's candid statements provided considerable insight not only into his policy at the Bosque Redondo but also into his overall attitude toward Indian-white relations. Many other persons in the West, particularly military officers, held similar views; thus Carleton's ideas represented the opinions of a powerful block of individuals. In time the government would adopt many of those ideas.

Doolittle first quizzed Carleton about the number of Indians in the nation. Did Carleton believe the Indians were decreasing in numbers, and if they were decreasing, from what causes? Carleton replied that the Indians had decreased in numbers very rapidly for several reasons. First, there were wars with the armed forces, and sickness generated by the change of climate, particularly for those Indians (Cherokees) removed from the East to the Far West. Second, the Indians as a whole were notoriously intemperate in their use and abuse of liquor. Third, venereal diseases constantly plagued them; Carleton incorrectly cited scrofula, a form of tuberculosis, as being caused by venereal disease. Fourth, smallpox, measles, and cholera, all diseases of the white man, wreaked havoc on the Indians. Finally, there were those causes which the "Almighty originates when in their appointed time he wills that one race of man — as in races of lower animals — shall disappear off the face of the earth and give place to another race." Carleton believed that God had traced out a great cycle of creation which went beyond the understanding of mortal man. The mammoths, mastodons, and great sloths had come and gone — and so "the Red man of America is passing away!"

How would Carleton curb prostitution among the Indians and the diseases associated with it? The best practicable remedy, he replied, lay in education, in teaching the people of the evils to which their type of life tended them. Indians had to be educated to the point where moral principles, Christian principles, could be taught them. The Indians committed acts of wrong out of sheer ignorance of the moral and physical consequences of those acts. "The natural decay incident to their race must find its remedy in a power above that of mortals," the General said.

What policy should be pursued when white settlements advanced and surrounded Indian reservations? Should Indians be removed to new reserves, or should the white encroachments be resisted? Carleton argued that Indians should be maintained upon their reservations, and white inroads prevented. Existing reservations must be made inviolate. In the great rising sea of "palefaces," these reservations were islands, and in time this "great sea" would engulf the Indian races one after another. In time they would be known "only in history and at length blotted out, of even that forever."

Doolittle then asked Carleton if he thought Indians were industrious. He responded by describing the young Navajos at the Bosque as being both docile and industrious. In contrast, the grown men seemed lazy and could not be prevented from "their savage desire to roam about and lead a life of idleness." The older Navajos must die off, Carleton observed, and the younger ones take their places before any marked improvement could be observed in the tribe.

Should reservations be established by treaties? The reservation system was necessary, Carleton said, for all wild tribes, and should be set aside by law and enforced by arms. He did not believe, however, in treaties. It was beneath the dignity of the United States to sign a treaty when the other party was not a legal nation. The government would have its own way, regardless of the Indians' desire, and to go through the form of making a treaty was theatrical. *"We can do right,"* he wrote, "without resorting to any theatricals simply for effect."[16] On this note the questions ended. Carleton's answers were indeed revealing of the motivations for his policies at the Bosque Redondo.

The Navajo exodus from the Bosque in mid-June caused waves of fear in the territory. Sharing the excitement, the Santa Fe *New Mexican* exaggerated the number who fled, setting the number between 900 and 2,500 Navajos. Even so, they did relatively little damage.

Most New Mexicans responded to Carleton's call to arms with eagerness. To some it seemed like a return to the old days of raiding the Navajos to secure women and children who could be sold for servants in the small communities. One party had come upon the camp of Manuelito, the leader of the Navajos remaining in Arizona. Although the Indians escaped, the disappointed New Mexicans managed to take horses and other booty which the Indians had hastily abandoned. A Navajo woman, captured in a different clash, reported that the life of the wandering Navajos was miserable and that most of them desired to go to the Bosque but feared that they would fall into the hands of the bands of New Mexicans who roamed the countryside looking for them. Another military force under Jesus Montoya intercepted part of the Navajos in southern New Mexico and skirmished briefly.[17]

The largest battle by far, however, took place only fifty miles southwest of Fort Sumner, when Captain Fritz overtook a band led by Ganado Blanco. Relentlessly pursued, these Indians already had lost many from thirst and starvation. In a violent clash, Fritz's soldiers killed Ganado Blanco and ten or twelve other Navajos and captured eight hundred sheep and forty horses. The fight marked the end of the campaign. The other refugee Navajos soon began returning to the Bosque. In determining the causes for the outbreak, Captain Ben Cutler, Carleton's Assistant Adjutant General, stated that the Navajos had "been tampered with by men who, for poltical purposes, have opposed the reservation."[18] Peace once again came to the Bosque.

In June at least 1,000 Navajos were still absent from the Bosque. In forwarding a monthly report to Carleton, McCleave explained that most of these were on the reservation but had not been counted. Some groups, working the outlying fields, lived at quite a distance from the main post. Twenty-four Indians lay ill in the hospital, and several were locked in the guardhouse. The Indians also failed to report deaths. Fortunately, the number of deaths had dropped substantially with the advent of warm weather. Jose Gallegos, who delivered several hundred head of sheep in mid-June, stated that he found most of the Indians satisfied and looking fit and healthy.[19]

Despite his optimistic pronouncement, McCleave placed a picket twenty miles northwest of Fort Sumner on the Rio Salado, a tributary of the Pecos. Lieutenant Cronin, First New Mexico Cavalry, commanded the outpost. Soon after locating there, he surprised and captured forty-two Navajos near his camp. One of his patrols spotted two lone Indians who showed their pugnacity by firing at the soldiers, slightly wounding a sergeant in the head. Although bleeding, the veteran soldier calmly raised his rifle and fired, killing his would-be assailant instantly. The other Indian fled. Cronin sent the forty-two Navajos back to Sumner where they were given a stern lecture by Captain Bristol. To his chagrin, Bristol discovered that the party had received permission to go out hunting, that they had never intended to run away, which accounted for the ease with which Cronin had "captured" them. Bristol ordered the group set at liberty.[20]

Conditions at the reservation deteriorated. In mid-July insects again swarmed over the Indian fields. The frustration of soldier and Indian alike was overwhelming. McCleave informed Carleton that all the crops were plentiful, "but the cursed insects seem to devour all the grain in the ear." The mature corn "was being devoured by worms." Moreover, torrential rains destroyed the wheat crop, sown in case the corn harvest failed, and turned the fields into bottomless pools of mud. When put into the fields, the reaping machines immediately sank into the nearly liquid earth and were useless. Captain William H. Bell, departmental commissary, declared that one million pounds each of corn and flour must be bought in the States to offset the destruction. Breadstuffs would again be scarce at the Bosque.[21]

Carleton frantically searched for ways to save the crop. After the last harvest, he had consulted with agricultural experts about the eradication of the "army" worm. When no solution was found he recommended that both soldiers and Indians be sent into the fields to pick the worms from the corn. This meant that they had to open the husks, carefully remove the insects, and then close the husks. He also suggested that large plates of molasses be placed at strategic intervals in the fields to attract the moths laying the eggs. In Kansas, farmers had used the remedy with some success. Before they laid the eggs in the corn ears, the moths would be drawn to the sweet syrup. When they settled in the sticky substance, they could be destroyed. Although pessimistic about its success, Carleton ordered McCleave to try these experiments.

The appearance of the worms in the Bosque fields prompted additional economy measures. Carleton ordered that cavalry horses and animals be fed unthreshed grain, and that all processed wheat go to the Indians. McCleave also detailed a soldier to search the reservation grounds in search of loose seeds. The seeds he found were to be counted, sorted, and stored for the planting of next year's crops. When hungry Indians invaded the fields and ate the ripening crops, he wrote McCleave to station guards in the fields. At the same time he ordered that every reservation Indian found off the Bosque without a pass be killed. In an effort to offset the shortage of corn, McCleave increased the meat ration to one and one-quarter pounds per person.[22] In the late summer the beeves were at their heaviest. More importantly, however, inexpensive Longhorn cattle had started to arrive from Texas, and the price of beef was dropping.

On July 17, 1865, McCleave issued an order that signaled the opening of a new avenue for supplying the Bosque with beef. On that day McCleave directed Captain John Thompson and Sergeant Sandoval, both of Company I, New Mexico Cavalry, to take a detachment of eight privates from Lieutenant Cronin's command and proceed down the Pecos River and meet a herd of cattle being driven to Sumner from West Texas. Hostile Comanche bands were known to prey on trail herds, principally for horses and mules. Thompson was to go as far as Emigrant Crossing on the Pecos in Texas and there relieve a military escort coming from a Texas post. Thompson drew thirty days provisions and a wagon for transportation, and promptly left for the south. The opening of this new "Pecos Trail" proved important, for in later years many thousands of cattle were driven over it.

Jim Patterson and Bill Franks probably owned the herd en route up the river. Patterson and Thomas L. Roberts, the latter having recently resigned from the California Volunteers, held an exclusive contract for supplying Fort Sumner with beef from September 1, 1865, to August 31, 1866.

Beef prices were extremely high in New Mexico, and the contractors had sought the cheapest cattle available. Patterson and his agents contacted cattlemen throughout west Texas in the early summer to furnish herds on his contract, and by July trail herds were plodding west to Fort Sumner and the Bosque. M. Smith, a Patterson employee, described trailing a herd of 1,500 Longhorns to the Bosque as the hardest drive he ever experienced.* The Texas cattle proved a great boon to the military, and the high beef prices soon fell as thousands of inexpensive cattle took the trail to the Pecos.[23]

---

*One cannot state for a certainty the owner of the cattle which comprised the first drive from Texas. They were not owned by Charles Goodnight, however, who had hoped to drive cattle to the Bosque in the summer of 1865, but was thwarted by the Comanches. Other Texas herds reached Sumner before Goodnight finally made his first drive. The Goodnight-Loving name seems to have been applied only in later years to the Pecos Trail, probably by Goodnight himself.

With the opening of the Pecos Trail, it became necessary to have better weighing equipment for the cattle, as Sumner rather than Union would be the delivery point. Carleton ordered Captain Bristol to have every animal weighed and gave instructions on how to make a crib for the scales. Each beef would be placed inside the stout crib bound by iron, situated upon the large scale. The crib would be strong enough to last for years, and it could be moved on and off the scales with ease.[24]

On July 28 Andres Dold signed another contract to haul one million pounds of corn from the States to Fort Union before the fifteenth of November "brought from the east side of the Arkansas river." Dold received $18.50 per hundred pounds, a discount of five dollars over the previous year, owing to improved conditions on the Plains and the time of year. Prices always rose higher in late fall and winter over late spring and summer levels.[25]

In addition to his other arguments, one reason that Carleton opposed the location of the Navajos in Arizona was the widespread belief that their land contained rich deposits of gold, silver, and other precious metals. He believed that miners would soon be attracted to the region, and the military should keep the Navajos out of the area. Otherwise, there might be bloodshed. Moreover, Carleton himself was far from immune to gold fever. It was not surprising that, on July 20, he gave Albert Case Benedict a power of attorney to "take up, locate and register, in accordance with the laws of said Terr., mining claims upon any ledge, lode or vein of gold bearing quartz, or of silver, copper, cinnabar, or any other material," in his name. Major Cutler and DeForrest witnessed the power of attorney, only one of several Carleton authorized.[26]

The Santa Fe *Weekly New Mexican* in July reported on a meeting of Carleton's backers in Dona Ana County. John Lemon, local probate judge, called the meeting, which adopted a resolution applauding Carleton's Indian policy. Lemon had been previously accused by the newspaper of receiving private contracts from Carleton for double the market bids. Strangely, both Lemon and Frank Higgins, who also held government contracts, had also supported the Confederacy in Mesilla.[27]

In late July the Indians watched with amazement as an immense bronze bell was unloaded from a wagon at the Bosque. Cast in St. Louis and purchased by drawing on the Indian fund, it weighed 1,000 pounds and was installed to summon the Indians. Its tremendous blows could be heard for miles. Sounded at specific intervals during the day, it informed the Indians to commence work in the fields, to eat, and to cease laboring in the evenings. To officers who had served or traveled in the ante bellum South, the similarity between the Bosque reservation and a plantation must have been apparent. Now a bell pealed at precise times during the day, like the slave horn which had regulated plantation life.[28]

Renegade Indians, as usual, caused major headaches at the Bosque. The return for July showed forty-nine Apaches absent from the reserve. Captain L. G. Murphy, Superintendent of the Apaches, had some difficulty in accounting for the Mescaleros, for they often left their camps without applying for passes. For example, while chief Cadette was away on a pass, twenty-eight Apaches fled the reservation. When Murphy questioned an interpreter about the Apaches, the men replied that all were present. When "break-outs" were discovered, Murphy stated that the Mescaleros would soon return. They had left to collect fruit and mescal, which they believed were necessary to their health. Murphy also issued passes to several Apaches in late July so they could contact those off the reserve. To Jose Mana, leader of one of the larger renegade bands, Murphy warned that if he and his people did not return to the reservation, troops must be sent out after them. Although a large part of the Mescaleros, perhaps four hundred, still lived in the Guadalupe Mountains near the Texas line, the military had no intention of bringing them to the reservation. It would require too many men and too great an expenditure. However, once an Indian had lived at the Bosque, he would not be allowed to return to his old home.[29]

Another band of Navajos now left the Bosque. This group, like most others, probably wanted to hunt game or look for mescal or fruit. When they departed without passes, they were listed in the monthly return as absent without leave. In July some two hundred were absent. The military had great difficulty in hunting them in summer because the Indians could subsist off the countryside and escape pursuit. Thus, the number of Indians on the reservation gradually declined during the summer and rose during the winter.[30]

On August 6 Carleton wrote Commissioner Dole concerning the $150,000 appropriation by Congress for the Navajos beginning July 1, 1865. Agent Dodd had gone east to make purchases and seemed determined that the jobbery which had taken place the previous year would not occur again. Carleton urged that goods be purchased immediately, so that some of them might reach the Bosque before winter. Expressing concern for the women and children having to suffer "for want of clothing," the General reminded Dole that 9,000 Indians at the Bosque were *"entirely dependent upon the Government for everything"* and that their health and comfort were at stake.[31]

Carleton made his hand felt in the most minor operations at the reservation. In early August he instructed McCleave to save all the grease which melted from bacon. In a futile effort to combat scavenger dogs that roamed in packs all over the post, McCleave announced orders from Carleton that "all dogs found at large, after today, will be shot." And, there was the problem of rations. "Laundresses" at the post had apparently been drawing rations, but Carleton decided to put a stop to the practice. Beginning on August 12 no woman would be furnished with a ration by virtue of being a laundress at the post, "unless she is lawfully married to the Soldier with whom she lives, and has the legal certificate, properly witnessed, of such marriage." Carleton seemed to be attempting to upgrade the moral fiber of his soldiers.[32]

In early August the little group of Coyotero Apaches at the Bosque requested permission to return to their homeland in eastern Arizona. As they numbered only twenty, Carleton granted their wish. It was only a matter of time, he reasoned, before a war would be waged against the Coyoteros. When the clash occurred, the twenty former residents of the Bosque perhaps would be advocates of acquiescence and would favor removal of the tribe to the Bosque. Carleton had learned an important lesson in conducting Indian warfare: a few influential Indian leaders who received proper benefits from the whites could persuade their people to follow the General's wishes.[33]

The size of the garrison at Fort Sumner mushroomed during the summer of 1865, largely due to the sizeable Navajo outbreaks. The number of companies varied between seven and ten, with the average as seven or eight. All were vastly understrength. At one time four companies of the Fifth Infantry, two of New Mexico Cavalry, three of California Cavalry, and one of California Infantry garrisoned Sumner.

On August 25 McCleave established a picket at the Agua Negra to prevent Indians from leaving the reservation. Agent Labadie had established an Apache agency in that vicinity, and Carleton feared the consequences of his tampering with the Mescaleros. Apaches occasionally had visited Labadie against the orders of Carleton. Lt. Shields, commanding the picket, sent out scouts to the east and west of his camp. His soldiers carried ominous instructions. "All grown male Indians," McCleave had instructed Shields, found off the reservation without a passport would "be killed." These orders would be universally applied in New Mexico, as they were in the past.[34]

The Indians in August received $1,462 for their fodder, a sum the military spent in their behalf. Nearly $1,000 went to purchase sheep to add to the flocks pastured on the grama grass on the rolling hills above the river valley. One hundred five dollars were paid for grape cuttings to start a vineyard, and sixty-six dollars were spent on tobacco and matches. Although the Indians seemed pleased at receiving the sheep and tobacco, the expenditures were too paltry to influence the course of events at the reservation.[35]

On September 9 Navajo Agent Dodd sent Commissioner Dole a list of nonedible supplies to be purchased from the most recent Congressional appropriation. He gave agricultural implements a high priority. On his list were five hundred turning plows, thirty-two horse plows, one threshing machine, one reaping machine, five hundred hoes, three hundred spades, and one hundred pitch forks. Dodd hoped the agricultural implements could be sent to the Bosque before the late autumn snow covered the plains. If planting took place in the winter, the wheat should be ready to harvest before the annual blight of insects took place. The agent also needed oxen to pull the plows. Perhaps they could haul the goods across the plains and then go to work on the farms.[36] In hopes of diversifying the crops at the Bosque, Dodd also requested seed to grow rice, apples, cotton, oranges, peaches, and tobacco. To eliminate the usual purchase of blankets for clothing, he suggested that $20,000 be spent in New Mexico to purchase wool, from which the Indians could weave cloth to make their clothes.

New Mexico Indian Superintendent Delgado, on September 10, 1865, recommended that the Jicarilla Apaches at the Cimarron Agency be moved to the Bosque. In what may have been nothing more than an effort to get the army to shoulder an Indian Department problem, he wrote the new Commissioner of Indian Affairs, D. N. Cooley, noting that the Jicarillas had caused a good deal of trouble in the last few months. Unable to support themselves, they were "the most worthless vagabond Indians in the Territory." When the Jicarillas learned of Delgado's proposal, they protested. Labadie, their agent since June, pointed out that these Apaches were intermarried with the Mohuache Utahs. He predicted increased turmoil if the government moved the Jicarillas to the Pecos. The subject subsequently was dropped.[37]

Indian Bureau purchases for the Navajos were entrusted to Agent Dodd. In late September he traveled to St. Louis from Washington to obtain Indian supplies. He scrupulously avoided the practices of Leavenworth the previous year, and by the end of October he had completed his purchases. Dodd spent $10,000 for fifty yoke of oxen and wagons for hauling the goods to the reservation. With a military escort to protect his supplies from the depredating Plains tribes, in mid-November, with his wagons, the agent headed down the Santa Fe Trail for New Mexico.[38]

In Washington a whispering campaign against Carleton had reached the highest circles of the government. In mid-September Theodore S. Kervet told William Seward, Secretary of State, that he had been a representative in the New Mexican territorial legislature in the winter of 1864–65, and he felt compelled to inform the government of the problems in New Mexico. Slavery had not been abolished in the territory; the traffic in Indian captives still continued, with the approval of Carleton. Governor Connelly, Kervet said, could be seen going to church every morning escorted by three or four Navajo slaves, "bought and sold and held as property."* Copperheads (southern sympathizers) and the regular army conspired to circumvent Mr. Lincoln's policy. Lincoln's friends in New Mexico had found Carleton to be a "regular" Copperhead, and his support of McClellan in the 1864 national election gave credence to the charge. Kervet informed Seward of the Indian slavery because he knew of Seward's well-known actions on the behalf of freedom. Unfortunately, Carleton, while issuing fine-sounding proclamations on the subject, was taking no action on the question of Indian slavery. Seward forwarded the letter to President Andrew Johnson, and another charge was added to the rumors of a contractor's scheme.[39]

Garrison life at Fort Sumner continued as usual. McCleave faced the old problem of discipline. Due to the heat many men failed to wear the proper uniform. Moreover, many absences had been occurring at roll call and drill. McCleave ordered a cessation of these offenses, and courts-martial followed.

On September 21 news of the death of Brigadier General Crocker arrived. McCleave issued an order to mark his passing. Then on October 7 Captain Joseph Birney of Company D, First New Mexico Cavalry, died of consumption, believed to have been complicated by a "very bad case of syphilis." Because Birney was regarded as an officer of great zeal and devotion to duty, the entire garrison was paraded in his honor.[40]

The Bosque Redondo finally was surveyed in the autumn, at the order of General U. S. Grant. Captain John B. Shinn, Third Artillery, was sent to the reservation to undertake the task. He completed the assignment early in 1866, and his map was submitted to the War Department by the end of the year.[41]

The autumn days brought more reports about depredations. A commentator in the *Weekly New Mexican* stated that Indian atrocities were "fast becoming the order of the day." In Rio Abajo County in northwestern New Mexico, the Navajos apparently had the upper hand. Bands entered small towns in broad daylight and stole whatever stock they pleased. These attacks merely served to increase the public outcry against Carleton's policy.[42]

---

*The 1860s showed a marked increase in the number of Navajos being baptized in the Catholic Church. By this method, New Mexicans prevented Navajo captives from being released and taken to the Bosque Redondo.

To combat the impending food shortage at the Bosque, Carleton took drastic action. In General Orders 11 he required all farmers south of Hart's Mill in east-central New Mexico to sell their grain to the government. They would be paid six dollars per fanega, considerably less than the twenty dollars per fanega that contractors were receiving for deliveries of corn from the States. Commenting on Carleton's actions, the *Weekly New Mexican* stated that contracts in the States had been let for four million pounds of corn at a cost of $750,000. If an equal purchase were made in New Mexico, it would run only $25,569. The newspaper overstated their case, but the true difference in prices was about sixfold. In contrast, the *Weekly Gazette* reported that the finest crop of corn was being harvested at the reservation, and it would greatly assist in feeding the Indians. The idea that the reserve was a poor site for farming could only be described as "ridiculous." As soon as the Indians and soldiers completed the harvest, an elaborate return would be compiled of the separate products of the Navajo and Apache farms. The *Weekly Gazette* also recommended that Indian fund money, growing by the continual sale of fodder, should be partly dispensed to noncommissioned officers and soldiers who had been employed working or supervising the labor on the Indian farms.[43]

In mid-October the post chaplain M. Fleurant asked to be granted a leave of absence for two weeks to journey to Mora, thirty miles north of Las Vegas. He also requested permission to take three bright Navajo children with him and place them in the school at Mora. The priest promised to pay for their education and be responsible for them. McCleave granted the leave but stated that orders forbade taking any Navajo children from the reservation except by permission from the Commanding General. Fleurant, who had requested the leave for his health, was angered by the response. He was too sick to dispute McCleave's order, however, and he died shortly thereafter.[44]

On October 29, Captain Bristol, Military Superintendent of the Navajos, left the Bosque Redondo. He had received orders assigning him to recruiting duty in New York. Bristol had worked diligently on the reservation since its inception, and was thoroughly instilled with Carleton's sense of mission for the experiment. The General deeply regretted the loss of the fine officer, and he wrote in a special order that "much of the success which thus far has attended the colonization of this powerful tribe" was due to this officer.[45]

McCleave informed Carleton on November 3 that Labadie had accused the officers at Fort Sumner of issuing diseased meat to the Indians, that the authorities at the post had always gone to great pains to ameliorate the condition of the Indians, and that some of the problems which the reservation had experienced were due to men of Labadie's stripe. McCleave noted that the previous day a harvest feast had been held for the Indians, but most of them refused to attend. Apparently someone had told them that the troops were going to use the occasion to poison them. He recalled that Labadie had not been removed from the reserve because of his protests over the Indians' rations, as Labadie argued, but because his personal herd contained government livestock. Labadie seemed to be a thief and a slanderer, according to Major McCleave.[46]

A measles epidemic struck the reservation in the fall of 1865. Cases had been reported in the summer, but they had been ignored. Although relatively harmless to the soldiers, the disease proved fatal to many Navajos and Apaches.

By late October, it had reached epidemic proportions, with more than four hundred Indians wedged into the small rooms of the Indian hospital. Throughout the reservation, others fell ill, developed the characteristic red spots, high fever, and a persistent cough. At this point, the Mescaleros decided that they had had enough of the Bosque. Quartered with an ancient enemy who outnumbered them twenty to one, they had seen their fields confiscated, their agent dismissed, and now their people were dying. In the darkness of night on November 3, the entire tribe silently left their camps. Their departure marked the beginning of the rapid decline of Carleton's grand scheme.[47]

The Mescaleros planned their escape well. They departed in small groups, scattering in different directions to prevent a successful pursuit by the military. Some went down the east side of the Pecos for more than fifty miles, others followed the west side for a similar distance, and still more struck out across the plains in different directions. They appeared to be heading toward their old homes near Fort Stanton.[48] Major McCleave personally led the scouting forces, but the task of catching the elusive Apaches was hopeless. While in the field, he saw no Apaches, although a small Navajo pursuit force did manage to kill two. The troops followed the Mescaleros for a distance of ninety miles away from the post. When the cavalry horses became exhausted near Bosque Grande, McCleave disgustedly gave up the chase and returned to the post. He stated in a letter to headquarters on November 6 that the removal of the Apaches apparently had been going on for several days. The first groups to flee went on foot. The horses had been saved for those who went last. The Navajos reported that two hundred of their horses had been stolen, enabling the runaways to make good time.

Upon his return to Sumner, McCleave ordered Captain Murphy to pursue the Apaches with a force of about one hundred men. Murphy left Fort Sumner on November 8 bound for Fort Stanton with two companies of cavalry: Company B, First California Volunteers, and Company M, First New Mexico Cavalry. Drawing sixty days' rations, Murphy carried orders to kill all male Apaches; only women and children would be saved. Murphy's expedition proved futile: the Apaches had vanished.[49]

In late November, McCleave established a picket of sixteen men on the Pecos River at a point known as Blue Water, some twenty-five miles south of the post. Second Lieutenant Joseph De Hague, First New Mexico Cavalry and Company L, commanded the picket. Several days later McCleave sent out standing orders to the various outlying pickets. If the soldiers saw any Indians, they would order them to stop; if any resistance was offered, the troops would attack and shoot them.[50]

By the fall of 1865, the operation of the Bosque Redondo had run into serious difficulties. In the midst of heightened Indian depredations, a Congressional committee had come to the territory to examine its administration. For the second year the insects destroyed the crops on the Indian farms. Finally, with measles rampant and food shortages looming, the Mescaleros fled the reservation. The foundations of the Bosque were crumbling.

7

Debating the Reservation's Fate

"This is the best place for us we know there is outside of our own country. We want to go back to that country. We have done wrong, but we have learned better and if allowed to return to our Mountain homes will behave ourselves well. Cage the Badger and he will try to break from his prison and regain his native hole. Chain the Eagle to the ground, and he will strive to gain his freedom and though he fails will lift his head and look up to the sky which is his home."

Navajo leader, unidentified

IN THE FALL OF 1865, criticism of the Bosque Redondo Reservation and its architect, General Carleton, continued to mount. The crop harvest was only a fraction of the amount needed to sustain the Indians, and depredations increased throughout New Mexico. In its fall term the territorial legislature petitioned the President to remove Carleton and abandon his policies. But top military leaders in Washington, believing the General had chartered the proper course, were not swayed by the memorial. At the reservation the problem of supply continued to plague its operations. The Navajos grew increasingly restless, and small bands repeatedly left their camps to live off the countryside.

At Carleton's insistence, McCleave in November of 1865 conducted an elaborate survey of Indian farm production. He wanted to determine the amount of money the Indians had saved the government during the previous year by their farming operation. The survey revealed that three crops had been planted: wheat, corn, and beans. The Navajos had raised 34,113 pounds of wheat, 373,909 pounds of corn, and 3,040 pounds of beans. The Apaches had grown 49,673 pounds of corn, and 475 pounds of beans. Applying standard rates to these products (wheat, 11¢ per pound; corn, 16¢ per pound; and beans, 8¢ per pound), the total value of the Indian crops came to $73,246.93. On the other side of the ledger, the number of rations came to 2,886,762 and cost $767,473.20. The rations averaged out to be 26.58¢ per day per individual Indian. The usual number of Indians subsisted was set at 7,909 per day. When the Indian produce was deducted from the overall subsistence cost, the amount of $694,226.27 was the actual cost of feeding approximately 8,000 Indians.

Despite the poor crop year for the Indians in 1865, the sum of roughly $700,000 for subsistence was considerably less than the figure of $1,250,000 projected by the Indian Bureau.

However, the figure of about $700,000 given by the army was strictly the cost of the rations and did not include the cost of distributing them. Several hundred civilian employees worked at the Bosque Redondo, and when their salaries were added into the equation, along with the cost of the post itself, the Fort Sumner–Bosque Redondo complex proved an expensive operation indeed. A final figure probably exceeded the Indian Department estimate.

Regarding the fodder the Indians raised and sold to the Quartermaster, the figures in 1865 were somewhat better than in the previous year. The Navajos raised 572,709 pounds of corn fodder, and the Apaches turned in 150,000 pounds. The fodder added $5,255 to the Indian Fund, but the military took $4,000 to pay the soldiers who worked as overseers. So, at the close of 1865, the Indians had banked only $1,096.[1]

As Carleton pondered the arithmetic of rations, McCleave's problems at the post continued. On the night of December 11, an Indian group stampeded a herd of government cattle; the next morning Lieutenant Robert Thompson, First New Mexico Cavalry, and ten men of Company L rode out in pursuit. Problems of discipline still existed with the volunteers. For example, Second Private Miles B. Andrews of Company A, First California Volunteers, was court-martialed on charges of conduct prejudicial to good order and military discipline. He failed to properly display shirts, drawers, and socks at an inspection. The court found him guilty and sentenced Andrews to fifteen days at hard labor and fined him ten dollars. Liquor was being sold on the reservation to Indians, and McCleave announced that anyone caught violating the law would receive the most vigorous punishment.[2]

On December 14, M. Lucero, the probate judge of Santa Ana County, reported to Carleton on a recent militia expedition he led in Navajo country. With thirty-two Hopis as scouts, his group had searched for Navajos far into the San Juan country — near what later would be known as the Four Corners area — but they had no success. Lucero particularly wanted to locate the chieftain Manuelito, leader of the last remaining band. The Navajos living in the San Juan country numbered fewer than forty, he said. The depredations recently committeed in Rio Abajo, northwest of Santa Fe, were believed to be the work of *ladrones*, or thieves, who secreted themselves in the Datil and Escudilla Mountains in west-central New Mexico.[3]

By January of 1866 Lucero had heard that on Thanksgiving Day Governor Connelly had issued a proclamation banning further civilian campaigns. The judge filed a vigorous protest. He wrote Connelly that the Bosque Redondo had many advantages; then he added that in mid-December a large number of Navajos, supposedly from the reservation, had driven off about 8,000 sheep belonging to Thomas, Jesus, and Luis Baca, killing four men in the process. Another man later died from wounds received in the clash with the renegades. One of Baca's herders reportedly had been captured with the Navajos and had been taken with them to the Bosque Redondo. Upon his release he testified that the marauders came from the reservation. Only the citizen militia could protect the territory, Lucero said.[4]

In Washington, the Bosque Redondo was a frequent topic of conversation. In mid-December, Secretary of War Stanton sent James Harlan, the new Secretary of the Interior, a copy of a letter from Amos B. Eaton, the Commissary General of the Army. Eaton recommended that the Interior Department assume the responsibility of subsisting the Apaches and Navajos at the Bosque. Secretary Harlan promptly replied that his department would "cheerfully undertake this duty," as soon as Congress granted the necessary appropriation, and he promised to present the request to the Joint Committee on Indian Affairs. However, he needed additional information concerning the number of Indians drawing rations, the annual cost for feeding and clothing them, and the projected expenses for the forthcoming year.[5] Stanton replied that if the farms at the Bosque managed to escape the destructive torrential rains and the insect plague, he thought the Indians could provide a large measure of their own subsistence. However, even though the subsistence costs could be greatly reduced, the Department of the Interior must not rely solely on the farms.

Thus, by December of 1865, both Interior and War departments came to the conclusion that it was time for the proper arm of the government to take over the reservation. The War Department had found the operation far too expensive, and with budget reductions following the close of Civil War hostilities in the spring, it was impossible for the army to bear the full burden of the reservation. Stanton did not regard this condition as a reflection upon Carleton and his commanders; they had been extremely dedicated and performed an outstanding job. But the fact remained that the reservation depleted funds too fast, so the military began the slow process of extracting itself from running the Bosque.[6]

New Mexican politicians had been unhappy with Carleton's Indian policy for a long time, and the Navajo and Apache outbreaks in 1865 provided abundant ammunition for their arguments. The Santa Fe *Weekly New Mexican* ran countless articles condemning Carleton and asking for his removal. On November 3 the newspaper requested that Carleton, "the brightest star in the constellation of American generals," be sent to some point where his greatness could develop itself. It was destined that he would "remain unappreciated in New Mexico."[7]

During the winter of 1865, the legislators drafted a memorial which called for the government to remove Carleton from command in New Mexico. The memorial caused heated debate, but on January 21, 1866, amidst rumors that many bribes had been taken, the memorial was passed and sent to President Andrew Johnson. The petition stated that Carleton had failed to reduce the hostile Indians in New Mexico. He had created a reservation that proved lucrative for sutlers and speculators, and worked against the best interests of the citizens of the territory. The General's military administration had been "a terrible calamity to the people of this Territory." In short, the document combined all of the charges that had ever been leveled against Carleton in his three years as the commanding officer of the New Mexico Military Department.[8]

Typical of the barbs hurled at Carleton was a sarcastic poem published in the *Weekly New Mexican* during the legislative session. Despite its crude rhymes, the verse repeated the charges against Carleton in the form of a dialogue between a small boy and his father.

The General's Greatness

Son:

O, General Carleton's great, papa,
    His paper calls him great,
The biggest man you ever saw,
    He stands so mighty straight.

Father:

Not so, my son, about as big
    As I or Uncle Jeff;
The people do not call him great,
    But the Santa Fe Gazette.*

Son:

But papers tell the truth, papa,
    So I at least suppose;
And from this paper one might think
    His fame to heaven rose.
And then, my dearest Pa, you know,
    From lowest degredation
He's raised the barbarous Navajo
    Above an angel's station.
He looks not like a man, papa,
    But brighter than the stars,
The people tremble at his name,
    He's wonderful in wars.

Father:

Man at the most is only man,
    This you must not forget,
The people call not Carleton more,
    His fame is bought — "you bet."
The Casa Blanca is the horn
    That sounds abroad his fame;
When facts are known to you, my son,
    T'will all seem wondrous tame;
He lives on government pap,
    And taxing contract meat,
Tis this that makes the Gazette say
    To all his praise amen.
The Governor's proclamation said
    The Navajos were beat,
But every day or two they steal
    Cattle and ten thousand sheep.
They murder all within their track,
    Though bound by Carleton's order,
The people can't give tit for tat —
    The General won't take the bother.

*John T. Russell, publisher of the pro-Carleton Santa Fe *Gazette,* lost the government printing contract to W. H. Manderfield and Thomas Tucker, owners of the rival newspaper, the Santa Fe *New Mexican.*

Son:

> But in the race for Washington,
>   Which Perea lately made,
> He used his military power
>   To force him through 'tis said.

Father:

> But then, my darling little son,
>   You know that Chaves beat.
> With all the force that Carleton run,
>   Poor General beat retreat.
> And have you seen the late Gazette?
>   Which Carleton's shrewdness runs,
> Its dying agonies were great,
>   Poor thing, it is undone.
> The Legislature's struck the blow,
>   And Carleton groaned aloud,
> His organ called them lousy men,
>   And these lice eaters proud;
> Then viper like he bit his side,
>   "O Russell, help!" he cried,
> "The lousy dose we've vainly tried."
>   He bit again and died.

Son:

> Then Carleton's a small man, papa,
>   I thought he was much greater;
> If fame like his is boughten fame,
>   He's but a small per-tater.
> I'm glad, papa, you've told me all,
>   And yet not told the best,
> For Andy is about to send
>   A general out here West.[9]

While the public outcry against Carleton swelled, disaster struck the wagon train hauling supplies from the Missouri frontier to the Bosque. The previous November a train of seventeen wagons left Westport, Missouri, heading down the Santa Fe Trail to New Mexico. General John Pope, commanding the Department of the Missouri, had warned that the season was very late for caravans starting west. Most military posts along the route were short on forage. But the supplies were urgently needed, so Agent Dodd gave the word to leave. Traveling with him on the train was Julius K. Graves, a Special Indian Commissioner en route to investigate the reservation.[10] Graves' appointment was in response to the Doolittle Committee's recommendation that the Indian Department conduct its own study of the Bosque. At Fort Zarah, four hundred seventy-five miles west of Kansas City, a heavy snowstorm halted the wagons. A number of oxen perished in the freezing weather. Deciding that it was impossible to continue at that time, Dodd parked the loaded wagons and returned to Kansas. He planned to renew the journey the following spring when there would be sufficient grass to support the livestock. Commissioner Graves, however, proceeded on to New Mexico, reaching the Bosque in late December bearing the forlorn news about the supplies.[11]

Graves inspected the Indian fields and camps; he was visibly impressed with the vastness of the enterprise. He commented particularly on the *acequia madre*, or main irrigation ditch, flowing from a diversion dam on the Pecos River in a big loop on the east side of the fields. At intervals, small lateral ditches branched and ran across the farms to the river. From the north, the road from Fort Union and Santa Fe entered the reserve, bisecting the fields. Called "The Avenue," this thoroughfare extended south for seven miles across the reservation to Fort Sumner. As he rode down The Avenue, Graves saw Indians engaged in a variety of tasks in the fields, but their major activity at that time of year was plowing.

The farming potential at the Bosque seemed virtually unlimited to Graves. Grapes, melons, vegetables, apples, peaches, and apricots grew in abundance. The Bosque produced beets weighing twenty-five pounds. There was also room for agricultural expansion. South of Sumner lay 2,000 acres of tillable ground on the east side of the Pecos. A large stand of cottonwoods provided shade for the livestock. Graves made a point to taste the water of the Pecos, as he had heard the Indian complaints about it. He found the water as potable as the Cimarron or the domestic water in Santa Fe. However, he learned that during the summer months the water had a distinctly brackish taste. The Bosque possessed many advantages. It had plentiful grass for grazing and good farm land. The fuel problem had been partially solved. Twenty miles north of the reservation, Indians were cutting wood in a large stand of piñon trees. They threw the wood into the Pecos, where it floated downriver to a boom which trapped the logs near the reservation. Here they cut, corded, and hauled the wood to the Indian camps. Several of the Navajos complained to Graves that they needed more animals to assist in the hauling, and he promised the use of the oxen from the next supply train.

The greatest impediment to the Bosque experiment, Graves found, stemmed from the superstitions of the Navajos. During the recent measles epidemic, many had blamed the disease on the location of the reservation. He saw no way of preventing such fears, but he believed that educating the children should eliminate superstition in the years to come.[12]

On December 31 Graves held a council at Fort Sumner with fifty or sixty Navajo headmen. Talking through interpreters, the Indians indicated their strong desire to return to their own country. They said that they had learned their lesson and would be obedient if they were allowed to leave the Pecos. One Navajo described himself as an eagle chained to the ground striving to gain his freedom. Even though the great bird failed to break the chain, he continued to "lift his head, and look up to the sky which is his home." Other Indians believed that the reservation was cursed and that if they remained they must all die in a short time. Graves disagreed. He strongly believed that if the Indians stayed at the Bosque for another two years, they would never consider leaving it. The traditional pipes were then smoked and the council ended.[13]

Traveling on to Santa Fe, Graves questioned members of the New Mexico legislature as to their opinion of the conduct of Indian affairs in the territory. In response, the assembly adopted a resolution declaring that the military "had done very little toward subjugating the Indians in New Mexico," and in handling the Navajos its acts had not been characterized "by efficiency or humanity." In fact, the condition of the tribes had not been improved in the slightest. Furthermore, the Bosque Redondo Reservation was situated too close to the settlements and should be moved to another location in the territory.[14]

During his stay in New Mexico, Graves contacted every person who could give information about the Bosque. Major Bristol made several recommendations. He suggested that land below Fort Sumner be given to the Navajos for growing vegetables and that the Indians be encouraged to raise sheep, goats, and cows rather than horses and mules. Once the Indians were dismounted, he stated, their presence on the reservation was assured. He also suggested that the government quit purchasing useless items.[15] When Graves returned to Washington, he reported that the experiment on the Pecos was progressing satisfactorily. Admittedly, the military had suffered setbacks, but Graves, like Carleton, felt that in the long run the reservation would succeed.

Throughout the length and breadth of the territory, the Navajos continued to raid. They stole thirty sheep from Francisco Narle, the former governor of the Jemez Pueblo. Pursuing the culprits Narle and ten men caugth eight Navajos and killed them. Two of the pursuers suffered wounds, one receiving an arrow in the forehead. They lifted the Navajos' scalps, and the men of Jemez undoubtedly held a celebration.[16] McCleave once more increased the number of picket stations to deter reservation Indians from leaving their camps. On January 30 Lieutenant E. C. Baldwin, First California Cavalry, with eight enlisted men, established a picket post at Yew Creek. Detachments established stations at Yew Creek (probably Yeso Creek), some twenty miles to the southwest, and at Point of Rocks. From these points, patrols went out every day to ride between the stations. For example, the picket at Point of the Rocks station would patrol to the east for a distance of ten miles and then return to its base.[17]

During the winter, military routine at Fort Sumner weighed heavily on the garrison. Soldiers continued to traffic in stolen government property. Captain Thompson discovered one of his men, Albert H. Smith, Quartermaster Sergeant of Company L, First New Mexico Cavalry, illegally disposing of corn, and had him court-martialed. Smith was reduced to private and confined at hard labor for twenty days, while wearing a twenty-four pound ball chained to his leg. The court also required him to forfeit one month's pay as a private.[18] An officer found Sergeant Franklin Sanchez absent from his company in the middle of the night; he investigated and located the man in bed with a Navajo woman in an Indian hut. A court found Sanchez guilty of conduct prejudicial to good order and military discipline and reduced him to private.[19] Learning that a group of Navajos had stolen and butchered several head of government cattle, McCleave sent Captain Martin Mullins, Fifth Infantry, to apprehend the guilty parties and move the camp closer to the post. Mullins performed this task successfully and without incident. To offset the critical shortage of wood at Sumner, McCleave sent a detachment of nine men and three wagons to Fort Stanton to procure wood from the mountains. The timber was ticketed for the construction of wagons, long desired by the Indians.[20]

Carleton's Indian policy continued to divide the citizens of the territory. During the last week in January of 1866 a serious incident occurred one night in the Fonda Hotel in Santa Fe between friends and foes. An unnamed assistant of Marshal Abraham Cutler, a Carleton supporter and friend for many years, issued a challenge to the editors of the *Weekly New Mexican*. The assistant publicly charged that the newspaper had been responsible for the recent legislative attack on the General which had culminated in the memorial of condemnation. He declared that he would like to service the editors with a cowhide whip in one hand and a pistol in the other. The editors on January 26 invited him to try, but he dropped the challenge. The newspaper again denounced Carleton, stating that the "country has suffered too long from his pet schemes which if successful would benefit the favored few and ruin the many."[21]

General Carleton continued to watch the Bosque Reservation closely. The planting of trees particularly interested him. McCleave in mid-February ordered a detail of men to preserve all cottonwood trees suitable for planting which stood in the farms, putting additional acreage under cultivation. He continued to urge on McCleave to greater efforts to make the reservation a success.[22]

On February 16 New Mexicans learned that three top territorial officials had been removed. The newspapers published orders from Washington for the removal of Governor Henry Connelly, a Carleton supporter, Chief Justice Benedict, and William F. Arny, Territorial Secretary. Benedict and Arny had long opposed Carleton's policies. Connelly's successor was Robert Mitchell, who had achieved fame as a major general and cavalry commander during the Civil War.

The shuffling of territorial officials reached the Indian Bureau. On February 17, A. Baldwin Norton, brother of Senator Daniel S. Norton of Ohio, replaced Felipe Delgado as Indian Superintendent for New Mexico. Graves had recommended to Indian Commissioner Cooley that Delgado be removed. He proved incapable of discharging the responsibilities of his office and could neither read nor write English, a decided handicap. A general feeling also existed that he had not taken a strong enough stand on the problem of Indian peonage.

Many citizens were surprised that General Carleton was not included on the list of removals. A primary reason was the support he was receiving from General Grant. Disagreeing with the New Mexico legislature's memorial to remove Carleton, Grant in mid-April wrote General William T. Sherman, who had succeeded Pope as commander of the Military Division of the Missouri, that it would be well to keep Carleton in command. The veteran officer had the right approach to Indian affairs, and his policy had been successful. Grant implied that only the cost of the Bosque really distressed him. He fully agreed with Carleton's basic objectives of attempting to civilize and humanize the wild Indians on the reservations by teaching them Christian truths and the white man's way.[23]

Major McCleave struggled vigorously to make Carleton's experiment a success. Believing that the soldiers could relieve the strain on the food supply by developing company gardens, he assembled the commanders, ordered each one to select a permanent company gardener, and divided the land into the garden plots. These were located directly north of the main post, about one quarter mile from the flagstaff. To expedite the logging operations on the Pecos, McCleave sent Captain Thomas Henderson, First New Mexico Cavalry, to oversee the Navajos who were cutting wood some twenty miles north of the post. Spring weather would cause mountain snows to melt and send a torrent of water down the river, providing a perfect means for transporting wood to the reservation.[24]

Contracting for the Bosque remained a major operation. The Santa Fe *Weekly Gazette*, on April 2, announced that Albert H. French, formerly a captain in the First California Volunteers, had been the low bidder for supplying beef to Fort Sumner. Over the next several months, French, now residing in Franklin, Texas, promised to deliver 6,000 head of beef to the post at 5.75¢ per pound, which was a third to a half lower than previous beef prices. The influx of Texas cattle was driving prices lower and lower.

The winter of 1865–66 was very severe for the Indians at the Bosque. The much-needed supplies failed to arrive from Kansas, and many Indians went cold and hungry. In April, Zadoc Staab, a prominent merchant-contractor in Santa Fe, wrote Commissioner Cooley that his firm could furnish blankets for the Navajos made by the "Peasantry of this Territory." The blankets weighed four to five pounds, were six and one-half to seven feet long, and three and one-half to four feet wide. He set the price at $2.50 per blanket. Carleton recommended the purchase from Staab in a cover letter to the Indian Department.[25]

In Washington, the Commissary General Eaton tried to improve military shipments to New Mexico. He wrote Captain Bell, the assistant commissary in Santa Fe, to be explicit in his annual subsistence requests. Bell should indicate the nature of the packages, and the kind of stores best adapted to the district. Moreover, he should stipulate when he wished stores to arrive. Bacon, for example, spoiled unless sent out during cool weather. In its preparations to feed the Navajos for another year, the military resolved to perform the operation with as little waste as possible.[26]

Almost gleefully, every issue of the Santa Fe *Weekly New Mexican* contained stories of depredations. The people of San Miguel County, the newspaper reported, regarded the Bosque Redondo Reservation as "a refuge and headquarters for the bands of roving Indians who have rendered life and property so uncertain in that country." At the ranch of Jose Rafael Martinez, the Indians killed all the livestock they could not run off, and they poured his flour on the ground. Elsewhere Navajos had killed eleven individuals in the last two weeks. Indians had attacked and killed a party of four men near Las Conchas in San Miguel County. One of the corpses was "hacked and mutilated in a manner that savage ingenuity only could invent."[27] The newspaper warned small parties to avoid travel unless well armed.

Apprehensive about conditions at the Bosque, General Carleton in early May visited the reservation with U. S. Marshal Cutler. Carleton still believed his course would prove the best in the long run. He realized, however, that the Indian Bureau must take control of the reservation. The military had already spent too much time in running the reserve. The hardest work had been finished, and the troops were needed to police the territory.

Shortly after Carleton's visit, McCleave ordered a court-martial for Private Martin Detrich, Company G, Fifth Infantry, for illegally disposing of government property. Time after time soldiers were court-martialed at Fort Sumner for this offense, but with the large Indian population willing to part with everything from their women to their sheep, the soldiers were sorely tempted. Detrich apparently had sold most of the uniform clothing he had been issued. The court found him guilty and confined him at hard labor.

Other obstacles arose at the reservation. In mid-May the Pecos River became filled with debris that came down from its headwaters; this blocked the firewood from floating to the reservation. McCleave sent out a force to clear the channel up to Gerhardt's dam, which formed a storage pond for the wood. At the same time he established a picket at Carretas to protect the government herd in the vicinity. Animals could not be left without guards, because the Navajos, hungry and anxious to increase their private herds, made constant raids on them.[28]

Despite the problems on the reservation, the military was still escorting Navajos from Wingate to the Bosque Redondo in May of 1866. On May 17 a macabre incident overtook one party. Captain Nicolas Hodt, First New Mexico Cavalry, was traveling with a party of Navajos toward the Pecos when two miles east of Cubero he pulled his pistol and discharged a bullet through his brain. The military preferred to call the suicide an accident. Hodt had been one of the strangest officers in Carleton's command and probably was insane. He had been arrested on previous occasions but had always managed to be cleared of charges.[29]

In late May, Lieutenant Charles T. Jennings, First California Cavalry, sent Carleton a unique description of the slaughtering procedures at the Bosque. The General had been impressed with these operations on his recent visit. Slaughtering, Jennings explained, was done on alternate days. Twenty to thirty beef cattle were brought to the slaughterhouse, a large sixty-foot-square building located one mile east of the main post, and shut up in a reception corral for some two hours. They then were driven into two strong bull pens that held from eighteen to twenty animals at a time. From each pen a door opened into the slaughter room in the building. The military generally selected about forty-five Navajos to do the slaughtering. These Indians were regarded as civilian employees and received a wage of fifteen dollars per month. From five to fifteen additional Navajos worked as government herders. Stripped to their breechcloths, the men were divided into four butchering groups, each with an American overseer. When everything was ready inside the building, an Indian on the wall above the corral lassoed a steer and attached the rope to a windlass in the building. The Indian at the windlass pulled the protesting animal, bellowing and kicking, into the building. Its head was then pulled into a floor ring, and an Indian stepped forward with an ax, knocked the steer down, and then proceeded to sever its throat. Four animals were killed and butchered at the same time.

Once the animal died, four Indians rushed forward, each grabbing a leg. One cut away the hide, while another chopped off the beast's head, and still another cut the brisket and removed the entrails. By means of a pulley, they hoisted the beef, stripped the hide from its back, split the beef open, quartered it, and passed the meat to the scales for weighing. At the same time, two Indians scooped up the blood on the floor and carried it to the rear of the building. Under a sergeant's watchful eye, they divided the blood into pans, buckets, cans, and other vessels, and distributed it to Indians who had gathered there for the treat. When mixed with cornmeal, the blood made a nourishing pasta.

Several Navajos took the entrails out the back door to three Indians assigned the task of cutting off the heart, liver, and lungs. Others opened the stomach and intestines and washed the contents in the nearby acequia. With sure aim, an Indian split the head of the animal in two, and took out the tongue for issue. Workers also severed the feet from the body and placed them in a pile to be issued in pairs. The steer hides were carried to the rear of the building to a sergeant who distributed them to those Indians in need of shoes. Lieutenant Jennings personally supervised the most important of all of these tasks — the weighing of the beef. Under his observation, a crew weighed the meat and hung it on meat hooks. A detail then washed the building with quicklime.

On the day after the slaughter, Indians arrived before dawn in groups, armed with axes and knives, to cut the meat into one and a half pound pieces, or two days rations. It was not "easy to chop thirty head of cattle into six thousand six hundred pieces and have all equally large," Jennings said, but the Indians took great care in the job. By six:thirty in the morning, they had the beef rations ready for issue. The Navajos then lined up in three long files in front of the three issue windows in the slaughter building to receive their meat.

An Indian crew carried the beef in a box with handles to the issue window and placed it on a shelf or table nearby. An Indian might draw several rations, or just one, depending on his tickets. Soldiers took the tickets and counted out the issue in the Navajo language, so that the Indians knew how many rations they were receiving. No favoritism whatsoever was shown in the issuing of rations. The Indians placed the rations in the blankets which were brought for that purpose. At the same time, an Indian with a cup, holding precisely two pounds of cornmeal, issued the breadstuffs. After receiving their rations, the Indians took the food to a point about twenty yards from the building where they put everything into bags for the return trip to their camps. The precision in issuing rations, Jennings said, was a tribute to the enlisted men on duty at the issue house, who spent hours perfecting their methods.[30]

At the Bosque, the regular routine continued. Large shipments of supplies arrived in May. The supplies purchased with the $100,000 appropriation rolled in from Kansas, and a month later four wagons loaded with precious agricultural implements appeared. Planting was well advanced by then, and a good harvest was anticipated. Commissioner Cooley hinted to Secretary of the Interior Harlan that thought might be given now to transferring the Bosque from the War Department to the Interior. The key problem was making arrangements to subsist the Indians. As the military had already let contracts, he suggested that the transfer be postponed another year.[31]

The spring of 1866 witnessed the usual increase in Indian depredations. The Santa Fe *Weekly New Mexican* stated that on April 27 a Navajo band had driven off some seventy mules of Jesus Maria Baca and headed for the Capitan Mountains. No one doubted that "the thieves belong to the Navajos at the Bosque Redondo." If the Indians reached the reservation there would be no way to reclaim the booty. In a recent case, two individuals visited the reservation and discovered some of their animals among the Indian herds, but it was dangerous to separate them from the Indian herds. The newspaper added that in some instances the Navajos carried passports to hunt. These passports constituted death warrants for the citizens and stockowners.

DAILY LIFE AT FORT SUMNER

Major McCleave, post commander, is surrounded by
Navajos in front of the Indian Issue House.

Navajos are gathered near their fields for corn-husking.

*Indians waiting to receive their ration tickets
from the Provost Marshal's office.*

According to the archival caption, the Indians seated on the ground were accused of counterfeiting ration tickets.

Front view of the enlisted men's barracks. In the foreground is the parade field.

An unidentified building, probably the Indian agency,
a few miles away from the main post at Fort Sumner.

Indians outside the officers' quarters on the left.
Post headquarters are on the right.

Men, officers, and tents of Company B, First New Mexico Infantry. Despite the size of the post, many companies lived in tents due to a shortage of permanent quarters.

Eastward view from the infantry quarters. In the foreground are sinks for company quarters, with a small acequia flowing in front. To the left rear is the Indian commissary, with storerooms. At the far right is the quartermaster corral and cavalry stables. Notice the corded wood to be used for fuel.

The sutler's store, a popular hangout for the Indians, soldiers, and civilians.

Scene inside the large quartermaster corral. Notice the lookout cupola.

Enlisted men assembled in front of the post hospital.

Westward view across Fort Sumner showing quartermaster corral and wagons.

Elsewhere in the same issue, Samuel B. Watrous, a prominent settler in the Mora Valley, stated that reservation Navajos had killed the majordomo of J. D. Tipton. Tipton supplied the reservation with beef and breadstuffs through the contracts of his son-in-law, William H. Moore. Watrous stated that he had always favored reservations but felt they should be conducted properly. He did not favor a reserve where Indians were kept on half rations, issued arms to hunt, and given opportunities to rob and murder citizens. Anyone who permitted such conduct must be totally indifferent to the welfare of the citizens. Watrous touched a sensitive nerve when he observed that if the contractors failed to support Carleton's experiment, his plan would fail.

Aware of the rising complaints over depredations, Carleton ordered McCleave to take action. The officer dutifully sent out another scout. He directed Captain Rufus C. Vose, First California Cavalry, to visit Anton Chico, Hatch's Ranch, and the other settlements to determine the extent of reported depredations. The soldiers must "kill all Male Indians found outside the Reservation without a passport."[32]

In early summer a dispute broke out over trading rights on the reservation. This conflict occurred when the military designated Oscar Brown to succeed J. A. La Rue as the post sutler. La Rue became sutler for the Indians, receiving his appointment from Commissioner Cooley. Brown, a former officer of the California Volunteers, had been selected by a board of officers the preceding February. As La Rue had constructed a large store on the west side of The Avenue, a short distance north of the post, he asked for time to dispose of some of his merchandise. The request was denied, and friction followed. Eventually Grant directed General Pope to issue an order allowing La Rue to sell to the soldiers for an additional one hundred days. Brown protested, stating that he had purchased supplies on credit and needed to sell them immediately in order to pay his bills. La Rue then sold his goods at cost and thereby drastically undercut Brown, who charged in turn that La Rue was trying to wreck his store and drive him out of business. Brown also said the move was part of the continuing dishonest actions by the Indian Bureau at the Bosque.[33]

While waiting at Fort Sumner for their discharge from war service, the volunteer troops posed many headaches for McCleave. Private Archibald McGregor of Company A, First California Infantry, was found guilty of severely beating his corporal. On the same day, Private Sension Salazar of Company B, First New Mexico Infantry, was found guilty of conduct "prejudicial to good order and military discipline." Several days before, Salazar, without provocation, violently struck and kicked a Navajo woman in the breast and "did otherwise shamefully and disgracefully abuse her person." This probably was rape. Salazar received a sentence of thirty days at hard labor, a mild punishment. This perhaps showed the attitude of many members of the garrison toward the Indians. In the past, failure to have a proper display of uniforms resulted in more stringent punishment than Salazar received.[34]

The *Weekly New Mexican* on June 15 resumed its series on Navajo depredations, crying that "a perfect reign of terror" existed in the territory. Unless the depredations were stopped, the citizens must organize to avenge massacred friends and relatives. If this happened, the Navajos remaining on the reservation would be more than happy to stay there. Roaming bands had been seen all over the territory, and many clashes had occurred. The newspaper concluded with the sarcastic refrain: "Great is Carleton and his glory, the Bosque."[35] The Indian depredations soon hit close to home. Comanches killed seventeen Navajos on the eastern edge of the reservation, prompting McCleave to send out scouting forces led by Captain William Brady, First New Mexico Cavalry, and Lieutenant E. J. Edgar, First California Cavalry. One party of thirty-two men scoured the countryside, but they found no Comanches.[36]

On June 22 Captain Vose returned from his lengthy scout. He had visited Gerhardts' Ranch, and on June 10 reached Las Colonias, where he learned that cattle belonging to Don Antonio Gallegos had been stolen by Indians. The people of the vicinity were gathering to search for the cattle and pursue the Indians, and they joined Vose. They eventually found the cattle but saw no signs of Indians. From evidence they found, Vose stated that he believed the Navajos used the area as a thoroughfare of some sort in and out of the country to the east of the Pecos.

While having his horses shod at Las Vegas, Vose heard about a Navajo ambush. A man named Gonzales on May 26 had walked three or four miles outside of town to a mesa to look for missing stock. Navajos hidden in bushes by the side of the trail sprang at him, beat him with clubs, then took his revolver and shot him in the head. They dragged the body into the bushes. Searchers had found a Navajo blanket, the cross poles of a loom, and the flat stick used in weaving blankets. The latter item had been used as a club in the killing and was covered with blood. Resuming his scout, Vose on July 17 found tracks of Indians and eighteen horses. He pursued the trail into a rocky area and lost it. He did recover a number of sheep which seemed to have been placed in a remote pasture by the Navajos who had stolen them. Upon his return to the post, Vose discounted the rumors of recent Indian depredations. The freshest Indian sign he had discovered was at least two weeks old.[37] He also brought in a squaw, who had been mistaken for a Navajo, but turned out to be an Apache. The woman said she would be glad to go to the reservation, as she had been mistreated by her Mexican captors.

During the summer of 1866, Texas cattlemen began supplying the Bosque Redondo regularly with beef. Taking the cue from the cattle drives to Sumner of the previous year, such men as John Chisum and Charles Goodnight drove large herds up the Pecos to the Bosque Redondo and sold their beeves to general contractors. The beef contractors enjoyed certain privileges. For Thomas L. Roberts and a few others, the contract for supplying the Bosque Redondo with beef involved little effort. For example, Goodnight arrived at Fort Sumner, found he could not sell directly, then agreed to turn the stock in on Roberts' contract. Roberts paid Goodnight eight cents per pound and received ten cents from the government. Other general contractors at Fort Sumner included William H. Moore and James Patterson. Moore's contract called for the delivery of four hundred head of cattle after April 30, 1866, while Patterson's was a true general contract and open ended. He could deliver as many head of cattle as the army needed and received ten cents per pound.

By this time many former army officers or personal friends of Carleton held large contracts. The contractors had hoped to maintain high prices, but prices sagged when herd after herd came up the trail from Texas. By the fall of 1866, it was clear that beef prices would fall to more reasonable levels in the following year.[38]

Carleton's most outspoken critic, the *Weekly New Mexican,* enjoyed pointing out the problems caused by the reservation. In Las Vegas a serious affray occurred between Agent Dodd's teamsters and a group of local citizens. At the time, Superintendent Norton, Delgado's replacement, was en route with wagons bearing presents for the Navajos at the Bosque. At a fandango, several citizens got into a violent brawl with Norton's teamsters. Pistols and knives were drawn and freely used, according to the reporter, and several of the combatants suffered serious injuries. The fight stemmed from some heated remarks about the Bosque and illustrated the strong feeling that the average individual held toward the Navajos at the Bosque.[39]

Beginning in 1864, bands of Comanches from the Texas plains started visiting the Bosque vicinity to steal from the government herds. In mid-July of 1866 these warriors became a serious threat. For three days, commencing on July 10, a large war party of over one hundred Comanches camped on the eastern edge of the reservation. They rode boldly into the Navajo herds, killed several Navajos, and drove off some two hundred horses. When he heard of the raid, McCleave immediately formed and personally led a force in pursuit of the Comanches. With the major rode approximately fifty men. The troops headed southeast and discovered a trail some twenty miles away from the post. At about two:thirty P.M. on July 14 the Comanches turned to give battle twenty-five miles east of Sumner. The soldiers attacked and the Comanches fled east, their ponies soon outdistancing the heavily weighted cavalry mounts. According to McCleave, the Comanches were extremely bad shots. The troops had closed to within one hundred yards of the Indians, who were well armed with guns and ammunition. The Comanches fired wildly and totally ineffectively, while the troopers proceeded to take a steady toll of the Comanches. McCleave noted that the Comanches had used a white flag as a ruse, a familiar ploy of that tribe.

Several days later, a New Mexican Comanchero, or trader, appeared at Fort Sumner with word that the Indians would return in fifteen days to "clean out" the Navajos. McCleave, having seen the Comanches flee before his troops, put little faith in the report. The Comanches apparently had a number of Comancheros with them, who hoped to instigate raids. Writing to Commissioner Cooley, Superintendent Norton stated that the traders were largely responsible for the Comanche raids. Holding illegal licenses to trade with the Indians, these men supplied the Comanches with ammunition and whisky, and encouraged them to raid the Bosque for livestock. The Comancheros then sold the stolen property elsewhere. As the Comanches were traditional enemies of the Navajos, they were easily persuaded by the traders. This uneasy situation further increased Navajo unhappiness with reservation life.[40]

In mid-July, General Pope visited New Mexico with the specific purpose of examining Indian problems. The *Weekly New Mexican* charged that Carleton had deliberately deceived Pope and other superior officers regarding the extent of Indian depredations. Pope interviewed several of the most prominent citizens at the Palace of the Governors in Santa Fe. Many persons indicated their hostility to Carleton's policies. Superintendent Norton urged the relocation of the Navajos on a reservation in their old country. Others who had formerly supported Carleton switched their allegiance, not wanting to be associated with what appeared to be a rapidly sinking experiment.[41]

McCleave continued to take steps to protect the territory and the reservation as well. He ordered the establishment of another picket post about ten miles east of Sumner, near a lake. Hopefully it would prevent Navajos from fleeing eastward. The principal task of the eastern picket, however, was to prevent future Comanche raids from the east. Always a realist, McCleave had started to doubt the value of his far flung picket network.[42]

Superintendent Norton, sometimes incapacitated for weeks by chronic illness, tried to contact the Mescalero Apaches who had fled the reserve. He hoped that he could negotiate a treaty with them and induce them to settle on a reservation in their own country around Fort Stanton in southern New Mexico. The man selected to find the Mescaleros and counsel with them was Lorenzo Labadie, who had been their agent from 1862 to 1865. Labadie still insisted that his actions in 1865 had been justified and that his unconventional methods had kept the Mescaleros from starving. Despite the agent's many-sided character and questionable transactions, Norton recommended that he be sent to deal with the Apaches. Labadie, Norton believed, was "the best man to get the Mescaleros together and on a reserve." Labadie's efforts, however, proved fruitless.[43]

In August of 1866, at Fort Sumner the regulars of the Fifth Infantry and Third Cavalry replaced the California and New Mexico volunteers. Lieutenant Colonel George Sykes, Fifth Infantry, became the new post commander; he replaced McCleave on September 1. The important post of Acting Commissary of Subsistence fell to Lieutenant Robert McDonald. McDonald was a dedicated, sensitive career officer who had started his service in the ranks. He would later receive a Medal of Honor for gallantry. Captain Mullins replaced Lieutenant Robert Edmunston, First California Infantry, as the Superintendent of Indian farms.

Secretary of War Stanton now decided that General Carleton should be replaced. Grant had fought his removal, but Stanton saw that the Bosque Redondo Reservation had cost the government an enormous amount of money. Prominent Republicans had been angered by the distribution of contracts for the Bosque. Carleton's habit of letting contracts to prominent New Mexican Democrats proved to be his undoing. He had spent nearly a million dollars a year for three years at the Bosque. With the reservation close to failing, the Navajos were far from being self-sufficient. Indian depredations during the last three years had increased at an alarming rate. The Mescalero exodus the previous November brought increasing criticism of Carleton's program. The New Mexico memorial in January calling for his removal had found a favorable audience in Washington.

Grant knew that the Bosque had been expensive, too expensive, but he also knew that Carleton had been motivated by the forces of humanitarianism rather than greed. He believed that the reservation was a qualified success. If conditions had been more favorable, it might have worked more successfully. Here, Carleton had presented a blueprint for the civilization of the American Indian.[44]

By the early fall, it was generally known that Carleton, along with many other generals, had been reduced to his line rank in the regular service.* He had received orders to report to his regiment — the Fourth Cavalry — as soon as a replacement arrived. The *Weekly New Mexican* on October 27, reviewed the General's record. New Mexico, wrote the editor, would soon be relieved of the haughty presence of "this man Carleton, who has so long, lorded it amongst us." During the three years he had commanded, little had been done to win the "gratitude of our people, or the confidence of the War Department." The General indeed had gained "the detestation and contempt of almost the entire population of the territory." With the vast resources at his disposal, he should have had no trouble in securing peace. Instead of placing troops where need dictated, he had put them where speculators could profit. His whole administration had been a failure, the paper charged, and his removal from the chief command in New Mexico would "redound to the profit of the Territory."[45]

---

*Carleton might have considered his reduction to the permanent rank of Lieutenant Colonel as indicating his superiors' approval on his Indian policy. Other volunteer generals found themselves as junior officers in the post Civil War army, while the lower ranking officers frequently ended up as enlisted men, if they stayed in the military.

8

Carleton's Control Ends

"I believe the only solution to our present Indian relations
is in the perfection of a system similar to that pursued by
you [Carleton], in reference to the Navajoes, whereby all
the tribes interfering with our settlements on great thoroughfares, may be placed on Reservations removed therefrom,
and under the control of the Military; are supported by the
Government, if necessary, until they have been taught so
much of husbandry, as may be necessary to provide them
with means of subsistence and clothing from material raised
by their own labor."

General Winfield Scott Hancock

"The War Department has performed its whole duty in having
brought these Indians into subjection, and now in my opinion stands ready to transfer them to the Department of the
Interior."

General Carleton

IN THE FALL OF 1866, conditions at the Bosque Redondo deteriorated further.
Despite great efforts, the harvest failed again, the third year in a row. Depredations reached new highs every month. It was generally known in New Mexico
that Carleton soon would be replaced and the control of the Bosque transferred
to the Department of the Interior. However, weeks turned into months before
these changes took place.

In his last months in command in New Mexico, Carleton strove to keep
order and to encourage farming on the Bosque. However, the production on
the Indian farms in 1866 was disheartening. Over fifty percent of the crops
failed. The officers at the reservation attributed this disaster to the change of
command, saying regulars had never held such responsibilities before. In
reality, the major reason for decline stemmed from the large number of Indians
absent from the reservation. During the previous year, 1,343 Indians had left
and not returned. In 1865 the Indian farms produced 34,113 pounds of wheat,
14,000 pounds of oats, and 2,740 pounds of sorghum; in 1866, none of these
products were planted. Corn production dropped from 423,582 pounds in
1865 to 201,420 pounds, while corn fodder declined from 411,703 pounds to

156,800 pounds. The quantities of pumpkins and beans also showed marked drops. The summer of 1866 had been worse than the two previous summers. The dismal reports of crop production for the three summers clearly indicated that the Navajos could not be self-sufficient in the near future.

While crop production had declined, the cost of feeding each Indian had risen. In 1865 an Indian could be fed for $94.55 per year; in 1866 the cost had increased by $2.44. Moreover, in computing these costs, the military based their figures solely on the cost of the rations, excluding the additional expenses. Lieutenant McDonald, the Commissary Officer, issued a warning about the dwindling supply of rations. He estimated that he had 683,483 pounds of breadstuffs on hand, making 911,310 rations at three-quarters of a pound. Considering approximately 6,700 Indians were on hand, the food would last for one hundred thirty-six days. Already the Indians were complaining about their rations, and McDonald wisely suggested that an increase to one pound be permitted. At the increased rate the food would last only one hundred two days. He also urged the purchase of additional breadstuffs to prevent a food shortage in mid-winter. About this time the Santa Fe *Weekly Gazette* noted that a shipment of watermelons had just arrived at the Bosque, indicative of the successful harvest. Few people were fooled, however.[1]

Beef contracting caused problems, too. Jesse Cantrill of El Paso, a friend and subcontractor to Albert French, reported that he could not meet his obligation. This forced Captain Bell, Commissary of Subsistence for New Mexico, to make purchases in the open market temporarily. On October 13, the *Weekly New Mexican* advertised for sealed bids on 5,000 head of cattle to be delivered on the hoof at Fort Sumner by January 1, 1867. Bids would be taken until November 24. While this procedure was in progress, John Chisum arrived at the Bosque from West Texas with six hundred head of his Jinglebob steers and proceeded to sell them at Fort Sumner in December.[2]

In the fall it was reported that the last sizeable Navajo band in Arizona had surrendered. Chief Manuelito and forty or fifty Indians had given themselves up at Fort Wingate and had started to the Bosque Redondo. Many persons believed that the surrender would make the Navajos at the Bosque forget about returning to their homeland, especially when they heard that Manuelito's band had been suffering for want of food. Perhaps the Navajos would now become content and happy and no longer gaze "wistfully towards the blue range near the golden sunset."

The Navajos at the Bosque, however, reacted more sharply to the pathetic harvest than to the news of Manuelito's surrender. They were greatly disappointed by the poor crops and grew restless. Superintendent Norton attributed the great decline in production on the Indian farms to "bad management on the part of the military and not chargeable to the poverty of the soil nor the scarcity of water for purposes of irrigation."[3]

On October 11 Commissioner Cooley wrote to Secretary of the Interior Orville H. Browning stating that Superintendent Norton had recommended that the Navajo agency try to sell its cattle to the military. To feed the cattle for the winter would cost one-half of their value. At the reservation there was fodder available for only two hundred oxen who had hauled supplies from the States, and the military refused to sell any fodder to the agency. If the Indian Department wished to feed their cattle through the winter, they had to buy fodder

Manuelito actively cooperated with the Americans at the Bosque Redondo after he decided that continued resistance would be futile.

from the Quartermaster. Browning consulted with General Grant on the matter and reached an agreement whereby the military agreed to buy the cattle at a fair and resonable price.[4]

The transfer of the Bosque Redondo Reservation to Indian Department control was discussed throughout the fall in Washington. On several occasions the topic even was mentioned at Cabinet meetings. Grant, like Carleton, wanted the reservation transferred to the Interior Department, but he argued that the season was too far advanced to make the change at that time. The army must maintain the Indians a while longer or there would be great suffering. Grant agreed that orders for the disposal of the Navajos should be drawn up as soon as possible. He knew that when released from nominal imprisonment they might become a great burden on the Indian Department, and perhaps they should be moved elsewhere. At one time Carleton had envisioned the Bosque as a holding point before the Navajos were sent to the Indian Territory. Grant believed the Navajos would inevitably clash with prospectors in search of mines on a reservation in their old country. He therefore recommended their removal "with the consent of the removed to the Indian Territory west of Arkansas." In that area they would be relatively safe from white encroachments. Secretary Stanton concurred with him.[5]

Stanton informed Secretary Browning on October 31, 1866, that the Indian Bureau should plan to take charge of the reservation at the earliest possible moment. The Indians legally belonged under that Department anyway. The military should confine itself to military problems. The Indian Department had a vast experience in contracting for reservations and might provide stricter accountability and economy in spending than the army had. In his removal of Carleton, Stanton possibly believed that contracts had been let at higher rates than could have been obtained, hinting at possible collusion. Certainly he did not want the army saddled with the enormous expense of the reservation for another year.[6]

The Santa Fe *Weekly Gazette* on October 20 also hinted at corruption in government contracting, but pointed to the Indian Bureau. The editor stated that it was generally understood that a large proportion of the appropriations made for the Superintendency never reached New Mexico. The money had not been expended for the Indians; it had gone into the pockets of swindlers. This allegation probably was a veiled reference to the notorious swindle of Leavenworth and friends in 1864. The newspaper hoped that, with new individuals heading the Indian Bureau and the Department of the Interior, the past practices would not be repeated.[7]

Another favorable report reached Carleton in early November from Fort Wingate. Barboncito, a Navajo leader who had fled the Bosque in the large outbreak in the summer of 1865, had turned himself in at that western post. He and twenty-one others had been persuaded by friends, perhaps Manuelito, to again make the long trek to the Bosque. Barboncito reported that the old Navajo stronghold of Canyon de Chelly was completely deserted. Hope blossomed that northwestern New Mexico would suffer no more depredations.

The Santa Fe *Weekly New Mexican* continued to publish stories of Indian raids. On November 13 it declared that a Navajo party near Galisteo, an Indian pueblo twenty-two miles southeast of Santa Fe, attacked the herd of a Mrs. Ortiz, killing the sheep and taking away all they could steal from the ranch. The next day Indians killed Jose Martin, a resident of Santa Cruz, and stole several horses. Local citizens recognized the culprits as Navajos and noted that they fled toward the Navajo country. The *Weekly New Mexican* charged that Navajo raiders traded their stolen livestock for sheep or different horses in their own country and then surrendered at Fort Wingate, where they received free transportation to the Bosque. First, of course, they were "paraded before the people they are constantly murdering and plundering for the glorification of the district commander."* The editor declared that the military had given the Navajos a passport to rob, murder, and steal, and as usual "within the magic bounds of the Reservation" they rested secure. "Though his hands may be reeking with the blood of our citizens," the writer added, "he is safe from all punishment."[8]

Desiring to unseat Carleton's friends, Territorial Secretary Arny in November sent the new Commissioner of Indian Affairs, Lewis Bogy, a memorial signed by over 2,000 citizens. They requested that drastic changes be made in the Indian policy in New Mexico. The memorial was addressed to Stanton, Grant, and President Johnson. "We are infested on all sides by hostile and discontented Indians," the memorialists stated. The Comanches, Navajos, and Apaches were murdering and robbing the people and must be punished and placed on reservations guarded by military posts. Most importantly, an Indian agent must be placed on each reservation.[9]

In a similar vein, George W. Nesmith wrote Commissioner Bogy that Carleton's policy of placing all of New Mexico's Indians on a single reservation was a mistake — as some people, such as Steck, had forecast from the beginning. The Mescaleros, since their escape, had caused more trouble than ever, and now they were better armed because they had acquired weapons while at the Bosque Redondo. Carleton's ultimatum that hostile tribes must go to the Bosque Redondo would not bring peace, especially in the southern part of the territory. Both the Indians and the non-Indians wanted peace, and Nesmith believed the answer lay in a new Indian policy.[10]

While critics argued for closing the reserve, others still hoped to reap profits there. Contractors Thomas Roberts and James Patterson in late November sent Carleton an unusual proposition. They requested that the Indian farms at the Bosque be turned over to civilian ownership. As the leading contractors for Fort Sumner, they desired to direct the labor of the farm and sell the products to the military. The many difficulties on the farms during the previous three years resulted from bad luck and mismanagement, they said. Roberts and Patterson planned to hire a team of civilians to supervise the Indian labor. They wanted the military to provide enough troops to guarantee that the Indians would do their assigned work. Roberts also wanted the irrigation ditches, now in a state of advanced deterioration, repaired before he and his associates took over the farm. He quoted prices which he expected to receive for farm crops, saying they were at a considerable discount to the existing rates. He would

---

*During the years of the Bosque experiment, residents of Santa Fe witnessed many "parades" of Navajo captives through the streets. Carleton apparently believed that the long straggling lines of wretched Indians somehow demonstrated to the New Mexicans the effectiveness of his Indian policy.

deliver corn, for example, at four dollars per hundred pounds. Carleton, however, turned down the suggestion, feeling that it would be unethical to allow the contractors to profit from the Indians' labor.[11]

At the reservation and fort, the soldiers began preparing for the monotony of another long winter. On November 16 the officers and men had an opportunity to place wagers on a horse race held at Sumner. The well-known horse, Joe, owned by an officer of the Fifth Infantry was matched to run against Frank, a thoroughbred owned by an officer in the Third Cavalry. A large number of Indians and soldiers witnessed the event, which had become a grudge race between the two undisclosed men, reportedly for a wager of $5,000. As the race course was along the west bank of the river, about one and a half miles south of the post, the large crowd had an impressive view. At three P.M. the word "go" was given, and Joe moved rapidly forward, getting a thirty-foot lead which he held for 1,200 yards. But the thoroughbred stallion was not to be defeated. Moving with graceful bounds, Frank easily passed Joe and won by more than one hundred yards. A quarter horse race followed, and everyone enjoyed the entertainment.[12]

Despite such diversions Carleton worried over McDonald's report of dwindling breadstuffs at the reservation. In the past McDonald had not issued wheat meal, as corn had been easier to procure. But the situation in 1866 was different. A large crop of wheat had been raised in the territory, so Carleton ordered McClure, the district Commissary officer, to advertise bids for one million pounds of wheat and 250,000 pounds of corn. McClure previously had requested 1,250,000 pounds of corn. Carleton was determined that in his last months as district commander the Navajos would have enough to eat. A setback occurred, however, when cattle purchased in Colorado and sent from Fort Garland to Fort Union arrived so emaciated from exposure they had to be kept at Union and fattened.[13]

Impatient with the Indian Bureau, Carleton again urged the Department of the Interior to assume immediate responsibility of the Navajos. He wrote Adjutant General Thomas that other tribes along the Gila in Arizona were murdering and committing robberies almost every week. His troops should not be embarrassed with the care of Indians who were no longer hostile. Carleton urged that orders or laws be drawn up to effect the transfer at once and that the proper officials be sent to take care of the Navajos. The military had done its job and should not be required to control and instruct the Navajos any longer. Troops should remain at Fort Sumner to preserve order and to protect the Navajos from the Plains Indians to the east. But military control, direction, and operation of the reservation must cease. Carleton was now an ardent crusader for transferring the Bosque to the Indian Bureau.[14]

In mid-December, Dr. John Brooke, assistant post surgeon, complained to Colonel Sykes, now commanding Fort Sumner, about the hospital building at the Bosque. The building was located in the middle of the Indian camps, over a mile away from the post. If the patients were put in beds, which they never were, the hospital could hold only twenty. This condition gave each individual less than four hundred cubic feet of air space. Moreover, the builders had divided the structure into so many small rooms that it required many fires to keep the place heated. Dr. Brooke stated that it was almost impossible to keep the Indians in the hospital until they recovered. If they became dissatisfied for any reason, they ran off, spreading their disease. Money spent in treatment was simply thrown away. Two years before, Dr. Gwyther had said that he had not cured a single case of syphilis among the Indians because, after two or three days treatment, they fled. The Indians also stole the bedding. Brooke closed by recommending that the building occupied by the soldiers' hospital be converted into the Indian hospital, as it had been when first constructed. Also, La Rue's old store was for sale and would make an excellent hospital for the soldiers.[15]

La Rue offered to sell his building for $9,000. He said that he had invested $10,145 in the adobe structure up until February 1866 and that it was in excellent shape. Sykes passed the recommendation on to Carleton, agreeing that the building was in good condition and that it could not be built for La Rue's price. He added that the soldiers suffered because a large number of sick Indians refused treatment, then proceeded to infect the garrison. Carleton sanctioned the purchase, and it was duly made.[16]

Carleton wanted the Indians at the reservation to be given sheep before he relinquished command. He sent Lieutenant McDonald orders to procure rams to be distributed among the various Indian flocks to insure their increase. McDonald balked at the orders. He stated that if he purchased the rams, they could not be placed with the ewes before January 15, which would mean that the ewes would drop their lambs too late in the season. By the time the rams could be obtained, the ewes either already would be shorn or would have begun to shed their fleece. Wool was of utmost importance to the Indians. In characteristic fashion, Carleton brushed aside these comments and ordered the commander at Fort Bascom, Colonel Andrew J. Alexander, to buy the required number of rams. He directed McDonald to go ahead and shear the ewes at the usual time of the year, adding that this would have little effect on the lambs, as the Bosque was a warm and sheltered place.[17]

In Washington, the War Department now issued orders transferring the Navajos at the Bosque to the Indian Department. On December 31 General Grant signed Special Orders 651, which instructed General Winfield Scott Hancock, commanding the Department of the Missouri, to turn over the control of the Navajo Indians "now held as prisoners" at the Bosque Redondo to the Indian Bureau. The agent who received the Navajos could make requisitions temporarily on the Subsistence Department for such supplies as could be spared. The cost for these supplies would be settled later between the Departments of War and Interior. Grant instructed the Commanding Officer in New Mexico to provide the usual military aid to the Indian Agent in his control of the Indians but "without going beyond the strict duties and administration of the military service, or interfering with those which belong to the Indian Department."

Clearly the transfer could not take place immediately, but the order was now on the books. The Department of the Interior immediately complained about insufficient funds to support the Navajos. When called upon for estimates to run the reservation for the coming year, Superintendent Norton stated that the superintendency needed $700,000 to operate the reservation.[18]

Carleton, anticipating a food shortage, in late December took steps to prevent it. On December 24 a contract for one million pounds of wheat at 5.85 cents per pound was signed with Vicente Romero, a long-time Carleton supporter, who had acquired great wealth and power in the past several years. It seemed fitting that one of Carleton's last acts as district commander was to sign yet another contract for an old friend and ally.

In late January of 1867, Hancock's order to transfer the Navajos reached Santa Fe. The Santa Fe *Weekly Gazette* stated that the transfer marked a return to the old days. As on many past occasions, the newspaper praised Carleton's "wise, military foresight," which had always been characterized by "boldness, independence, determination, and success." When the General finally relinquished command, he would not be forgotten. The success of his Indian policy stood as an honor to his memory, and in the future the Bosque Redondo would be pointed to as "an example worthy of imitation." The newspaper echoed statements made by many high-ranking military officers. General Grant believed that Carleton's act of subduing the Navajos and placing them on the road to civilization at the Bosque was an enormous feat. The Indian Department now could carry forward this great work.[19]

Statistics for the Bosque in January of 1867 again showed a decrease in the number of Navajos there. Navajo men numbered 2,039, while there were 2,125 women, 2,685 children, and 131 infants — a total of 6,980. Nine Apaches still made the Bosque their home. Shortly thereafter, an additional 430 Navajos arrived from the old country. This sizeable group was an indication that after four years a number of Navajos still resided in their homeland. The garrison at Sumner contained 15 officers, 564 enlisted men, and 15 laundresses. The civilian employees at the post numbered several hundred. The reservation and fort were an enormous operation by the standards of the time.[20]

The Santa Fe *Weekly New Mexican* still criticized the reservation. In mid-January, news of a reported Mescalero depredation came from Las Cruces. Fourteen Apaches had made an attack upon Anastacio Ascartes' herd of mules and horses, stealing fifty head and two small boys. An unnamed man was shot in the leg. Sarcastically, the editor stated that the army controlled the Mescaleros about as much as it controlled their breathing. He then pitched into Carleton's recent contract with Vicente Romero, stating that the citizens of Las Vegas received more favors from the government in a week than the residents of Santa Fe get in a month. The *Weekly Gazette* countered that the cost of the reservation would be cut in half in 1867. Texas beef dropped in price by more than half, that is, from 12¢ per pound to 5¢ per pound. Wheat meal was much lower, and the cost of corn plunged by two-thirds. In short, the opponents were hard pressed to charge that the Bosque was a contractor's scheme. Commodity prices in New Mexico were lower than they had been in six years.[21]

Carleton confirmed beliefs that the expenses of the reservation could be cut by more than half in the coming year. Besides obtaining rations at more reasonable rates, he altered the size of the ration at the proper time. He informed General Hancock that rations must always be reduced during the summer, and especially during harvest. Furthermore, during the warm months the Indians raised small gardens, growing melons, corn, and beans. Despite the best efforts of the soldiers to prevent it, the Navajos invariably stole large quantities of food from the ripening fields. The Indians should always be put on three-quarter rations during those months. Then in the winter they could be given a full ration.

Carleton still believed that the Indians could make themselves self-sufficient at the Bosque. The main reason they had failed to do so was for want of the proper equipment and technical knowledge about farming. Now that the Indian Bureau would soon be providing for them, the major question was whether or not Congress would appropriate the necessary funds to feed the Navajos. During the Civil War, the large military expenditures for the tribe had been buried in the enormous war expenses. After the war Secretary Stanton began to realize that a vast amount of money was being spent on Navajos; he felt that this burden belonged to the Indian Bureau. Carleton agreed. The architect of the Bosque then noted that a large portion of the money which Congress had appropriated in the past for Indians, such as the infamous appropriation of 1864, had disappeared into the pockets of the Indian Bureau and those individuals connected with it. In conclusion he stated that every officer under him and involved in the reservation business had looked after the government's interest as well as after the "health and comfort of the Indians." He had acted on a course that he knew was right, and he believed he had been successful.[22]

Carleton remained intimately involved in the operations of the reservation until the last day of his command in New Mexico. He received a requisition from Captain James R. Kimble, Third Cavalry, for fifty-five Remington Revolvers to replace those lost by men. The men apparently had sold their revolvers and were then charged twelve dollars for them. Carleton informed Hancock that a company of eighty-eight men could not possibly lose fifty-five guns. In New Mexico the pistols commanded a high premium, and he recommended that any man who lost a pistol be charged fifty dollars, as was being done in Texas. In this manner soldiers could not profit by selling the scarce pistols to Indians and settlers.

General Carleton also advised that the Indian Bureau not buy blankets for the Navajos. Such a purchase had been the cornerstone of the 1864 swindle. Instead, the money should be used to purchase sheep from which the Indians could obtain wool and weave their own blankets, superior in quality to anything made in the States. Carleton explained to Hancock that food held the Navajos at the reservation like a great magnet. By issuing food only once every two days, they could not get enough at any one time before hunger drove them back, preventing outbreaks. They clustered around the issue house "like steel filings around a loadstone." Of course, there would always be a few "vagabonds" who would steal and commit some outrage from time to time. Fortunately these acts had become less frequent.[23]

The campaign by New Mexico politicians to discredit Carleton bore additional fruit in late January of 1867. General Grant ordered Colonel Alexander, commanding at Fort Bascom, to make a thorough investigation of the District of New Mexico. He was to pay special attention to the contracting methods and would describe any maladministration in detail. Upon completing the task, Alexander would report in person to General Grant's headquarters in Washington. Commenting on Grant's orders, the *Weekly New Mexican* hoped that the investigation would result in the closing of the Bosque reservation and the other endeavors of his "pseudo military highness," General Carleton. The newspaper was certain that a great scandal of corruption would be uncovered. Alexander's report was delayed for many weeks, however, as he scrupulously gathered material.[24]

General Hancock firmly believed that Carleton had pursued a proper course. He wrote that letters and statistics received from New Mexico indicated that expenditures for the coming year would be much lower. Congratulating the General, he stated that "the management at the Bosque Redondo has been the best effort in the direction of humanity and wisdom which has yet been inaugurated for the benefit of our Indians." Hancock believed the only solution to present Indian problems was the perfection of a system similar to one which Carleton had followed with regard to the Navajos. All tribes raiding the settlements or interfering with the great thoroughfares should be placed on reservations or removed from the region. Then, like the Navajos, they should be placed under military control and supported by the government until they learned the arts of husbandry. They must be taught how to make themselves self-sufficient. Hancock agreed with Carleton that the older men would not learn much, but great hopes should be placed in the education of the young. In short, Carleton now saw his policies being adopted by his superiors.[25]

Superintendent Norton found himself questioning his superiors in Washington about supplies for the Bosque. On February 6 he complained to Commissioner Bogy that his critical statements regarding the Bosque Redondo had been deleted from his last annual report, and in the version presented to Congress, the favorable views of Investigator Graves had been substituted. A month later Norton advised Nathaniel G. Taylor, who had replaced Bogy as Commissioner, that the Congressional appropriation for the next fiscal year was much too small to support the Navajos. He urged Taylor to insist that the next Congress increase the appropriation. Thus, the Indian Department was already wrestling with the high cost of the Bosque, as the military had done earlier.[26]

At Fort Sumner, Sykes maintained an uneasy control over his men. His officers were lax, allowing their men to buy alcohol from the sutler for cleaning purposes, a privilege they abused. Occasionally liquor fell into the hands of the Indians with sad consequences. Appalled by the drunkenness, Sykes directed that the most alcohol an individual could procure would be one gill, and the officers of the post must supervise its use. Sykes also kept his garrison active. During March pickets were maintained at Yew Creek, Rio Salado, Cedar Springs, Carretas, and the Lake.[27]

During the early spring of 1867, the Navajos returned to the fields to plant and put in a crop. They diligently dug new irrigation ditches and broke the sod for seeds. Fifty Navajos were assigned to build adobe-walled gardens for use as nurseries to raise seeds for the farms. The walls also prevented the Indians from stealing the young plants. Other Indians began work repairing the diversion dam on the Pecos, an annual task. Each spring the river, fed by runoff from melting snows, swelled and broke the dam in several places.[28]

In Washington, New Mexico's delegate, J. Francisco Chaves, a long-time foe of Carleton's, attacked the Bosque in a letter on March 27 to Secretary of the Interior Browning. The "alleged mismanagement" at the Bosque Reservation, Chaves said, "came very near at the last Session of Congress of being the cause of the defeat of all the Indian appropriations throughout the country." Navajo Agent Dodd had not been directly to blame because the military controlled the reserve. However, Dodd always supported the military. As a former officer, the agent seemed to put the Indian office endorsement on the reservation operations.[29]

Chaves resumed his attack on April 2 in a letter to Commissioner Taylor, urging that the Navajos be relocated. He suggested that the Indians be returned to their own country, and that the government provide them with sheep. The Navajos could subsist on small flocks. The wool provided clothing, and the animals gave milk for the children. A Navajo, stated Chaves, was "as much attached to a sheep or goat . . . as an Arab to his camel, or an Irishman to his pig. . . ."[30]

The proud and haughty General Carleton relinquished his command of the District of New Mexico in late April with a feeling of pride in what he had accomplished. He rightly believed that he had started a new era in government policies toward the Indians, which in the years to come would prove to benefit both the Indians and the entire country. Carleton remained in Santa Fe on leave through July, attending a railroad convention in Albuquerque and publishing articles on local mining — before departing for his family home in Maine.*[31]

General George W. Getty, Carleton's successor, inherited a complex Indian problem. Getty, who had been colonel of the Thirty-seventh Infantry, possessed a distinguished Civil War record, serving admirably in many battles in the Eastern theater. However, he lacked the determination of his predecessor. For the most part, Getty ignored the vast enterprise on the Pecos, believing that the operation would soon be turned over to the Indian Bureau.

Fort Sumner continued to attract more than its share of problems. In mid-May, the post suffered an outbreak of scurvy. The disease spread rapidly among the troops, and the post surgeon reported that a near epidemic existed. Company commanders ordered men to gather all the vegetables and wild greens they could find in the vicinity of the post. Officers made certain that anti-scorbutics were cooked and eaten. A problem also arose when such Indians began reporting to the hospital. An Indian would report in, complaining of some feigned malady; he then would pass his ration ticket to his comrades. While in the hospital he would be well fed, and his friends could eat heartily drawing his extra ration. Sykes quickly caught on to the ruse and ordered that any Indian admitted to the hospital had to turn in his ration ticket.[32]

Like former post commanders, Sykes tried to stop the depredations. On May 22 he ordered Brevet Major Elisha W. Tarlton, Third Cavalry, to scout the Pintada Canyon, some sixty miles northwest of the post. Reportedly, renegade Indians lived in the canyon, and Tarlton was to destroy the ranches or huts of Indians that he found there. If any warriors were spotted, Tarlton's men should immediately attack them. Any Indians found in that region knew that they had no business being off the reservation. Sykes ordered Tarlton to kill any Indians without a passport and to return all captured livestock to the

---

*Carleton's leave was extended through December 31, 1868. He then served in the Department of Texas, where he died of pneumonia on January 7, 1873.

post. The expedition had been prompted by the murder of several Mexicans near Mesa Leon, sixty miles west of Fort Sumner. To augment the force, forestall private expeditions, and keep vengeful citizens under the eyes of the military, Tarlton was to encourage Mexicans to join his soldiers. Despite the preparations Tarlton's force was singularly unsuccessful.[33]

Commissioner Taylor on May 25 complained to Acting Secretary of the Interior William T. Otto that the recent Congressional appropriation was far too small for the Navajos. Congress had simply made the usual $100,000 appropriation, which in the past had been expended for sheep and clothing. Superintendent Norton had recently declared that the appropriation for the fiscal year ending July 1 was too small. Taylor advised the Indian Department to refuse to accept the Navajos, until the government forced their transfer, because of the expense. Norton had estimated that an appropriation of $720,000 would be necessary to sustain the Navajos. A contract had been let for three hundred head of beef at ten cents per pound, a sizeable mark-up over the going rate. The contractor, John B. Brown, was a close friend of ex-Commissioner Bogy's son. Taylor also informed Secretary Otto that proposals had been received from J. A. La Rue to furnish daily rations of one pound of meat and one pound of breadstuffs at from 15¢ to 20¢ per ration. This made the total cost per year between $480,000 and $644,000, depending on whether there were 6,000 or 7,000 Indians at the reservation.

Taylor castigated Congress for failing to appropriate adequate funds for the reserve. His estimates were less than one-half of the amount paid by the military in the previous year for the Navajo subsistence, and he stated that the transfer of control was advisable only if an adequate appropriation were available. The Indian Department was balking at the prospect of acquiring large numbers of Indians when little money was available to feed them.[34]

Because Superintendent Norton, an extremely sick man, had been absent from New Mexico for several months, Indian Commissioner Taylor had great difficulty learning about the Navajos. On June 1 he proposed to Acting Secretary Otto that a special agent be sent to New Mexico to examine the matter fully and enter into the contract with La Rue for feeding the Navajos. He suggested the name of Colonel William P. Davis of Indiana. Two days later Otto replied that Agent Dodd was more than competent for the job. Since Norton was absent from his post, Dodd should report directly to Taylor.[35]

Taylor disagreed, believing that the situation constituted an emergency, and he went over Otto's head to President Johnson. Taylor informed the President that Otto did not appreciate the nature of the situation. The Navajos were soon to be turned over to the Indian Bureau and no arrangements had been made to feed them. If Dodd received the Navajos in July, supplies would have to be purchased on the open market. Taylor stated that the law provided for the appointment of agents, when necessity demanded that appointment.

He then explained why it was impossible for Agent Dodd to perform the duties of the special agent. In addition to his ordinary duties, Dodd soon would be required to appraise and receive from the War Department all farming implements, stock, and other personal property, while providing for the Indians. The War Department had many employees at Fort Sumner, but the Indian Department had only one agent. Taylor stated that he was perfectly convinced that unless the president appointed a special agent, great wrong would be done to the Navajos and great suffering would ensue. Apparently Johnson reacted to Taylor's suggestion by following a simpler course. He ordered that the transfer of the Navajos to the Indian Department be delayed until that arm of the government was able to receive them.[36]

General Getty, the new district commander, found he had to deal with problems of Indian affairs, inherited from Carleton. In mid-June of 1867 he received an order from General Hancock, an order for the transfer of the Navajos. It was basically the same as his previous order to Carleton, but this time Hancock stipulated that military authorities continue to send any Navajos found at large to the Bosque. In contrast to Carleton, Getty rarely communicated with the Bosque. Gradually, the officers at the reservation came to answer only to themselves. Getty failed to realize the danger which lay in ignoring the reservation. He did, however, try to prevent Indian depredations. St. Vrain recently had lost forty-two mules to Comanches and Mescaleros, and Indians also stole a number of horses in the Los Alamos area. Five shepherd boys had been carried off, and Rumaldo Baca was killed. The *Weekly New Mexican* continued to list the names of people who had been victimized by "fugitives from that pandemonium of breech clouts and red skins, the Bosque Redondo."[37]

On June 30 Theodore Dodd submitted his second annual report as Navajo agent at the Bosque Redondo. He noted that one of the major problems which existed between the Navajos and the New Mexicans resulted from the Comanchero trade. In May, Navajos killed a New Mexican because they had found some of their horses in the possession of local citizens. The animals had been purchased from Comancheros, and the new owners refused to part with them. Dodd stated that trouble of this sort would continue so long as citizens (Comancheros) were permitted to trade with the Comanches.

Hardly a day passed at the reservation, he noted, in which Comanche signs were not observed. Recently Comanches had killed a Navajo man and taken a boy prisoner within fifteen miles of the post. Lately the Navajos had become disappointed and had grown fearful of the Comanches. Saying that the Comanches would annoy them so long as they remained at the Bosque Redondo, they expressed a desire to be relocated in their old country. There they could live in peace, raise good crops, and have better grazing.

Dodd noted that the buildings belonging to the agency had fallen into great disrepair since Agent Labadie had left. In fact, when he arrived at Sumner there was not a single place where he could transact agency matters or store goods and tools. The two-room dwelling occupied by Labadie and his family was unfit to live in. For a time he stored goods with the military until suitable buildings were constructed. To make matters worse the post commander informed him that the military needed the buildings which Dodd occupied. Consequently, the Navajo agent put a number of Indians to work making adobes, took others south to the Capitan Mountains for timber, and managed to repair the old structure. Dodd also made an addition to the agency building, constructed a corral sixty feet square, and enclosed ten acres of land adjoining the agency for planting. The Indians performed all the labor except the carpentry and were paid by receiving full rations (they generally drew three-quarter rations in summer) and occasional presents.

Dodd stated that the Navajo Agency had received many light and useless goods. The Navajos differed from the Plains tribes and did not need expensive light-weight blankets. If provided with wool, they could make their own blankets at half the cost. He again urged that the Navajos be provided with sheep.

The increasing scarcity of wood on the reservation presented a problem. If the Indian Department planned on making the Bosque a permanent reservation, Dodd suggested that every family be furnished with a condemned wagon or a burro to haul wood. During the previous winter the Navajos had to travel as much as twelve miles to dig mesquite roots, and many suffered acutely from the cold. The shortage of wood could lead to more dissatisfaction.

In concluding his lengthy report, Dodd stated that if the government desired to make the Navajos self-sufficient, they must have more cultivable land. In their crude way, the Indians raised very good crops. They understood the principles of irrigation and had built excellent acequias. They were an intelligent and industrious people, and Dodd believed that if placed upon an efficient reservation they would soon become self-sustaining.

The farming operations looked disheartening. Roughly 3,000 acres lay under cultivation, but the crops probably would be a "total failure." Noncommissioned officers and privates acted as overseers; they knew little about farming. Those who possessed some knowledge of agriculture failed to use it because "they were not enlisted for this purpose." Dodd recommended that if the Navajos were transferred to the Indian Department only 1,500 to 2,000 acres should be planted. The rest of the land should be allotted to the Indians themselves. The Navajos had great difficulty in understanding that they labored on the government farm for themselves.

Another major problem was the earthen dam on the Pecos. If the site were to be a permanent reservation, the dam should be moved farther north and constructed of stone so it would not wash away in the spring floods. Dodd stated that he had recently had the Indians dig another acequia below the post, running for a distance of three and one-half miles and opening up a new area for cultivation. The agent then gave some revealing figures. The number of animals owned by the Navajos were: 950 horses, 20 mules, 940 sheep, and 1,025 goats. The once mighty tribe had seen its wealth of sheep reduced to virtual extinction. The fall harvest had been ruined by hailstones, and a sizeable part of the livestock had died from eating poisoned herbs. It was a dismal report.[38]

After a prolonged search for a contractor, Commissioner Taylor recommended to the Department of the Interior that Elijah Simerly of Kansas be appointed to supply the Bosque Redondo. Several proposals had been received, but Simerly's appeared the best. He agreed to furnish rations of one pound of beef, one pound of corn or wheat, and four quarts of salt per hundred rations, at a price of 19 cents per ration. Acting Interior Secretary Otto approved the recommendation, and the government let the contract. Perry Fuller, Simerly's representative in New Mexico, would handle all of the details.[39]

Commissioner Taylor was somewhat upset by the rebuff from Interior Secretary Browning on the matter of a special agent. In July he again told Browning, who had returned after an absence, that if Agent Dodd attended to the receiving and issuing of subsistence at the reserve he would have to neglect important duties. Of especial importance was Dodd's supervision of the farming.

His duties were more than a full-time job for one man; in fact, in the past the army had detailed a team of soldiers for the task. Taylor recommended that one man be appointed to supervise the food issue, and a third person to act as a go-between for the agent and the contractors. This third individual would insure that the proper price was made on the Indian Department contracts, and he would act as an overseer of the entire operation. Commissioner Taylor also addressed Secretary Browning on the question of the appropriation. The recent $100,000 bill would last the Navajos for approximately three months. The new contract with Simerly would reduce the expense of the reservation by six cents per ration, but the department required more money. Sounding like Carleton, Taylor stated that the Navajos had to be supported until they became self-sufficient.[40]

While the military waited to turn the reservation over to the Indian Bureau, one of the most serious incidents that ever occurred at the Bosque took place in early July. The result of a misunderstanding between the soldiers and Indians, coupled with drunken officers, a clash occurred between troops and Navajos, and five soldiers were killed. A lengthy investigation into the incident revealed that the reservation had taken a decided change for the worse since the volunteer forces had departed.

For several weeks there had been rumors that some Navajos had been stealing horses. On July 8 Agent Dodd received word from two Navajos that indeed a party of unreconciled Indians had been hiding horses in a canyon, twenty-five miles south of the post. Dodd carried the information to Major Tarlton, temporarily in command of the fort. The two Indian informers agreed to guide troops to the hidden canyon on the night of July 8. Tarlton selected Second Lieutenant Henry Bragg to head a detachment of twenty-one men from Company I, Third Cavalry. The men left Fort Sumner at 9:00 P.M. under orders to bring the stolen horses into the post but not to use force unless it became absolutely necessary. They arrived near the camp and waited until morning.

Early on the morning of July 9, Bragg entered the Indian camp and told the Navajos the reason for his visit. There was no trouble, and the soldiers rounded up one hundred and fifty horses. The Indians agreed to go to the fort with the herd. The interpreter Jesus accompanying the force noted that the horses did not appear to belong to the government, as they lacked the distinctive "U. S." brand. Jesus realized that the animals probably belonged to the Navajos. At nine o'clock Lieutenant Bragg sent Sergeant Terrell with four men to escort some one hundred horses back to the fort, while Bragg and the rest of the party continued to round up the animals.

The Navajos already had decided upon a plan of action. Assuming that the soldiers had come to steal their animals, the Indians decided to stampede the horses on the way back to Fort Sumner. When the sergeant and his party were about half-way back to the post, the Navajos accompanying him started to yell and scream, striking the horses. The handful of soldiers, who were greatly outnumbered, watched helplessly as the Indians drove off the herd. The empty-handed soldiers then returned to the post.

Unaware of the deliberate stampede, Bragg had rounded up some fifty horses and started for Sumner. When he reached a point five miles from the post, he fell victim to the same trick. Still uncertain as to what was happening, he sent Sergeant Myers and two privates to recover the herd. As the men approached the villages on the river toward which the Indians and the horses had fled, the three troopers were fired on and beat a hasty retreat back to Bragg. Puzzled by the Indians' behavior, Bragg lined up his men and charged forward, only to be confronted by nearly two hundred Navajo warriors drawn up in a rough skirmish line. The Indians were determined to make a fight, and Bragg realized that it would be suicide to resist with sixteen men. The soldiers wheeled their horses and galloped back to Fort Sumner.

When the first detachment reached Sumner, Sergeant Terrell hastened to find Major Tarlton and report the stampede. He found the post commander and Lieutenant Charles Porter drinking heavily. Tarlton ordered his drinking companion, Porter, to take a small detachment and find the horses. He obviously did not realize the seriousness of the situation.

Guided by Sergeant Terrell, Lieutenant Porter and his men drew up in sight of the Navajos who had stampeded the herd. Porter yelled at the Indians in Spanish, but he could get no answer from them. They were young and recently from the Navajo country, and quite possibly did not understand Spanish. No interpreter was present. The Navajos were obviously hostile. They made threatening gestures and motioned Porter to return to Fort Sumner. The Indians had their bows drawn and leveled at Porter's party.

Porter decided to retreat to favorable ground, but in the tenseness of the situation a soldier fired a shot. Immediately the Indians charged, and Porter fired his pistol, screaming at his men to look out for themselves. Heavy firing ensued, and the twenty troopers tried to retreat to the fort. In the melee five soldiers were killed and four others seriously wounded, one dying shortly thereafter. Many soldiers had a near escape in the clash that took place at the river's edge. Porter himself was wounded in the side by an arrow, and another splintered the hilt of his pistol. The Indians still did not know why the army was stealing their horses. Porter later stated that he had requested an interpreter, but Tarlton did not think one was necessary.

Frightened and confused, Porter and his shattered detachment retreated to the post, pursued by the Indians. Soldiers at Sumner stared in amazement at the sight of troops riding desperately over a hill with the Indians behind them in hot pursuit. At the top of the hill south of Sumner the Navajos stopped and turned back to the river and their herds. Soldiers and Indians alike at the post were shocked. One Navajo leader, Narbono, said that it was like two brothers fighting. At this point Lieutenant McDonald, who had many friends among the Navajos, decided to go to the Indians at the river and reason with them. He believed that the entire incident resulted from a misunderstanding that could be cleared up if he could talk to the Indians. Major Tarlton accompanied the group, but his inebriated condition prevented him from being of much assistance. As the group left the post, Manuelito, who only recently had stopped fighting the government, grabbed the reins of McDonald's horse, fearing that his friend would be killed. When the soldiers, augmented by several Navajos who were preparing to fight with the troops, reached the river, they saw the hostile Navajos on the opposite bank. Drawn up for war, the Indians kept their women and children behind them. They were clearly determined to make a stand.

At a great risk to his life, McDonald with Manuelito went forward to talk. The soldiers had not been stealing the horses, the officer stated through Manuelito, but merely wanted to inspect them, as there had been rumors that some were stolen. Manuelito, standing by the side of a brave officer, was a powerful symbol to the truth of the officer's words. The Indian also was one of the most respected Navajos on the reservation. No one could accuse him of being a white man's Indian, a charge leveled against Delgadito. The Indians on the far side of the river were convinced, and the incident which might well have resulted in several hundred deaths was closed. The young Navajos, new to the reservation, who had been the backbone of the resistance, fled the reservation.

News of the incident at the Bosque reached Washington. Lt. Col. John W. Davidson, investigating officer, declared that the trouble "arose from a drinking and indiscreet officer Bvt. Maj. Tarlton." The officers who executed his orders "had no more discretion than he had." According to Davidson, the testimony against the officers was vague enough that they probably would not be convicted in a court-martial. Sherman was especially angry when he learned of the incident, and although the three officers remained in the army for several more months, their careers were at an end. General Getty, Carleton's successor at Santa Fe, received a severe reprimand for leaving such an important post "in the hands of incompetent officers." The only bright spot in the incident had been the performance of Lieutenant McDonald.

The Santa Fe *Weekly New Mexican* tried to use the incident to discredit Carleton's policy. However, if he had been in command of the district, such an occurrence might not have taken place. With several exceptions, the regulars at Fort Sumner did not equal the caliber of the volunteers, and the series of pathetic commanders who followed McCleave indicated the fact in no uncertain terms. Tarlton was replaced with Major Charles J. Whiting, and a new order concerning liquor was promulgated. The post sutler was forbidden to sell spiritous liquor to any soldiers (including officers), to government employees, or even to citizens. However, this change would not solve the problem of incompetency. The Indians sensed the change in the nature of the reservation, and when it appeared that the summer crops for 1867 would be a total failure, rumors began that another large outbreak was in the offing.[41]

9

Closing the Bosque Redondo

"I found the Bosque a mere spot of green grass in the midst
of a wild desert, and that the Navajos had sunk into a condition of absolute poverty and despair."

General Sherman

"When we saw the top of the mountain from Albuquerque
we wondered if it was our mountain, and we felt like talking
to the ground, we loved it so, and some of the old men and
women cried with joy when they reached their homes."

Manuelito

AFTER THE TRAGIC CLASH in July of 1867 between reservation Navajos and
troops, the army held several councils with the Navajo leaders. Although they
showed no hostility toward those who had confined them to the reservation, the
Navajos pleaded to be allowed to return to their old country. The harvest at
the end of the summer was a total failure, and a general depression had settled
over the Indian camps. With the councils proving of no value, younger Navajo
leaders began urging action, and in the fall Manuelito and Barboncito led their
bands off the reservation. Their absence, however, was temporary. Too many
New Mexicans and soldiers swarmed over the countryside looking for renegades. After months of discussion, the Navajos in a dramatic council meeting
convinced a group of visiting Peace Commissioners to permit them to return
to their old country. Five frustrating years of exile at last came to an end.

Following the battle at the Bosque, Superintendent Norton visited the
reservation in July to conduct a council with the Indian leaders. He questioned
them closely about their feelings concerning the reservation. One prominent
leader, Herrero, stated that since their arrival on the Pecos the Navajos had
been constantly hungry and their large flocks of sheep had been decimated.
They also feared the Comanches. Ganado Mucho stated that the Plains raiders
had killed his son and captured his daughter. Herrero added that the Comanches "told me the land belongs to them. The water belonged to them. The hunting grounds belonged to them. The wood belonged to them. And I believe it

Ganado Mucho (center), Tiene-su-se (left), and Mariana (right): prominent Navajo leaders at the Bosque Redondo.

now because they [the Comanches] come here every day and steal our stock." Every time the Indians made the long trek for wood, he feared they would never return "because our enemies are all around us." Herrero said he had thought more and more about his home country. He reminded Norton that if the government put them back there, it could still exercise authority over them. "Even if we starve there, we will have no complaints to make," the leader added. All his people longed to return to the lofty mesas and red sand country in Arizona. In conclusion, Herrero asked: "What does the government want us to do — more than we have done? Or more than we are doing?" Superintendent Norton, who had seen nothing but failure at the Bosque, was impressed with the Navajos' words.[1]

The Navajo farms had failed again at the Bosque, but the diet of the Indians had changed somewhat. Many Navajos had developed a taste for beef, since it was now a major item in their rations. The price of Texas beef continued to be low. Andy Adams had won the new contract effective July 1, 1867, agreeing to supply the reservation with cattle at 2½ cents per pound, undercutting Patterson and Roberts by a large margin. Adams had contracted with cattleman J. D. Hoy to drive several thousand head of cattle to the reservation, but disaster struck when the Comanches drove off the herd. Adams' luck had run out. For Oliver Loving and Charles Goodnight the theft seemed a blessing. The two men arrived with a herd of Texas steers and sold them to Roberts and Patterson, who were back in the government's favor. W. J. Wilson also drove a small herd to the Bosque, preceding Goodnight, and John Hittson reached Sumner with cattle in August. John Chisum also started a herd over the Pecos Trail that summer, but before he reached the Bosque a Navajo band stole his herd of eight hundred head.[2]

Shortly after Norton concluded his conference the military called the Navajos together for another larger council. Several important army officers attended. These included General Getty, Carleton's successor; Lieutenant Edward Hunter, Getty's aide-de-camp; General Randolph B. Marcy, Inspector General of the Army; Captain Robert Barnard; and the Navajo agent, Theodore Dodd. The Navajo leaders were Manuelito, Ganado Mucho, Delgadito, Narbono, and Barboncito, along with fifteen lesser leaders. Getty opened the council by stating that when he visited the Bosque in May he had been very pleased by what he had seen. At that time the fields and crops prospered, and he had seen no reason to make changes. Now, there had been the regrettable fight with the troops, and the scarcity of rain had killed the crops.

Delgadito was the first Indian to speak. Recently he had lost favor with his brothers because he had worked so closely with the soldiers in the early days of the reserve. Delgadito stated that his head and heart were "for the

Smithsonian Institution

Navajo leaders with interpreters. In the front row are Carnero Mucho, Mariana, Juanita (Manuelito's wife), Manuelito (head chief), Manuelito Segundo (son of Manuelito and Juanita), and Tiene-su-se. In the back row are "Wild" Hank Sharp (interpreter), Ganado Mucho, Barbas Hueros, W. F. M. Arny (territorial secretary and, later, Indian agent), Kentucky Mountain Bill (interpreter), Cabra Negra, Cayatanita, Narbona Primero, and Jesus Arviso (interpreter).

right." When he had come to the reservation he had been told that the ground and water belonged to the Navajos. He had made up his mind to live at the Bosque and do right. He planted seeds but could raise no crops. Three more times he tried to grow corn and failed. Now he did not believe that crops could be raised at the Bosque. The ground on the Pecos was not the best land for the Navajos. Delgadito admitted that he had plenty of food and clothing, but he found it impossible to secure two of anything. In the old country, abundant crops and numerous herds were commonplace. He was deeply saddened by not owning sheep or cattle, and he regretted that he would never again see the large flocks of the old days.

At this council, as on so many past occasions, Jesus Arviso, the Navajo translator, played a key role. Apaches had captured Arviso, a Mexican, in his youth; later they traded him to the Navajos, whom he now called his people. He had been involved in almost every major event that had taken place at the reservation since the Navajos arrived. As none of the Navajos at the council spoke fluent Spanish, except possibly Delgadito, and none understood English, Jesus Arviso played an extremely delicate role.

Barboncito, considered the best of the Navajo speakers, then registered his complaints about the reservation. A small wiry man with a drooping mustache and weary eyes, Barboncito said he was glad that the meeting was being held in such a large room where everyone could be heard. He emphasized that the Navajos did not like the ground at the Bosque. When he first reached the reservation, he had thought that all land was alike, but the Pecos country had shown him otherwise. Like all the other Navajos, Barboncito stated that in their old country they had raised plenty of corn and cattle. Even a leader like himself now had become a pauper. He owned no stock, and his only possession was his body. Before he became too old, he hoped to see his children in their own country. Barboncito asked that his words be carried to the Great Father in Washington so it could be known that crops could not be raised at the reservation. Even a great number of livestock had died from eating some mysterious root which grew at the reservation. All the Navajos wished to return to their old country. When the conference ended, the Navajos believed that something had been accomplished.[3]

On July 4 Commissioner Taylor informed Superintendent Norton that control of the Bosque would soon pass to the Interior Department. A contract had been let to Elijah Simerly of Kansas to furnish cattle and other supplies to the Bosque. Norton relayed the information to General Getty. Supposedly Simerly would begin supplying the reservation on September 1, 1867, but Norton doubted if all responsibilities could be turned over to Agent Dodd by that date. Getty replied that he had received no new directives concerning the transfer, and he advised that the War Department was sending a group to investigate the reservation.[4]

In his annual report to Commissioner Taylor, Norton called for the removal of the Navajos to their homeland. He had predicted the failure of the reservation in his report of the previous year, but Taylor's predecessor, Cooley, had ignored his advice and published garbled extracts, with the favorable views of Inspector Graves substituted for his own. After his experiences the previous year, Norton had little inclination to write a report this year. He cited all the arguments against the reservation. The crop had been a failure, the water was brackish, the soil was impregnated with alkali, and the Indians had to carry firewood for twelve miles on their "galled and lacerated backs." He noted that disease had swept away one-fourth of the Indian population. With great sarcasm, he added: "What a beautiful selection is this for a reservation." The Bosque had cost millions of dollars, and the sooner the government abandoned it and removed the Indians, the better off everyone concerned would be. Altogether, he estimated that the government had spent nearly $10,000,000 on the Bosque, and he hinted that speculators had been at the bottom of the experiment.

Norton said that the Bosque lacked the three essential ingredients for a successful reservation — wood, good soil, and pure water. The Navajos remained on the reservation only because the garrison kept them there. To subject human beings to "such torture" was a disgrace to the "age we live in and to the government we support." No matter how successful the Indian Department might be in realizing Carleton's plan to civilize and Christianize the Navajos and to teach them mechanical arts, they would always have to be held at the Bosque by force. Norton stated that the government should either let them go back to their old country or move them to some place where they would have cool water to drink, wood to keep them from freezing to death, and soil that would produce something to eat. Although some objections had been raised to removal of the Navajos because of the amount expended on buildings, acequias, and corrals, Norton believed that supplying the Indians with two years of fuel would equal the cost of all the post buildings. They should be removed, but where should they be relocated? Norton suggested that they be taken to their old country, or perhaps to the Maxwell grant which was for sale, or to the area around Fort Stanton.[5]

At about the same time, Norton heard from Labadie, the former Mescalero agent, whom he had sent on a mission to the Plains Indians in the early summer. Labadie had been unable to obtain a treaty with the Comanches and Kiowas. He had talked with the few Comanches he could find, but they said they lacked the authority to make a treaty. When questioned as to the whereabouts of the majority of the tribe, they replied that three hundred were on an expedition to raid the Navajos at Fort Sumner.[6]

In late August General Getty ordered an inventory of all items to be transferred to the Indian Department. He instructed Lieutenant McDonald and Agent Dodd to appraise that portion of the working stock, wagons, and implements owned by the Quartermaster Department being used for the benefit of the Indians. If they could not agree, a third party could be added to their board. Getty also requested that a close check be kept on the sutler for tax purposes and to insure that contraband was not being dispensed on the reservation.[7]

Acting Indian Commissioner Mix in early September told Acting Secretary Otto that General Getty had not received an order for the final transfer of the Navajos to the Indian Department. Getty refused to release the Indians until he received a specific order to do so. Mix urged that the order be given. Simerly's representatives shortly would be driving cattle and hauling breadstuffs to the reservation in compliance with his new contract.[8]

Norton held a council meeting in Santa Fe to hear Indian complaints. Ten Navajo leaders rode from the Bosque to confer with Superintendent Norton. The Indians again made known their complaints about the reservation, and Superintendent Norton undoubtedly told them that the government would soon take action. The Indians at the reservation, however, could see no sign that the government had heard their pleas at the recent councils.

Then, unexpectedly, the Comanches again struck the Navajo camps on the reservation. A raiding party of more than two hundred warriors stormed through the outlying camps while Lieutenant McDonald rode to Sumner for aid. Colonel Whiting quickly ordered Captain Thomas to take what troops he could find to beat off the attackers, but in the confusion the orders became garbled. McDonald watched while the Navajos battled the Comanches, with the army never taking a step to assist the Navajos. With few arms the Navajos somehow managed to beat back their ancient enemies.

At Santa Fe General Getty soon heard of the Comanche raid and the fact that his troops had made a poor showing. He asked Whiting if Captain Thomas could be court-martialed. Whiting stated that it would not be possible because in the confusion of the situation, it was difficult to pinpoint the blame. Getty fumed. Matters were becoming more tenuous each day. This raid, combined with the July clash with the soldiers, crop failures, and what the Indians regarded as poor faith on the part of the whites, pointed toward trouble.

On the morning of September 28, Lieutenant McDonald gloomily reported that between two and three hundred Navajos had left the reservation. Leading them were Manuelito, Barboncito, Ganado Mucho, and Muerto de Hambre. The Navajos picked an opportune time to bolt the Bosque. Detachments were away looking for the Comanche raiders, and Colonel Whiting at Sumner had only forty-five cavalrymen in garrison. Captain Thomas was under arrest and Major Tarlton faced a court-martial. Lieutenant Lambert Mulford was gone on a scout of the Puerto de Luna region. Realizing the cause of the outbreak, Whiting optimistically stated that an officer who knew the Indians could probably coax them back.[9]

The Navajos apparently left the Bosque to strike a party of Utes, known to be in the vicinity. The Utes had permission to go to a point forty miles from Sumner to search for some horses they thought were being secreted there. They decided that as long as they were in the neighborhood they should pay their respects to their old enemies, the Navajos, by stealing a few horses. After the recent fight with the Comanches, the Navajos were not about to allow the lowly Utes to steal their few remaining horses. Scouts were sent out from Fort Bascom, Fort Union, Fort Stanton, and even Fort Wingate. When the citizens heard of the outbreak, the New Mexican militia also took to the field, hoping to encounter the Navajos.

First Lieutenant William P. Bainridge, Third Cavalry, returned to Fort Union on October 4 and reported on his fruitless scout for Navajo renegades. He had left Fort Union on September 27 heading southwest along the Pecos. On Sunday September 30, he struck an Indian trail. The trail appeared five or six days old, but he could learn little of the Indians who had made it. The guide with the detachment of twenty-five soldiers stated that the signs spoke of many Navajos. When Bainridge learned of the large outbreak, he realized that the tracks which he saw belonged either to the Navajos who had jumped the reservation or perhaps to the Utes who were returning to their home country.[10]

Numerous scouting detachments had failed to find any Navajos by October 6. Whiting ordered Tarlton to take all the available men of companies I and G, Third Cavalry, and try to catch the Navajos and induce them to return to the reservation. He directed Tarlton to kill every male adult who refused to return to the Bosque. Tarlton must prevent the Indians from crossing the Rio Grande.

At the head of Yeso Creek, Tarlton found Muerto de Hambre and his Navajo family on their way back to the Bosque. He then met Ganado Mucho and his people heading for the reserve. Troops and small bands of Mexicans were swarming over the countryside looking for Navajos. Still missing, however, were Manuelito and Barboncito. The Navajos stated that both bands were bound for their own country. Tarlton rode west toward the Rio Grande trying to intercept the two families.[11]

Inaccurate reports circulated wildly about the whereabouts of the Navajos. A weary detachment reported they had seen Navajos near Tipton's ranch. From Fort Bascom Captain John V. Dubois headed northwest toward the Mesa Rica area, forty-five miles away. His horses and pack mules soon showed fatigue. "The post blacksmith is a miserable workman," Dubois angrily wrote, and many horses were unshod. The operation also was tedious because the pack mules had wild dispositions and required several men to load them. On September 29 Dubois crossed the trail of some Indians (probably the Utes) heading north. Tired and disheartened, Dubois outspokenly wrote Getty that he could not "catch Indians with such pack mules as are furnished me." Another scout should be sent out, but he gloomily forecasted that they would find nothing. Shortly thereafter, Tarlton returned to Fort Sumner. In the last few days his men had suffered greatly from thirst, heat, and lack of sleep. Men, horses, and mules had gone for twenty-eight hours without water. Upon reaching Sumner, Tarlton discovered to his chagrin that Manuelito, Barboncito, and the other Navajos had all returned. There had been too many New Mexicans scouring the countryside, hoping to catch them off the reservation.[12]

The Indians complained continually about the lack of wood for fuel. The government hired a wood contractor to provide the reservation with fuel, but his contract was let too late in the season, and he found it impossible to float the wood down the shallow river. He either had to haul the wood in wagons, a time-consuming process, or wait until the spring floods. In the meantime the Indians dug mesquite roots for fuel.[13]

While the Navajo band was off the reservation, General Getty prepared to transfer the Indians to civilian control. On September 30 he wrote Norton that in compliance with General Orders 651, 1866, and Special Orders 10, the Navajos would be transferred as soon as the Indian Bureau designated someone to receive them. Getty apparently had received a letter from the States concerning the situation. Unbelievably he wrote Norton that he "was not aware of the existence of these orders until today." Norton suggested October 11 as a possible date for counting and transferring the Indians to Agent Dodd. The agent must give the military a receipt for everything he received. Norton, in a burst of sarcasm, ridiculed Getty for not being aware of the orders. He considered them the most important issue concerning the District of New Mexico in the preceding year. General Getty disliked Norton, and he wrote that October

11 was too early to arrange the transfer. The military always counted the Indians on the last day of each month, and the Navajos would be alarmed by a head count during the middle of the month. Moreover, the details of the transfer required additional time. Getty suggested the date, October 31, and Norton agreed to the arrangement.[14]

In Washington, General Grant found himself involved with the Bosque issue again. Colonel Herbert M. Enos, Commissary officer for New Mexico under Carleton, had applied for a court of inquiry. The investigation of the Bosque made by Colonel Alexander at Grant's direction had generated many rumors, and Enos' name had been mentioned frequently. Getty had ordered Enos to be court-martialed if the alleged corrupt contracting practices were true. However it appeared that Enos, like many others before him, had heard too many stories, and Alexander's investigation had absolved him of any wrong doing.[15]

While top officials in both the War Department and the Indian Bureau weighed the pros and cons of removing the Navajos from the Bosque Redondo, work went ahead on the public buildings. In October the post commander at Sumner received authorization to hire a team to expedite this work so the buildings could be completed before the coming winter. The new personnel included a superintendent at $300 per month, a carpenter and two first-class masons at $75 per month, nine second-class masons at $55 per month, five third-class masons at $35 per month, and eighty-five Indians as adobe makers. Despite the possibility that the Indians were to be removed, the military continued to erect more buildings at the reservation.[16]

On November 29, 1867, Lieutenant McDonald, a consistent friend of the Navajos, received orders to join his regiment in Kansas. He turned over all the commissary property to his successor, Lieutenant Royal E. Whitman. The commissary position was important at the reservation, as the officer had the closest contact with Indian leaders, and subsequently understood the shortcomings of the experiment better than any other individual. The Indians officially passed into the civilian hands on October 31, 1867. The military, however, still directed the rationing. In general, while the Indians nominally remained under Agent Dodd's authority, the military retained much of the responsibility for the reserve. The agency had too few employees to direct the enormous operation. Consequently Whitman was involved daily with the Indians. He learned their ways and sympathized with their problems.[17]

The military authorities in late October let a large contract for corn to be delivered at Fort Sumner. From the size of the delivery, General Getty probably believed the Indian Bureau might not be able to feed the Navajos during the coming winter. The contract called for 1,700,000 pounds of corn to be delivered at Fort Sumner. Should Simerly be unable to fulfill his contract, the army could furnish the food and request that the Department of the Interior reimburse it. John Dold received the sizeable contract, agreeing to a price of $3.80 per hundred pounds. The demand for corn had lessened in New Mexico because Indian purchases had been recently made in the East. Consequently the price had dropped markedly on the New Mexican market. Recent events seemed to indicate that hoarding by corn speculators had driven up the price during the difficult days of 1864 and 1865.[18]

The Navajos, because they were so dissatisfied with the Bosque, often worked against their own best interests. On November 17 they attacked the wagons hauling timber to the post. The Indians drove off the mules and disappeared. Lieutenant Mulford took all available men in pursuit. His party returned to the post six days later, after searching for two hundred miles without catching a glimpse of the thieves.[19]

Like Colonel Enos, Carleton — now at San Antonio — also requested that a Board of Inquiry be appointed to review his command in New Mexico. In late December General Grant informed him that Secretary Stanton had refused the request, believing that no good for the service could result. Grant also said he had heard unfavorable reports on military affairs in New Mexico the previous winter and had directed Colonel Alexander to make a thorough inspection of the district. Quoting from Alexander's report, Grant praised Carleton's Indian policy. Evidence did not sustain the grave charges leveled by the citizens against Carleton. During Carleton's tenure it was understood that his principal objective had been the subjugation of the Navajos. In this endeavor, Grant declared, Carleton "was perfectly successful." The advantages from his policy were incalculable. It was true that Indian agents and contractors had opposed the Bosque Redondo Reservation and had heaped abuse upon him. With few exceptions, Grant continued, these agents had been "utterly worthless." Their whole object had been to plunder the Indians. They had purposely overestimated the number of Indians running wild in the mountains and had often failed to deliver their goods. On a reservation one could not falsify the number of Indians to receive annuities when the authorities on a reservation counted them regularly and reliable officers supervised the operation. Thus Carleton saw his policy fully vindicated and praised by the man who many persons believed would be the next president.[20]

Effects of the change of command in New Mexico could be seen on the streets of Santa Fe. Carleton had authorized Colonel McClure to distribute government food to the many orphans of the city, but when Getty took control he discontinued this policy. Like so many of the officers who had been deeply involved in Carleton's experiment, McClure was undaunted. He personally launched a crusade to raise food for the unfortunate children, and he contacted many prominent persons, probably the old Carleton supporters. He raised more than one thousand dollars. Several years before, when the Sisters of Loretto had first opened their home for orphans, Carleton had brought the first Navajo girl to the home. The Sisters named her Mary Carleton in honor of the General.[21]

The Department of the Interior continued to remain quite reluctant to shoulder the great expense of operating the Bosque. On January 10, 1868, Acting Commissioner of Indian Affairs C. E. Mix wrote Secretary of the Interior Browning that his Bureau was feeding 7,111 Indians at the Bosque. Of the $100,000 appropriated by Congress, $41,792 had been paid Simerly in November, which left a balance of $58,207 to subsist the Navajos from December 1, 1867 to June 30, 1868. Mix estimated that it would cost $295,876 to provide food for the Navajos for that period, giving the Indian Department a deficit of $237,668. To prevent great suffering among the Indians he urged that Congress take speedy action to appropriate more funds. The Indians, he added, "cannot be expected to remain on the reservation to starve." If permitted to leave the reserve, they would head for their old haunts and commit depredations upon the whites. If the Navajos remained at the Bosque, necessity demanded that immediate steps be taken to make them self-sustaining.[22]

Responding to a request from Secretary Browning, Commissioner Mix drew up a report on how the Navajos had lived in their home country. Before they were brought to the Bosque Redondo, he said, the Indians had subsisted themselves from the land, without government assistance. They had hunted, cultivated corn and wheat, and raised livestock. They had owned thousands of horses and sheep and were acknowledged to be one of the richest tribes in the country. Their blankets were some of the best that could be made. The important point, however, was that they had been able to support themselves without government expense!

The Indian Department understood that a great sum of money was necessary to keep the Bosque operating. As the expenses of the reservation became felt in the budget of the Indian Bureau, sentiment in Washington to remove the Navajos crystalized. But at this critical juncture, on January 10 Superintendent Norton succumbed to his chronic illness.[23]

In late January, Lieutenant McDonald, a former Commissary Officer, filed a report on the reservation. He informed his superiors in Washington that the location of the reservation had been unwise. He concluded that the Navajos could never be self-sustaining at the Bosque, and he recommended their removal.

After reading his report, Commissary General Eaton sent the document to Secretary of War Stanton. The whole experience of the subsistence department, Eaton stated, had shown that the attempt to accommodate the Navajos and Apaches on the Bosque had been a long unfortunate experience, which should be ended. A more suitable location must be found and the Indians transferred to it.

McDonald's report also showed that the reservation farm had been a total failure. Almost 2,500 acres had been planted. The farm had been divided into three sections; and a noncommissioned officer, with four private soldiers as assistants, directed the labor of eighteen Indians on each section. Usually one hundred to two hundred Indians labored constantly to keep the irrigation ditches in order. Why had the farm failed? First, a spring flood had washed away the river bank next to the dam. At great expense the army had strengthened the dam, and it was believed that the river could not wash it away again. However, on many days no water flowed in the acequias because of the large crevasse gouged around the dam. Other problems developed. Little rain fell during the summer, and the sun scorched the crops. Replanting had been attempted in July, in the hope of saving something, but the rains failed to come. As matters then stood, McDonald stated that a new expensive dam was needed and that a larger canal should be built.

From his experiences, however, McDonald argued that the government should not undertake the construction. "At no distant day the government will be compelled to seek a more suitable location for a permanent reservation," he believed. Although Getty, like Carleton, had collected a variety of seeds and shipped them to the reservation for planting, the results had been miserable. Any effort to ameliorate the Indians' condition at the Bosque, McDonald

argued, would have only a temporary effect. The want of timber both for building purposes and for fuel was "an inseparable barrier to the permanency of
the Bosque as a reservation." The Navajo leaders had told him time and time
again that unless the government provided them with a suitable location they
would leave the reservation. McDonald believed the Navajos were near the
point of fleeing the reservation, "even if assured of perishing in the attempt."
In conclusion the lieutenant reiterated that the Navajos only required a suitable
location with plentiful wood, grass, and water to make them the equal of the
Pueblos. McDonald's report received widespread circulation in Washington
and was another milestone leading toward the removal of the Navajos.[24]

On February 19, 1868, New Mexico's delegate to Congress, Charles P.
Clever, urged Secretary of the Interior Browning to consult with Governor
Mitchell as to citizen opinion in the territory on the Navajo question. He noted
that Mitchell was an influential man and that the Indian Bureau needed support. Clever believed there should be a harmony of opinion between the people of the territory and the federal government.[25]

In mid-February Commissioner Taylor sent a frantic note to Secretary
Browning. It was imperative that Congress appropriate special funds for the
Navajos. The regular $100,000 appropriation had been exhausted, and the
Indians on the reservation were becoming restless. If the government allowed
them to straggle back to their home country, another war would soon erupt.
The resulting expense to the government and the loss of many lives could not
be permitted. Congress must act promptly. From the viewpoint of economics
Taylor echoed Carleton, stating that it was much cheaper for the Indian Bureau
to keep the Indians under control, "than it would be to turn them loose and
fight them."[26]

Finally the federal government early in 1868 took definite steps to end
the problems concerning Indian-white relations in the West. To expedite this
program, a special Peace Commission was created. The members included
Senators J. B. Henderson, John B. Sanborn, and Samuel Tappan, representatives of civil government. Generals Sherman, Alfred H. Terry, William S.
Harney, and Christopher C. Augur represented the military. Indian Commissioner Taylor was the chairman of the group. Another aspect of the program
was the decision by Congress to revive the Indian treaty process. Because
many persons believed that the Navajos would be one of the first tribes to
sign a treaty, the Peace Commission made plans to send representatives to the
Bosque. The Navajo agent and the troops at Sumner frequently told the Navajos
that special emissaries of the White Father soon would be coming. The words
apparently had the effect of preventing outbreaks from the reserve during the
winter. However, as the spring months of 1868 wore on and no emissaries
appeared, the Navajos began to grumble.[27]

For the first time in years, the army was not buying breadstuffs in New
Mexico. In early March the Santa Fe *Weekly New Mexican* carried a curious
advertisement. The quartermaster at Fort Sumner announced that the army
was selling nearly 400,000 pounds of wheat meal to anyone who cared to buy
it. This apparently was the breadstuff that Getty had ordered to be bought in
case the Navajos fell back under the control of the military. It now appeared
that Congress soon would make a special appropriation for the Navajos, so the

army's wheat meal had to be sold. In unloading it on the market, the military undoubtedly took a loss on the transaction.

Other interesting actions took place at the Bosque. Major Whiting, commanding at Fort Sumner, issued several important orders. To rectify the problems created by persons obstructing the passage of water through the acequias, he declared that any soldier caught doing this would be court-martialed. If the culprit were a civilian, he would be expelled from the reservation. In another vein, Whiting sought to clean up his post. In recent months the grounds had become filthy due to a proliferation of pigs. Henceforth, he ordered, "all pigs found running at large" would be shot on sight. Animals of this sort must be kept in a pigpen. In late March of 1868, Whiting was replaced as commander of Fort Sumner by Brevet Brigadier General Benjamin S. Roberts.[28]

Following the tragic death of Superintendent Norton, a new Indian superintendent was named for New Mexico. L. E. Webb, formerly an agent for the Chippewas, took the appointment. About this time, Congress appropriated $150,000 to remove the Navajos to another location where they could become self-sufficient. The Santa Fe *Weekly New Mexican* noted that the Peace Commission soon would arrive to observe firsthand the fruits of Carleton's Indian policy. The editors strongly opposed returning the Navajos to their homeland, for the whites now needed that region. Echoing the sentiments of Arny and Carleton, the paper stated that the "mineral wealth of that region, would not be developed for years to come" if the Peace Commission placed the Navajos there. Yet, dramatic changes were forthcoming for the Navajos.[29]

Late in April of 1868, Manuelito, Barboncito, and several other Navajo headmen, accompanied by interpreter Jesus Arviso, were taken by Agent Dodd to Washington, D. C. They talked in person to President Andrew Johnson, but the Great Father refused to make any promises. The Navajos wanted to return to their ancestral lands, but the president explained to them that the Peace Commission would make that decision. Upon returning to New Mexico, the Navajos came to feel that if the commission did not give them justice (return them to their homeland), the entire tribe would bolt the reservation. Manuelito and Barboncito spoke in favor of fleeing, if the talks should fail. Delgadito had been shunted aside as a Navajo leader, perhaps because of his role in encouraging the tribe to move to the Bosque in the first place.[30]

From reports which had reached them in Washington during the winter, both General Sherman and Samuel Tappan, who were sent to the Bosque Redondo, had already decided to remove the Navajos. Upon reaching the reservation in late May they conferred with everyone trying to learn about the basic nature of the Indians. The Peace Commissioners had several alternatives. If they believed the tribe was peaceful and industrious, they would recommend that the Navajos be allowed to return to their homeland. If they reached that conclusion, continuing government support would be necessary. If the Indians seemed hostile, the commissioners would urge that they be sent to a new home in the Indian Territory.

Sherman was shocked when he saw the Bosque Redondo Reservation. Reports that he had read while in the East did not accurately describe the dismal state of affairs on the Pecos. "I found the Bosque a mere spot of green grass in the midst of a wild desert," he wrote, and the once proud and wealthy Navajos "had sunk into a condition of absolute poverty and despair." After conferring briefly with General Roberts, Sherman held a lengthy conference with Agent Dodd. The dedicated agent told the tragic story of the Indians working diligently every year only to find their fields ruined by insects, floods, or drought. He emphasized that until 1867 the Indians had worked well with the military. They understood the principles of irrigation and were good farmers. But after so many frustrating experiences, the Navajos now refused to work in the fields, and Dodd stated that he did not blame them. Probably half of the acreage along the river could be cultivated, but the soil in the remainder of the area possessed too much alkali. Dodd also explained the fuel problem to Sherman and Tappan.

Dodd wanted Sherman to know the extent and depth of the Navajo dissatisfaction and despair. The Indians had grown to hate the reservation because of the frequent Comanche raids, the unproductive soil, scarcity of fuel, bad water, and general unhealthfulness. For at least a year the Navajos had been begging to be returned to their homeland, where they promised they could look after themselves and be at peace. If the Indians were not moved to a reservation west of the Rio Grande, Dodd stated, they would return there by stealth and in so doing commit depredations upon the people of New Mexico. The only place that the tribe would be content was in their ancestral land. Dodd believed that the Navajos were generally hard-working and industrious Indians. The Bosque had taught them a lesson, and if they were allowed to go back to their own country they probably would never pose a problem again.[31]

Enormous expenditures overshadowed the entire venture at the Bosque. When Carleton had been in command, Sherman was aware of the high cost of the reservation; now he felt curious as to whether or not the Indian Department had been able to reduce expenses. The results were disappointing. Since it acquired control of the Navajos in November of 1867, seven months before, the Indian Bureau had spent $280,000 for subsistence. The monthly expenses had averaged $42,000. The Bureau was doing somewhat better than the military, but the expense remained far too high.[32]

Several days prior to the long-awaited arrival of the Peace Commissioners, the Navajos held a coyote ceremony at Fort Sumner. Barboncito directed the proceeding. First, a sizeable number of Navajos scattered in various directions until they encountered a coyote. Next, the animal was encircled. Walking forward to the coyote, Barboncito placed a shell bead in the animal's mouth. Then, slowly, the coyote walked away to the west. Barboncito had been given the power to speak convincingly to the white leaders, and the coyote ceremony guaranteed that the Navajos would be returned to their homeland.

The Peace Commissioners held the first of a series of councils with the Navajos at the Bosque on May 28. The meeting took place in the Indian council room with the principal headmen present. General Sherman opened proceedings by stating that the commission had come to Fort Sumner to investigate the conditions of the Navajos. He and Tappan desired to hear only the truth. Sherman then recited what he knew of Navajo history. He said that he was impressed with the amount of work the Navajos had done at the reservation, but it distressed him to see that no permanent progress had been made. The

Navajos appeared as poor as when they first came to the Bosque. Sherman invited the Navajo leaders to give their views of the Bosque. Barboncito eloquently stated the Navajo position. His words were translated from Navajo to Spanish by Jesus Arviso, and from Spanish to English by James Sutherland.

Smithsonian Institution

Barboncito, eloquent Navajo leader who was designated head chief of the Navajos by General Sherman in 1868.

Barboncito replied at length about the horrors of the reservation. Many Navajos, and many of their animals as well, had died. "Our grandfathers had no idea of living in any other country except our own," he said, and he was sure that they had been right. Barboncito explained the Navajo myth of creation. When the Navajos had first walked, First Woman had told them that their country was bounded by four mountains and that they must never move east of the Rio Grande or west of the San Juan, or disaster would befall the tribe. Their life at the Bosque Redondo had fulfilled the legend.

While at the Bosque the Navajos had always done as they were told. However the ground was not productive. They had planted every year, but it did not yield. All the stock they had brought to the reserve had died. Every year their labor had been in vain, and for that reason his people had "not planted or tried to grow anything this year." They had put seed in the ground, but it would not grow more than two feet high. Barboncito did not know why, except that the ground had never been intended for Navajos. At one time, he stated, there had been many *ricos* among the Navajos, but now they had nothing to sleep on except gunny sacks. He was very sad, his mouth was dry, and his head hung in constant sorrow to see his people, who were once so well off, now so poor. Barboncito stated that he could no longer sleep at night because of the condition of his people, and he hated the trip to the commissary for food because he did not like to be fed like a child.

The small vocal Indian told how rich the Navajo homeland used to be, how they had raised bountiful crops. At the Bosque, the land itself did not like the Navajo, and whatever they did seemed to cause death. Many sickened and died, while others drowned in the river. The Indian doctors could not practice their art because the necessary herbs did not grow this far to the east. Barboncito declared that in the old days he used to raise his head and see flocks of sheep in every direction. Now he could see none. Moreover, both the New Mexicans and Comanches hated them and frequently attacked his people. In their homeland they had never even heard of a Comanche. If the white men returned the Navajos to their homeland, the Indian leader said, the Indians would call them father and mother. They would do anything the government wished.

Although he realized that the Navajos had their hearts set on returning to their former homes, General Sherman decided to broach the topic of a possible Navajo reservation in the Indian Territory. It had been General Carleton's desire that the Indians eventually reside there, and Sherman felt that he should obtain their reaction to the idea. He told the Navajo leaders of how the Cherokees and other tribes had settled on productive reservations south of the Arkansas River, and that he would like some of the leading Navajos to visit the Indian Territory to see the country for themselves. He was aware that Grant and Commissioner Taylor both had stated that any removal must require the "consent of the removed" if it were to succeed. If the Navajos did not want to go to the land of the Cherokees, the commissioners would consider returning the Navajos to their homeland.

If they returned home, the government would draw a boundary and the Navajos would not be permitted to cross that line except to trade. They must live at peace and must not fight even with other Indians. If trouble occurred, it would be reported at the nearest military post. In the future the army would do the fighting. No Navajos would be allowed to raid the Utes; however, if the Utes or Apaches came into their country they could drive them out. The choice as to the location was up to the Navajos. The government would remove them either to the Indian Territory or back to their own country. Finally Sherman asked the Navajos to select ten leaders who would stand responsible for the actions of their people.

Barboncito's response was predictable. He hoped that the Navajos would not be asked to go to another country, as it might turn out to be another Bosque Redondo. They had been told that the Bosque was a good place, but it had been horrible. If allowed to return to their homes they would obey every order that was given them. "We do not want to go to the right or left, but straight back to our own country," the Navajo leader concluded.

On the following day, May 31, General Sherman appeared before a huge crowd of Navajos outside headquarters. He asked if ten leaders had been selected, and was told they had. The General then declared that the government recognized Barboncito as the head chief of the Navajos. In the future every Navajo must obey him. The military would return them to their homeland, but strict discipline must be maintained and there must be no incidents of raiding.

Sherman then explained to the leaders the government's plans for the new reservation. Basically the process of Christianizing and civilizing which Carleton had started would be continued. There would be churches and schools for the purpose of educating the children. Federal laws declaring slavery to be illegal must be enforced in New Mexico, particularly regarding those Navajos being held captive by New Mexicans. The Indians seemed pleased.

On June 1, 1868, Sherman and Tappan presented the Indian leaders with a treaty. Article One bound both the government and the Navajos to keep the treaty on their pledge of honor; the Indians also agreed to turn over to the proper authorities anyone who committed a serious crime. Article Two defined the limits of the reservation, and Article Three stated that the government would build an agency. The agency would consist of a warehouse, agent's residence, carpenter shop, blacksmith shop, schoolhouse, and chapel. Article Six, which would have pleased Carleton, pledged that the Indians would compel their children between the ages of six and sixteen to attend school and be taught English, among other subjects.

Most of the remaining articles pertained to specific arrangements. The government promised that the head of each Indian family would receive seeds and agricultural implements during the first year. Annually goods valued at not more than five dollars per Indian would be sent to the agency for distribution. These goods would consist of necessary items which the Navajos could not make themselves. Certainly the Navajos would not be given shoddy blankets for the benefit of contractors. Each Indian would receive ten dollars in cash, and both the gifts and the cash could be increased in the future. Furthermore the Indians must never oppose the construction of a railroad through their land, another point for the old Carleton backers in Santa Fe. Finally, the United States agreed to appropriate $150,000 for various expenses. It would be disbursed as follows: roughly $50,000 would be spent on removing the tribe from the Bosque, $30,000 would be allotted for sheep and goats, and a major part would be ticketed for cattle and corn to be held by the agent and given to the needy during the coming winter. If any money remained after these expenditures, it would be spent by the agent for their benefit. The Navajos were well satisfied with the plans. The headmen stepped forward and inscribed their signatory marks on the document.[33]

Sherman realized that if the Navajos were to reach their country to plant crops, they must leave the Bosque quickly — even before the Senate could review the treaty. On the same day the leaders signed the treaty, June 1, he issued orders to General Getty to prepare to remove the Navajos. The Commissary Officer would arrange subsistence for them until the funds under the treaty were made available. The army would later be reimbursed. If no funds were received by the time the Navajos reached their old country, Getty was to issue food to the Indians. However, in no instance should he issue more than the $150,000 as provided for in the treaty. Sherman also told Getty that Fort Wingate would have to be moved closer to the new reservation.[34]

Before the removal began, a serious incident occurred at the Bosque, threatening the entire removal project. On June 6 Lieutenant John W. Jordan led a detachment of men to Twelve Mile Creek where he discovered the bodies of four men who had been murdered by Navajos. They were found floating face downward in the water. Upon hauling the first body from the creek, the soldiers saw two Navajo arrows plus three bullet wounds in the body. The corpse also had a severe cut in the head, probably administered by an axe. The second victim had been shot by four arrows, one piercing his heart. The third man had his feet tied together with a rope, he had been shot by four arrows, and his face had been severely disfigured by an axe. The body of the last individual contained two arrows in the abdomen and two gruesome hacks in the face. Jordan's party buried the bodies, and in scouting the nearby area they saw the sign of a severe bloody struggle between the four white men and an overwhelming number of Indians. Sherman, who had not yet left New Mexico, was angered by the report.

General Roberts, the commander at Fort Sumner, immediately sent for Barboncito, Manuelito, and Delgadito. He told them that General Sherman would not be satisfied of their good faith under the treaty unless the guilty Indians were turned over to the authorities. The Navajo leaders found that the murderers had fled the reservation, but they gave Roberts the names of the men and their probable direction of flight. Lieutenant Monahan, the post adjutant, with a sizeable mounted force, rode off, taking with them interpreter James Sutherland, who would recognize the Indians. Manuelito had been right. Near Apache Springs, twenty miles south of Las Vegas, the soldiers found the Indians asleep. As Monahan made plans to surround them, Juh Sanchez, their leader, discovered the troops, and fired upon them. A furious fight ensued. The soldiers drove the Indians into a nearby ravine, killing two of them and mortally wounding Sanchez. After daylight a large number of the renegade Navajos surrendered. The Navajos at the reservation desired that these men be punished, for they wanted no interference with their return home. The Comancheros, who had an interest in keeping the Navajos at the Bosque Redondo, probably were involved in the affair.[35]

By June 7 General Getty informed Sherman that the orders for removing the Navajos had been given. Major Charles J. Whiting at Fort Sumner directed the operation. A train of fifty six-mule wagons was en route from Fort Union to Fort Sumner. Whiting would use them to transport stores for the troops and Indians and rely on them to carry the sick and feeble of the tribe who were unable to walk. The route marked out was via San Jose, Tijeras Canyon, Albuquerque, and Fort Wingate. Getty hoped that Whiting would be able to get the grueling march under way by June 15.

Getty also sent Sherman a lengthy letter describing the reasons for the removal of the Navajos. In Washington, Sherman wanted material available to press approval of the Navajo treaty. He wanted everyone connected with the tribe and interested in their removal to make detailed reports so that he would have plenty of ammunition. Actually, when General Grant gave his support to the removal on June 18, Sherman had little to worry about.[36]

Whiting and a soldier escort started a major part of the Navajo tribe on the road back to Arizona in mid-June. The Navajos had strict orders to stay near the road or trail and to obey the soldiers at all times. The ten Navajo leaders assumed the responsibilities of watching the conduct of the tribe. In late July several smaller groups of Navajos left the Bosque. These groups, normally accompanied by one or two soldiers, carried passes signed by General Roberts. The pass instructed civilians to refrain from molesting the Navajos while on their way west. The *Weekly New Mexican* reported that the Navajos were going to their homes in a peaceful fashion. By July 14, Fort Sumner had been reduced to a two-company post, and the vast Bosque was a quiet wasteland.*

In late July of 1868 the Navajos began arriving in the Fort Defiance area, and shortly thereafter they dispersed to the various parts of the reservation. Great excitement occurred on the march, when the Navajos first came into sight of Mount Taylor, a familiar landmark. Many Indians had to be restrained by their companions from going into a state of thankful hysteria over the sight of their sacred landmark. A few Navajos had died due to the hardship of the journey. For many the trip had a near carnival atmosphere. The Navajos who returned to their homeland in the summer of 1868, however, were a far different people from the seminomads who had gone east to the Pecos in the winter of 1864. Never again would these proud people pose a threat to the peace of the Southwest.[37]

---

*A small detachment of soldiers remained at Fort Sumner for a year following the departure of the Navajos. On February 24, 1871, an act of Congress transferred the building and property of the post to the Department of the Interior for sale, and only the military cemetery was retained by the War Department.

10

A Successful Failure

"In their appointed time He wills that one race of men — as
in the races of lower animals — shall disappear off the face
of the earth and give place to another race, and so on in
the Great Cycle traced out by Himself, which may be seen,
but has reasons too deep to be fathomed by us. The races
of the Mammoths and Mastodons, and the great Sloths,
came and passed away: the Red Man of America is passing
away!"

General Carleton

"The country in which they [the Navajos] live is described as
beautiful, and it is reported that the mountains contain as
rich deposits of gold as can be found on this continent."

William F. M. Arny

THE BOSQUE REDONDO RESERVATION, a unique military experiment to alter
Navajo culture, flourished in New Mexico for five years. In two instances the
reservation had proved a failure: (1) It failed to make the Navajos self-sufficient. (2) It did not solve the age-old problem of Indian depredations. However, reservation life caused many changes in the Navajos' way of life. In the
future the lesson of the Pecos reservation would serve as a milestone in the
government's ongoing attempt to civilize the American Indian.

Food was the key to the success of the Bosque. The availability of food
did more to keep the Indians on the reservation than did the guns of 10,000
soldiers. Due to the sizeable quantities of foodstuffs needed for the Bosque,
military purchases notably affected commodity prices in New Mexico. The
military pursued two avenues in procuring supplies for the Bosque: open
market purchases and low-bidder contracts. If an emergency arose, supplies
or foodstuffs were purchased immediately. The time factor did not allow for
running newspaper advertisements calling for bids and then examining those
bids. The abuses of the open market system were obvious, for the buyer usually
made his purchases from a friend or crony.

Even when time permitted the taking of bids, abuses still resulted. Certain individuals were not allowed to make offers — for example, former Confederates. Charles Goodnight had been prevented from receiving a contract under this law. Bids could be ignored, even though they might be the lowest, if the potential contractor had previously experienced any type of contractual difficulties with the government. In the end, the friends of the military commander still received the contracts. If the commander were honest, the system functioned smoothly; if he were corrupt, the results could be disastrous.

Contractors who hoarded precious foodstuffs presented a nearly insurmountable problem. During the time of martial law in New Mexico, Carleton issued edicts making the practice illegal, but the offense continued. Large-scale farmers and speculators naturally reasoned that it made good sense to hold back a portion or all of their grain until the winter months. Then market prices peaked, as States' grain could not be obtained for several months when the Santa Fe Trail was closed by winter storms. If the military had been making purchases only for troops, the dramatic fluctuations in prices would not have occurred. However, by purchasing subsistence for ten thousand Navajos, the military controlled the New Mexican market. Carleton would not see the Navajos starve, and high prices resulted. The charge that feeding the Navajos had driven the cost of corn so high as to be prohibitive for purchase by a New Mexican laborer was undeniably true.

In the administrative realm, the conflict between the departments of War and Interior over New Mexican Indian affairs clearly indicated a lack of proper

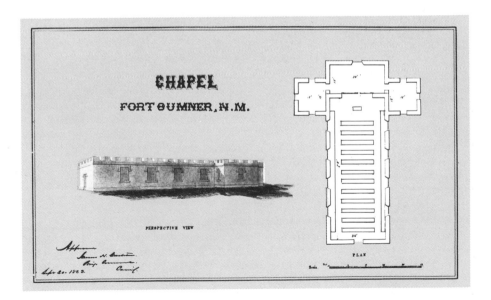

National Archives

Carleton's elaborate chapel for the Indians at the Bosque Redondo emphasizes the importance he attached to Christianity for the Navajo experiment.

definition of the responsibilities of the two arms of the government. As commanding general in New Mexico, Carleton had created Indian policy rather than implementing the program of the Department of the Interior. Policy-making decisions of this magnitude fell outside of the prescribed limits of his authority, but the temper of the times permitted him to carry them through.

Although the Bosque Redondo was a military reservation, a civilian agency tried to function there. Labadie attempted to conduct his Mescalero Apache agency as if he took orders from the New Mexico superintendency rather than from the military. Labadie's actions appeared to be working against the overall plan for the reservation, and Carleton jumped at the first opportunity to remove him. Navajo Agent Dodd, from the first, cooperated fully with the military authorities.

When control of the Bosque passed to the Department of the Interior on October 31, 1867, the lines of responsibility were better drawn. The army engaged solely in military duties, with the exception of supervising ration issues to the Indians. The reservation and its associated tasks now were under the control of the Navajo agent. However, because of the peculiar history of the Bosque, the line of authority there remained cloudy, setting a precedent for future reservation authority. Hostile Indians as prisoners of war clearly fell under the control of the military. However, if reservation Indians made a "hostile" action, an administrative conflict became almost inevitable. In such a case the military emerged in full command.

At the Bosque the military exercised crucial power. The post commander set the tone of both the garrison and the reservation. When a dedicated individual like Crocker or McCleave held the spot, he imbued his officers with the same sense of mission and responsibility that he himself possessed. If an incompetent or careless man commanded the fort, tragic results might occur. Other positions of importance on the Bosque were those of Commissary Officer, Quartermaster, Rationing Officer, and Superintendent of Farms. Possibly more important than the position of Post Commander was that of Indian Superintendent (held by Henry Bristol, for example), a vital assignment. The latter officer maintained a direct contact with Carleton, circumventing the chain of command, and often acted to implement Carleton's ideas. The Indian leaders worked closely with the Superintendent and later with the Commissary Officer in order to protect the welfare of their people. The Navajos at the reservation were fortunate in that almost all of the men who occupied these positions interested themselves in the welfare of their charges. Changing responsibilities, however, plagued the reservation, and administrative positions were created, dissolved, and combined from time to time.

In any study of the Bosque Redondo Reservation, the personality and aspirations of General Carleton must be kept clearly in mind. Carleton believed that every step taken at the Bosque to bring the Navajos into the fold of the white man's world would prove to be of benefit to both Indians and whites. During the years of his command, he dominated the daily life of the reservation. Nothing was too small to escape his attention. He maintained an iron-handed direction of the experiment. Convinced of the absolute righteousness of their cause, Carleton and his dedicated officers lived as if they were engaged in a holy crusade.

The Bosque had been a unique experiment, but like most experiments it failed to realize many of its objectives. Carleton knew that widespread opposition would develop if the reservation were supported by large public expenditures for any length of time. Consequently he bent every effort to make the Navajos self-sufficient farmers. Unfortunately every element of nature combined to ruin the farming operations. Long before 1868 it was clear to many that the Bosque was the wrong location for a giant self-sufficient reservation. In later years the area would be dotted with splendid farms, but only after the construction of a permanent dam on the Pecos and the introduction of chemical insecticides to prevent the swarms of insects that had devastated the crops.

A second objective of the Bosque — curbing Indian depredations — also was not realized. Not every Navajo went to the Bosque, and those remaining in their homeland continued to raid. Furthermore, Navajos on the Bosque came and went as they pleased. Measuring forty miles square, the Bosque was too large to be guarded effectively. The Indians had to be persuaded to stay there. Carleton's opponents played on the continuing depredations. Most of these reports were documented, but some had the ring of fiction.

Despite certain failures at the Bosque, there was a positive side to its operation. The prime goal of the army in placing the Navajos on the reserve was to start them on a path leading to assimilation. The officers and men who labored with them achieved certain successes in their efforts. As the Navajos walked back the long trail to their homeland, they were a different people from those who came eastward four years before.

The Navajos now comprehended the white man's world much better. The Indian Fund transactions taught many Indians the value of money and its relation to such everyday items as clothing, horses, wheat, corn, liquor, women, trinkets, and blankets. Admittedly, the Indians were not accountants when they left the Bosque, but they had a better grasp of material desires and values in the white man's world. Few Navajos who had lived at the Bosque would be easily duped by unscrupulous whites in the future.

Carleton had hoped to teach the Navajos the value of real estate, but he failed. At the Bosque the Indians had labored for the most part on a large communal farm rather than on individual plots. Due to the nature of the operation, it was impossible to explain the concept of real estate to them. Owning land did not seem possible by Indian religious teachings. An individual could no more own the land than the stars. As the years followed, the Indians' inability to comprehend the white man's fascination with "owning" mother earth led to great misfortunes for many tribes.

Through daily contact with white men, the Navajos learned that many whites truly were interested in the Indians' welfare. A feeling of mutual trust developed between soldiers and the Indians. The extent of the trust can be seen in the Indian-white camaraderie photographs of the post and reservation and the fact that the Indians were permitted to roam the reservation armed with rifles. The reservation experience thus was a step toward easing the tension between the two races. Unfortunately, subsequent writers who wished to dramatize the suffering at the reservation ignored this success.

Carleton was a fanatic about Indian education. At first the Indians had been lukewarm to the idea of sending their children to school, but in time they

Navajos were permitted to carry arms at the Bosque Redondo.

adopted an equally strong faith in the wonders of education. Christianity also made some inroads into traditional Indian belief (particularly among the children), but its greatest success came later. Most of the schooling at the Bosque, however, was under the supervision of the Catholic Church.

The Bosque Redondo experiment worked a great change in Navajo material culture.[1] With regard to farming, the Navajos returned to their homeland with a mature knowledge of irrigation. Navajos now farmed with hoes, shovels, plows, and rakes; they had learned farming techniques that caused greater crop production. This further lessened the desire to return to the old days of raiding and stealing.

Many Navajos also had learned the art of smithing. In years to come these Indians became the finest metal workers of the American West, their silver jewelry becoming known worldwide. This knowledge of smithing can be traced partially back to the Bosque Redondo. The counterfeiting of the metal ration tickets required delicate painstaking labor, and the Navajos learned the skill well.

Prior to the Bosque Redondo the Navajos had transported their belongings by the ancient travois. Now they used the wagon. The impact of the wagon on Indian society cannot be overestimated. The old army wagons which the Indians received as free gifts permitted whole families, with all of their belongings, to travel relatively long distances. Trips to call on distant friends, visit

Two Navajo boys of the Bosque Redondo era.

Navajo man, armed with bow and arrows, and hatchet.

The son of Navajo Chief Barboncito.

trading posts, and attend council meetings and celebrations, became regular occurrences. Supplies could be hauled for long distances. The wagon helped to alter Navajo life.

The years at the Bosque had even changed the traditional Navajo dwelling. In the past the Navajos had lived in the forked-pole hogan, a conical mud-plastered structure of limited size. At the Bosque the Navajos apparently watched the soldiers erecting the buildings at the post, and new types of hogans resulted. The cribwork hogan had a small log-cabin base, with the logs rising for several feet. Then branches arched over the cribwork, forming a domed roof covered with mud. The four-legged hogan also traced its origin back to Fort Sumner. These buildings contained more space, and they tended to replace the traditional dwelling.

Even the clothing the Indians wore had changed. The Navajos gave up clothing made from the skin of game animals and plants, in favor of the cloth material. For a time the quality of Navajo weaving declined as the Indians turned to government blankets and clothing. For many years after the Bosque experience, Navajo men continued to dress in the long white trousers they had first worn at the Bosque. The Navajo women also changed their styles. The long fluted calico skirt, world famous today as a "squaw dress," also traces its birth to the garments made by the Navajo women at the reservation.

The Indians at the Bosque received lessons in American justice. Occasionally offenders found themselves being punished for offenses which under the Navajo code might have demanded death, but lesser sentences were imposed. More importantly, however, the authorities at the Bosque turned over the Navajo criminals to the Indians themselves for trial. A jury of peers, generally a council of Indian leaders, tried Navajos accused of crimes. In most instances the Indians' decisions were just, by the white man's standard. For the first time in Navajo history a member of one clan became responsible for punishing an individual who had committed an offense against another clan. The responsibility of administering justice to their own people surely must stand as one of the great achievements of the Bosque. Allowing the Indians the responsibility of policing themselves would not be long in the offing.

At the Bosque Redondo, the Navajos had destroyed another myth: the old idea that Indians naturally were lazy and would not work. At the reservation, the Navajos on most occasions tried hard to make their farms successful, despite obstacles that would have sent a white farmer searching for a new home after the first disastrous summer. The Navajos, as much as General Carleton, wanted the Bosque to be a success. When the reservation finally failed, the Indians could certainly state that they had tried their best.

Most importantly, the reservation fostered a sense of tribal unity. For the first time in their history, some eighty to ninety percent of the various clans lived together at one location, working with each other. In the past, clan membership meant more to an individual Navajo than the fact that he was Navajo. Now a change had occurred. The Indians distinctly saw that they constituted a numerous powerful tribe. By cooperating with each other and confronting the whites as a unit, the Navajos gained an important sense of tribe which they had never possessed before.

At the Bosque it appeared that Carleton had shown that the nature of the Indian could be changed. Under favorable conditions, progress toward civilization and assimilation would be much more rapid. Many individuals believed that the Bosque had been a success. U. S. Grant, after he became president, tried to implement an Indian policy combining the best features of the Bosque experiment.

The administrative problems relating to reservation economics played a decisive role in the Bosque's history. From the very start of Carleton's new Indian program in 1862, critics charged that the experimental reservation was too expensive. As yearly budgets in excess of $1,000,000 occurred, officials in Washington gave credence to their charges. Finally, in the summer of 1868, the government ordered the abandonment of the reserve. The Navajos were returned to their homeland because the program had been so costly, not due to the military's humanitarian desires.*

The traumatic experience at the Bosque Redondo had caused a remarkable change in the Navajo people. In the years that followed they became one of the most peaceful, hard-working tribes in the country. The Bosque Redondo had been one of the first great steps taken by the government down this new road of civilizing and then, hopefully, assimilating the Indian. Dedicated individuals had achieved a partial success on a miserable piece of land where the forces of nature seemed to oppose their every effort. For the numerous other Indian tribes who felt the civilizing hand of the federal government over the next fifty years, it was unfortunate that the experiment on the Pecos had managed to succeed so well.

---

*Lynn Bailey, author of *The Long Walk* (Los Angeles: Westernlore Press, 1964) and *Bosque Redondo: An American Concentration Camp* (Pasadena: Socio-Technical Books, 1970) emphasizes the suffering of the Bosque, and called it a total failure. This writer does not disagree with Bailey in condemning the reservation system spawned in the 1860s, but unfortunately governmental leaders and humanitarians of that day regarded the Bosque experiment as a success. Few historians today would argue that the reservation program did not have a dramatic impact on the lives of countless American Indians.

Appendix

Officials of New Mexico Territory and Personnel of Fort Sumner and the Bosque Redondo*

Territorial Governor
Abraham Rencher	1857–61
Henry Connelly	1861–66
Robert B. Mitchell	1866–69

Commander, Military Department (District) of New Mexico
Col. E. R. S. Canby (Brig. Gen., U.S.V.)	June 1861
Maj. James H. Carleton (Brig. Gen. U.S.V.)	Sept. 1862
Col. George W. Getty (Bvt. Maj. Gen.)	April 1867

Territorial Indian Superintendent
James L. Collins	1857–63
Michael Steck	1863–64
Felipe Delgado	1864–66
A. Baldwin Norton	1866–67
Luther E. Webb	1867–69

Mescalero Apache Agent
Lorenzo Labadie	1862–65

Navajo Agent
Theodore H. Dodd	1865–69

Commanding Officer
Capt. Joseph Updegraff, 5th Inf.	Dec. 1862 (11 mo)
Maj. Henry D. Wallen, 7th Inf.	Nov. 1863 (5 mo)
Capt. Henry B. Bristol, 5th Inf.	April 1864 (5 mo)
Brig. Gen. Marcellus Crocker, U.S.V.	Sept. 1864 (5 mo)
Maj. William McCleave, 1st Cal. Cav.	Feb. 1865 (18 mo)
Lt. Col. George Sykes, 5th Inf.	Aug. 1866 (2 mo)
Capt. John V. Dubois, 3rd Cav.	Nov. 1866 (1 mo)
Lt. Col. George Sykes, 5th Inf.	Sept. 1866 (7 mo)
Capt. James S. Casey, 5th Inf.	Mar. 1867 (1 mo)
Capt. Elisha W. Tarlton, 3rd Cav.	April 1867 (1 mo)
Lt. Col. George Sykes, 5th Inf.	May 1867 (1 mo)
Capt. Elisha W. Tarlton, 3rd Cav.	June 1867 (1 mo)
Maj. Charles J. Whiting, 3rd Cav.	July 1867 (8 mo)
Lt. Col. Benj. S. Roberts, 3rd Cav.	Mar. 1868 (4 mo)
Capt. Ezra P. Ewers, 37th Inf.	July 1868

* Military ranks are those at the time the office was assumed.

Abbreviations Used

A and W   *Arizona and the West*
AGO   Office of the Adjutant General
AHS   Arizona Historical Society
CE   Records of the Chief of Engineers
CIA   Report of the Commissioner of Indian Affairs
DAB   *Dictionary of American Biography*
DNM   Department of New Mexico
GAO   General Accounting Office
HED   *House Executive Document*
LC   Library of Congress
LRNMS   Letters Received, New Mexico Superintendency
M   Microcopy
NA   National Archives
NMHR   *New Mexico Historical Review*
NMTP   State Department Territorial Papers, New Mexico
OIA   Office of Indian Affairs
QMO   Office of the Quartermaster General
RBOIA   Report Books of the Office of Indian Affairs
RG   Record Group
RMP   Returns From U. S. Military Posts
SED   *Senate Executive Document*
UA   University of Arizona Library
USACC   United States Army Continental Commands

Notes to Chapters

CHAPTER 1 *Notes to pages 2–7*

1. John Upton Terrell, *The Navajos* (New York: Weybright and Talley, 1970), 1–7, 12–16; Jack Forbes, *Apache, Navajo and Spaniard* (Norman: University of Oklahoma Press, 1960), xiii–iv.
2. Lawrence L. Mehren, "A History of the Mescalero Apache Reservation, 1869–1881," (M.A. Thesis, The University of Arizona, 1968), 1–3; Donald E. Worchester, "The Navajo During the Spanish Regime in New Mexico," *New Mexico Historical Review* [*NMHR*], 26 (April 1951), 101–106.
3. Edward H. Spicer, *Cycles of Conquest* (Tucson: University of Arizona Press, 1962), 210–12; Hubert H. Bancroft, *History of Arizona and New Mexico* (New Edition; Albuquerque: Horn and Wallace, 1962), 162–63.
4. Worchester, "Navajo During the Spanish Regime," 107–108; Frank D. Reeve, "Navajo Foreign Affairs, 1795–1846, Part I," *NMHR*, 46 (April 1971), 103; John P. Wilson, *Military Campaigns in the Navajo Country* (Santa Fe: Museum of New Mexico Press, 1967), 7.
5. Bancroft, *Arizona and New Mexico*, 285–87; Wilson, *Military Campaigns*, 7–25; Reeve, "Navajo Foreign Affairs, I," 104–125; Reeve, "Navajo Foreign Affairs, II," *NMHR*, 46 (June 1971), 223–45.
6. Grant Foreman, *Advancing the Frontier* (Norman: University of Oklahoma Press, 1933), Preface; Irvin M. Peithman, *Broken Peace Pipes* (Springfield: Charles C. Thomas Publisher, 1964), 41–60; Dee Brown, *Bury My Heart at Wounded Knee* (New York: Holt, Rinehart, and Winston, 1970), 3–9; Mary E. Young, "Indian Removal and Land Allotment: The Civilized Tribes and Jacksonian Justice," *American Historical Review*, 64 (October 1958), 31–45.
7. William A. Keleher, *Turmoil in New Mexico, 1846–1868* (Santa Fe: The Rydal Press, 1952), 22–26; Bancroft, *Arizona and New Mexico*, 421–23; Frank McNitt, *Navajo Wars: Military Campaigns, Slave Raids, and Reprisals* (Albuquerque: University of New Mexico Press, 1972), 95–123.
8. Keleher, *Turmoil in New Mexico*, 46–56; Charles J. Kappler (ed.), "Indian Affairs, Laws and Treaties, II," *Senate Executive Document* [*SED*] *452*, 57 Cong., 1 Sess. (Serial 4253), 432–34; McNitt, *Navajo Wars*, 124–56.
9. Howard Roberts Lamar, *The Far Southwest, 1846–1912* (New Haven: Yale University Press, 1966), 92–97. See also Annie Heloise Abel (ed.), *The Official Correspondence of James S. Calhoun* (Washington: Government Printing Office, 1915).
10. Keleher, *Turmoil in New Mexico*, 56–66; Maurice Frink, *Fort Defiance and the Navajos* (Boulder, Colorado: Pruett Press, 1968), 15–32.
11. Mehren, "Mescalero Apache Reservation," 7–10.
12. Frink, *Fort Defiance*, 33–42; David M. Brugge, *Zarcillos Largos* (Window Rock, Arizona: Navajo Parks Publications, 1970), 1–34; McNitt, *Navajo Wars*, 256–68.
13. Frink, *Fort Defiance*, 43–50; J. Lee Correll, "Ganado Mucho – Navajo Naat'- aani," *The Navajo Times*, November 30, 1967, 24–25, 27. McNitt, *Navajo Wars*, 341–62.
14. Lamar, *The Far Southwest*, 97–99; Frink, *Fort Defiance*, 47–62. McNitt, *Navajo Wars*, 363–84.

15. Max L. Heyman, *Prudent Soldier, E. R. S. Canby* (Glendale: The Arthur H. Clark Company, 1959), 115–125; Keleher, *Turmoil in New Mexico,* 102–108; Ralph Twitchell, *Leading Facts of New Mexico History* (2 vols., New Edition; Albuquerque: Horn and Wallace, 1963), II, 320–21, fn. 245. McNitt, *Navajo Wars,* 384–429.
16. Keleher, *Turmoil in New Mexico,* 143–191.
17. Lawrence C. Kelly, *Navajo Roundup* (Boulder, Colorado: Pruett Press, 1970), 1–11.

CHAPTER 2

1. William F. Arny to William P. Dole, January 17, 1863; James L. Collins to Dole, February 18, 1863, Letters Received, New Mexico Superintendency [LRNMS], Microcopy [M] 234, Roll 551, Records of the Office of Indian Affairs [OIA], Record Group [RG] 75, National Archives [NA].
2. Arny to Dole, January 6, 1862; Collins to Dole, December 7, 1861; Joseph G. Knapp to Dole, December 5, 1862; Henry Connelly to Edwin Stanton, March 12, 1864, LRNMS, M-234, Rolls 551–52; Carleton to Henry Halleck, May 10 and June 14, 1863, in Joint Special Committee on Indian Affairs, *The Condition of the Indian Tribes* (Washington: Government Printing Office, 1867), 110, 113–14.
3. Kelly, *Navajo Roundup,* 10–11.
4. Edward L. Sabin, *Kit Carson Days* (2 vols., New York: The Press of the Pioneers, 1935), II, 700–04.
5. Frank McNitt, "Fort Sumner: A Study in Origins," *NMHR,* 45 (April 1970), 108–09; Kelly, *Navajo Roundup,* 12–13; T. M. Pearce (ed.), *New Mexico Place Names* (Albuquerque: University of New Mexico Press, 1965), 9.
6. Aurora Hunt, *Major General James H. Carleton 1814–1873: Western Frontier Dragoon* (Glendale: Arthur H. Clark Company, 1958), 11–253.
7. Richard E. Crouter and Andrew Rolle, "Edward Fitzgerald Beale, and the Indian Peace Commissioners in California, 1851–54," *Historical Society of Southern California Quarterly,* 42 (June 1960), 107–32; Clarence Cullimore, *Forgotten Fort Tejon* (Bakersfield: Kern County Historical Society, 1941), 65–85.
8. Special Orders 193, November 4, 1963, Military Department of New Mexico, in *Condition of the Tribes,* 238; McNitt, "Origins of Fort Sumner," 109–15; Edwin V. Sumner briefly commanded the Department of the Pacific in 1861. F. Stanley, *E. V. Sumner* (Borger, Texas: Jim Hess Printers, 1969), 236–88.
9. Mehren, "Mescalero Apache Reservation," 11–12; C. L. Sonnichsen, *The Mescalero Apaches* (Norman: University of Oklahoma Press, 1958), 100–01; John C. Cremony, *Life Among the Apaches* (San Francisco: A. Roman and Company, 1868), 199–201; Carleton to Joseph West, October 11, 1862, Papers and Memoirs of William McCleave, Bancroft Library, University of California, Berkeley; Francis B. Heitman, *Historical Register and Dictionary of the U.S. Army* (Washington: Government Printing Office, 1903), I, 978.
10. McNitt, "Origins of Fort Sumner," 112; Cremony, *Life Among the Apaches,* 201–202; Post Returns, December, 1862, Fort Sumner, New Mexico, Returns from U.S. Military Posts [RMP], M-617, Roll 1241, Records of the United States Army Commands, RG 98, NA.
11. Carleton to Kit Carson, November 25, 1862; to Joseph Updegraff, November 26, 1862, in *Condition of the Tribes,* 101–02; McNitt, "Origins of Fort Sumner," 110; Cremony, *Life Among the Apaches,* 199–202; Stanley, *Sumner,* 319.
12. Cremony, *Life Among the Apaches,* 201–05.
13. John B. Shinn, "Map of a part of the Reservation for Navajo Indians, at Fort Sumner, N.M.," Sheet 47, Fortifications File, Drawer 142, Records of the Chief of Engineers [CE], RG 77, NA; McNitt, "Origins of Fort Sumner," 112.
14. General Orders 3, February 24, 1864; Carleton to Thomas, February 1, March 19, 1863, in *Condition of the Tribes,* 104–06, 247; Cremony, *Life Among the Apaches,* 208–10.
15. Carleton to James A. Doolittle, July 25, 1865, Letters Received by the Office of the Adjutant General, Main Series, 1861–1870 [AGO], M-619, Roll 561, Records of the AGO, RG 94, NA; Carleton to Thomas, March 19, 1863, in *Condition of the Tribes,* 106.
16. Collins to Dole, April 12, 1863, LRNMS, M-234, Roll 551.
17. Collins to Dole, April 18, 19, 1863, *ibid.;* Lansing B. Bloom (ed.), "Historical Society Minutes," *NMHR,* 18 (July 1943), 270; Henry P. Walker, *The Wagonmasters* (Norman: University of Oklahoma Press, 1968), 179–200.
18. Labadie to Dole, June 30, 1863, LRNMS, M-234, Roll 551.

19. Labadie to Collins, June 18, 1863; John S. Watts to Dole, December 8, 1863, LRNMS, M-234, Rolls 551–52. Military Board of Survey, Fort Stanton, August 13, 1863, U.S. Army, District of New Mexico, "Miscellaneous administrative papers from Fort Sumner and various other New Mexico Army Posts," Special Collections, University of Arizona Library [UA]; Charles F. Coan, *A History of New Mexico* (3 vols.; New York: The American Historical Society, 1925), I, 394; Jim Berry Pearson, *The Maxwell Land Grant* (Norman: University of Oklahoma Press, 1961), 16–17, 21, 65.

20. Military Board of Survey, Fort Sumner, July 17, August 16, 1863, "Fort Sumner Papers," UA. Information on Hinckley is from State Historical Society of Colorado and Denver Public Library.

21. Ralph Twitchell, *Old Santa Fe* (New Ed.; Chicago: The Rio Grande Press, 1963), 329; Carleton to John B. Lamy, June 12, 1863; to Updegraff, June 23, 1863, in *Condition of the Tribes,* 112, 116–17; Carleton to Doolittle, July 25, AGO, M-619, Roll 561.

22. Carleton to Updegraff, June 11, September 5, 1863; in *Condition of the Tribes,* 112, 133; Labadie to Dole, June 30, 1863, LRNMS, M-234, Roll 551. Helen Haines, *History of New Mexico from the Spanish Conquest to Present Time, 1530–1890* (New York: New Mexico Historical Publishing Co., 1891), 447; Updegraff to Carleton, August 29, 1863, Letters Sent and Received, 1862–69, Fort Sumner Records, Department of New Mexico [DNM], United States Army Continental Commands [USACC], RG 393, NA.

23. Updegraff to Carleton, August 29, 1863, Fort Sumner Records, DNM, USACC.

24. Pearce, *New Mexico Place Names,* 29, 105; Steck to Labadie, September 5, 1863, LRNMS, M-234, Roll 551.

25. Carleton to Updegraff, September 5, 1863, in *Condition of the Tribes,* 133; Steck to Carleton, September 6, 1863; Ben Cutler to Steck, September 7, 1863, LRNMS, M-234, Roll 551.

26. Carleton to Thomas, September 6, 1863, Appendix, to Carleton's "To the People of New Mexico" (Santa Fe: Publisher unknown, 1864), 12–13; Carleton to Doolittle, July 25, 1865, AGO, M-619, Roll 561.

27. Steck to Labadie, September 5, 1863; to Updegraff, October 29, 1863, LRNMS, M-234, Roll 551; Carleton to Thomas, November 15, 1863, in *Condition of the Tribes,* 143.

28. Carleton to William McMullen, November 15, 1863, in *Condition of the Tribes,* 143–44; Lynn R. Bailey, *The Long Walk* (Los Angeles: Westernlore Press, 1964), 157–58.

29. Santa Fe *Weekly New Mexican,* November 7, 1863.

30. Carleton to Thomas, November 15, 1863, in *Condition of the Tribes,* 143; George W. Cullum (comp.), *Biographical Register of the Officers and Graduates of the United States Military Academy* (Third Ed., 9 vols., Boston: Houghton, Mifflin, and Co., 1891–1950), II, 55–56.

31. Labadie to Steck, November 25, 1863, LRNMS, M-234, Roll 551.

32. Labadie to Steck, November 25, 1863, "Annual Report of the Commissioner of Indian Affairs [CIA] 1864," *House Executive Document [HED] 1,* 38 Cong., 1 Sess., (Serial 1220), 353.

33. Steck to Dole, December 10, 1863, John A. Clark to Steck, October 21, 1863, LRNMS, M-234, Roll 552. Clark to President Abraham Lincoln, June 15, 1863, *ibid.,* Roll 551.

34. Steck to Dole, December 14, 1863, *ibid.,* Roll 552.

35. Henry Connelly, Second Annual Message of the Governor, December 9, 1863, State Department Territorial Papers, New Mexico, 1851–72 [NMTP], M-T, Roll 2, Records of the Department of State, RG 59, NA; Lamar; *The Far Southwest,* 48.

36. J. Valdez to the Editor, Santa Fe *Weekly Gazette,* January 2, 1864.

37. Steck to Dole, December 20, 1863, LRNMS, M-234, Roll 552; Carleton to Wallen, December 24, 1863, in *Condition of the Tribes,* 152–53.

38. General Orders 8, February 24, 1864; Carleton to Thomas, December 23, 1863, in *Condition of the Tribes,* 254, 151; Labadie to Steck, October 22, 1864, *HED 1,* 38 Cong., 1 Sess., 346–48; Pearce, *New Mexico Place Names,* 19, 112; Valdez, Santa Fe *Weekly Gazette,* January 2, 1864.

39. Carleton to Wallen, December 24, 1863, in *Condition of the Tribes,* 152–53; Post Returns, Fort Sumner, December, 1863, RMP, M-617, Roll 1241.

40. Labadie to Steck, October 22, 1864, in *HED 1,* 38 Cong., 1 Sess., 346–48; Wallen to Cutler, January 5, 1864, in Santa Fe *Weekly New Mexican,* January 23, 1864; Cremony, *Life Among the Apaches,* 277–80; Henry P. Walker (ed.), "Soldier in the California Column: The Diary of John W. Teal," *Arizona and the West [A and W],* 13 (Spring 1971), 81.

41. Bailey, *The Long Walk,* 158; Carleton to Thomas, December 12, 1863, LRNMS, M-234, Roll 552.

42. Bailey, *The Long Walk,* 158–64; Santa Fe *Weekly New Mexican,* February 6, 1863; Stephen C. Jett, "The Destruction of Navajo Orchards in 1864: Captain John Thompson's Report," *A and W,* 14 (Winter 1974), 365–78.
43. Carleton to J. Francisco Perea, January 12, 1864, in *Condition of the Tribes,* 155; Twitchell, *Leading Facts of New Mexico History,* II, 399.

CHAPTER 3

1. Kelly, *Navajo Roundup,* 70–71, 107–09, 110–11; George W. Getty to Chauncey McKeever, August 24, 1867, AGO, M-619, Roll 484.
2. Kelly, *Navajo Roundup,* 107–09, First Lieutenant George W. Campbell to Carleton, February 2, 1864, AGO, M-619, Roll 283; Wallen to Ben Cutler, February 12, 1864, *ibid.*
3. Carleton to Thomas, February 23, 1864, *ibid.,* Santa Fe *Weekly Gazette,* September 21, 1864.
4. Santa Fe *Weekly New Mexican,* January 31, 1864; Cutler to Wallen, February 14, 1864, in *Condition of the Tribes,* 158; Steck to Dole, February 16, 1864, in "Report of the CIA, 1864," *HED 1,* 38 Cong., 1 Sess., 353–55.
5. Cutler to Wallen, February 25, 1864, in *Condition of the Tribes,* 158–59; Carleton to Wallen, February 25, AGO, M-619, Roll 283.
6. Carleton to Thomas, February 27, in *Condition of the Tribes,* 160–61; Santa Fe *Weekly New Mexican,* February 27, 1864.
7. Santa Fe *Weekly New Mexican,* February 27, 1864; Twitchell, *Old Santa Fe,* 322; Allen Johnson and Dumas Malone (eds.), *The Dictionary of American Biography* [*DAB*] (20 vols.; New York: Charles Scribner's Sons, 1935), xvi, 305–06.
8. Testimony of Henry B. Bristol, in *Condition of the Tribes,* 343; Heitman, *Historical Register,* II, 246; Carleton to Wallen, February 28, 1864, in *Condition of the Tribes,* 161; Bailey, *The Long Walk,* 178–80.
9. "Appropriation for the Navajo Indians," *HED 70,* 38 Cong., 1 Sess. (Serial 1193), 2–3.
10. Dole to Usher, March 4, 1864, in *HED 1,* 38 Cong., 1 Sess., 353–55; Dole to Usher, March 4, 1864, Report Books of the Office of Indian Affairs, 1838–85 [RBOIA], M-348, Roll 14, Records of the Bureau of Indian Affairs, RG 75, NA.
11. Santa Fe *Weekly Gazette,* March 5, 1864; Carleton to Wallen, in *Condition of the Tribes,* 163–64. Steck to Dole, October 10, 1864, in *HED 1,* 38 Cong., 1 Sess., 328.
12. Carleton to Thomas, March 12, 1864, in *Condition of the Tribes,* 166–67; General Orders No. 7, March 8, 1864, Department of New Mexico, AGO, M-619, Roll 286.
13. Carleton to Thomas, March 12, 1864, in *Condition of the Tribes,* 166–67.
14. Bristol to Baker, March 17, 1864; Carleton to Thomas, March 19, 1864; Baker to Dole, March 27, 1864, LRNMS, M-234, Roll 552.
15. Garrison to Taylor, March 26, 1864, AGO, M-619, Roll 286.
16. J. C. McFerran to General Thomas, March 27, 1864, Telegram, AGO, M-619, Roll 283.
17. Carleton to Thomas, March 19, 1864; to Wallen, March 20, 1864, in *Condition of the Tribes,* 169, 173.
18. Carleton to Wallen, March 25, 1864; General Orders 8, March 25, 1864, in *ibid.,* 170, 257.
19. Labadie to Carleton, April 1, 1864, AGO, M-619, Roll 286; Santa Fe *Weekly Gazette,* March 26, 1864.
20. "Abstracts of All Provisions Issued to Captive Indians," in *Condition of the Tribes,* 270; Santa Fe *Weekly Gazette,* March 26, 1864; Carleton to Edwin Rigg, April 1, 1864, in *Condition of the Tribes,* 172; Steck to Dole, March 28, 1864, in *The War of the Rebellion; The Official Records of the Union and Confederate Armies* (139 vols.; Washington: Government Printing Office, 1891–96), Series I, Vol. XLI, 899–900; Santa Fe *Weekly New Mexican,* April 2, 1864; Labadie to Carleton, April 1, 1864, AGO, M-619, Roll 286; Wallen to Carleton, April 1, 1864, *ibid.*
21. Dole to Usher, April 4, 1864, RBOIA, M-348, Roll 14; Dole to Usher, April 4, 1864; in John P. Usher, "Report on the Navajo Indians," *HED 65,* 38 Cong., 1 Sess., 1–2. Stanton to Usher, March 31, 1864, LRNMS, M-234, Roll 552.
22. McNitt, "Origins of Fort Sumner," 115; Usher to Dole, January 16, 1864, LRNMS, Roll 552.
23. Carleton to Wallen, April 9, 1864, in *Condition of the Tribes,* 175.
24. Dole to Usher, April 11, 1864, RBOIA, M-348, Roll 14; Albuquerque *Rio Abajo Weekly Press,* April 12, 1864.

25. Quartermaster General to Stanton, April 13, 1864, AGO, M-619, Roll 283; Wallen to Carleton, April 15, 1864, *ibid.,* Roll 286.

26. Steck to Dole, April 11, 1864, LRNMS, M-234, Roll 552.

27. Carleton to Thomas, April 24, 1864, in *Condition of the Tribes,* 179.

28. Bristol to the A.A.G., May 13, 1864, Fort Sumner Records, DNM, USACC; Bristol to A.A.G., May 1, 1864, *ibid.*

29. Labadie to Steck, May 18, 1864; Miguel Romero y Baca to Steck, June 23, 1864, *HED 1,* 38 Cong., 1 Sess., 349–50, 359–61; Henry Wallen to Carleton, May (?), Fort Sumner Records, DNM, USACC.

30. Santa Fe *Weekly Gazette,* September 21, 1864; Labadie to Steck, May 1, and May 18, 1864, LRNMS, M-234, Roll 552.

31. Wallen to Labadie, March 27, 1864, Fort Sumner Records, DNM, USACC.

32. "Abstracts of Purchases," in *Condition of the Tribes,* 272; Pearson, *The Maxwell Land Grant,* 15; Santa Fe *Weekly New Mexican,* March 5, 1864.

33. "Abstracts of Purchases," in *Condition of the Tribes,* 270–71.

34. Santa Fe *Weekly Gazette,* June 11, 1864; Santa Fe *Weekly New Mexican,* November 7, 1863; Heitman, *Historical Register,* I, 731.

35. Steck to Dole, May 28, 1864, LRNMS, M-234, Roll 552. Frank Waters, *The Book of the Hopi* (New York: Ballantine Books, 1970), 342–48.

36. Steck to Dole, May 30, 1864, LRNMS, M-234, Roll 552; Carson to Carleton, July 14, 1864, *Official Records,* Series I, Vol. XLI, Part II, 192.

37. Post Returns, Fort Sumner, May, 1864, RMP, M-617, Roll 1241. "Abstracts of Purchases," in *Condition of the Tribes,* 273.

38. Carleton to Amos F. Garrison, June 21, 1864; Garrison to DeForrest, June 22, 1864 and June 21, 1864, AGO, M-619, Roll 286.

39. Special Orders 22, June 23, 1864; Report of the Board, June 23, 1864; Garrison to Taylor, March 26, 1864, *ibid.*

40. Carson to Carleton, July 14, 1864, *ibid.*

41. Carson to Carleton, July 14, 1864, *ibid.;* Harvey L. Carter, *Dear Old Kit* (Norman: University of Oklahoma Press, 1968), 23.

42. Bristol to Carleton, July 15, 1864, AGO, M-619, Roll 286.

43. Labadie to Steck, October 22, 1864, *HED 1,* 38 Cong., 1 Sess., 347.

44. Dole to Usher, July 16, 1864, RBOIA, M-348, Roll 14; Bailey, *The Long Walk,* 188.

45. Cullum, *Biographical Register,* II, 622; Steck to Dole, June 20, 1864, *HED 1,* 38 Cong., 1 Sess., 357–58; Steck to Dole, June 25, 1864, LRNMS, M-234, Roll 552. Stanton to Usher, June 4, 1864, LRNMS, Roll 552; Baker to Dole, July 13, 1864; Steck to Dole, March 20, 1864, LRNMS, M-234, Roll 552.

46. Steck to Dole, July 24, 1864, LRNMS, M-234, Roll 552.

47. Romero y Baca to Dole, June 23, 1864, *ibid.*

48. Carleton to Bristol, July 17, 1864, in *Condition of the Tribes,* 187–88.

49. "Abstracts of Purchases," in *ibid.*

CHAPTER 4

1. Santa Fe *Weekly Gazette,* July 30, 1864.

2. Return of Indian Captives, July 31, 1864, AGO, M-619, Roll 286; Pearce, *New Mexico Place Names,* 1, 148, 62.

3. Santa Fe *Weekly New Mexican,* August 12, 1864.

4. Santa Fe *Weekly Gazette,* August 20, 1864.

5. Testimonies of Percy Ayers, George Gwyther, and Epifano Vigil, in *Condition of the Tribes,* 335, 339, 354–55; Carleton to Usher, August 14, 1864; Cutler to Wallen, August 22, 1864, in *ibid.,* 189–91; Bristol to A. A. G., August 5, 1864, Fort Sumner Records, DNM, USACC.

6. Santa Fe *Weekly Gazette,* August 15, 1864; "Abstracts of Purchases," in *Condition of the Tribes,* 278–79.

7. Carleton to Usher, August 27, 1864, LRNMS, M-234, Roll 552; Santa Fe *Weekly Gazette,* August 15, 1864.

8. Bristol to A.A.G., August 12, 1864, Fort Sumner Records, DNM, USACC; Carleton to Thomas, October 30, 1864, in *Condition of the Tribes,* 207–08; Santa Fe *Weekly Gazette,* November 12, 1864.

9. Proceedings of a Board of Survey, Special Orders 92, August 30, 1864; Bosque Redondo File, Consolidated Correspondence File, 1794–1890, Records of the Office of the Quartermaster General [QMO], RG 92, NA.

10. Carleton to Thomas, October 30, 1864, in *Condition of the Tribes,* 207–08; Testimony of Charles L. Warner, in *ibid.,* 342.

11. Labadie to Steck, October 22, 1864, in *HED 1,* 38 Cong., 1 Sess., 347–48.

12. Calloway to Carleton, September 14, 1864, Fort Sumner Records, DNM, USACC.

13. Santa Fe *Weekly New Mexican,* September 1864; Carleton to Wallen, March 30, 1864, in *Condition of the Tribes,* 171.

14. Santa Fe *Weekly New Mexican,* September 9, 1864.

15. Carleton to Bristol, September 12, 1864, in *Condition of the Tribes,* 196–97. Carleton to Dole, September 16, 1864, *LRNMS,* M-234, Roll 552.

16. Crocker to Carleton, September n.d., 1864, Fort Sumner Records, DNM, USACC; Special Orders 37, September 19, 1864, in *Condition of the Tribes,* 242; Crocker to Cutler, September 28, 1864, *LRNMS,* M-234, Roll 552.

17. Carleton to Crocker, October 9, 1864, in *Condition of the Tribes,* 109; Report of S. S. Gorham, May 1, 1865, in *ibid.,* 321–22.

18. Crocker to Carleton, September 30, 1864, Fort Sumner Records, DNM, USACC.

19. Crocker to Carleton, October 7, 1864, *ibid.*

20. "Abstracts of Purchases," in *Condition of the Tribes,* 279, 281.

21. Steck to Dole, October 10, 1864, in *HED 1,* 38 Cong., 1 Sess., 327–28, 330.

22. Robert Lusby to L. G. Murphy, October 15, 16, 1864, Fort Sumner Records, DNM, USACC.

23. Henry Bristol, Indian Fund, October, 1864, *ibid.;* Keleher, *Turmoil in New Mexico,* 502, fn. 105.

24. Crocker to Cutler, October 21, 1864, Bosque Redondo File, QMO; Crocker to Cutler, October 20, 1864, Fort Sumner Records, DNM, USACC; "List of Indians Who Delivered Fodder," November 6, 1864, *ibid.;* Kelly, *Navajo Roundup,* 145.

25. Labadie to Steck, October 22, 1864, in *HED 1,* 38 Cong., 1 Sess., 347–49.

26. Labadie to Carleton, October 22, 1864, Bosque Redondo File, QMO.

27. Carleton to Crocker, October 22, November 6, 1864, in *Condition of the Tribes,* 201, 210; Bristol to Taylor, May 9, 1865, in *Official Records,* Series I, Vol. XVIII, Part II, 378; Davis to Cutler, March 25, 1865, in *ibid.,* Part I, 1259. Carleton to Carson, October 23, 1864, in *Condition of the Tribes,* 202.

28. Carleton to Crocker, October 28, 1864, in *Condition of the Tribes,* 203–04.

29. Crocker to Cutler, October 28, 1864, Fort Sumner Records, DNM, USACC.

30. J. C. McFerran to H. M. Enos, October 29, 1864, Bosque Redondo File, QMO.

31. Carleton to Crocker, October 31, 1864, in *Condition of the Tribes,* 208–09.

32. Carleton to Thomas, October 28, 1864, Bosque Redondo File, QMO.

33. Crocker to Calloway, October 31, 1864, Fort Sumner Records, DNM, USACC; Crocker to Labadie, October 31, 1864, *ibid.*

34. Lamar, *The Far Southwest,* 124–31.

35. Steck to Charles E. Mix, November 5, 1864; to Dole, October 22, 1864, LRNMS, M-234, Roll 552.

36. Carleton to Crocker, November 6, 1864, in *Condition of the Tribes,* 210.

37. Cutler to Crocker, November 9, 1864, in *ibid.,* 211; Santa Fe *Weekly New Mexican,* November 11, 1864.

38. Crocker to Cutler, November 10, 1864, Fort Sumner Records, DNM, USACC.

39. Santa Fe *Weekly New Mexican,* November 11, 1864.

40. Crocker to Carleton, November 11, 1864, Fort Sumner Records, DNM, USACC; Dole to Usher, October 20, 21, 1864, RBOIA, M-348, Roll 14.

41. "Abstracts of Purchases," in *Condition of the Tribes,* 282–83; Baker to Usher, August 18, 19, 1864, January 15, 1865; to Dole, August 17, 19, 1864; to H. J. Blow, June 30, 1866; Leavenworth to Dole, July 29, 1864, LRNMS M-234, Rolls 552–53.

42. E. D. Townsend to Carleton, November 22, 1864, Fort Sumner Records, DNM, USACC.

43. Santa Fe *Weekly New Mexican,* November 25, December 9, 1864; Pearce, *New Mexico Place Names,* 135.

44. Robert Lusby to Faringhy, December 1, 1864, Fort Sumner Records, DNM, USACC.

45. Cutler to Crocker, December 9, 1864; Carleton to Bell, December 10, 1864, in *Condition of the Tribes,* 212–13.

46. Crocker to Carleton, December 2, 1864, Fort Sumner Records, DNM, USACC; Kelly, *Navajo Roundup,* 135–36.

47. Henry Connelly, Third Annual Message of the Governor, December 6, 1864, NMTP, M-T 17, Roll 2.

48. Steck to Dole, November 16, 20, 1864, LRNMS, M-234, Roll 552.

49. Baker to Blow, June 30, 1866, LRNMS, M-234, Roll 553.

50. Steck to Dole, December 11, 1864, LRNMS, M-234, Roll 552.
51. Special Orders 123, December 20, 1864; Report of Bristol and Murphy, December 28, 1864; Steck to Dole, January 13, 1865; Captain Robert Lusby to Cutler, January 3, 1865; Purchase orders (n.d.) from Carney and Stevens, LRNMS, M-234, Roll 552; Baker to Usher, January 15, 1865; to Blow, June 30, 1866, *ibid.,* Rolls 552–53; William E. Unrau, "The Civil War Career of Jesse Henry Leavenworth," Montana, *The Magazine of Western History,* 12 (April 1962), 74–83; "Resolution of the Legislature of Kansas," *Sen. Misc. Doc.* 34, 39 Cong., 2 Sess. (Serial 1278), 1.

CHAPTER 5

1. Lamar, *The Far Southwest,* 126–30; Carleton, "To the People of New Mexico," December 16, 1864, AGO, M-619, Roll 561; Gerald Thompson, " 'To the People of New Mexico' General Carleton Defends the Bosque Redondo," *A and W,* 14 (Winter 1972), 347–66.
2. Crocker to Carleton, December 20, 1864, Fort Sumner Records, DNM, USACC.
3. Indian Census of December 31, 1864, in *Condition of the Tribes,* 264; Testimony of Epifano Vigil in *ibid.,* 355; Return of Indian Captives held at Fort Sumner, January, 1865, LRNMS, M-234, Roll 552.
4. Steck to T. W. Woolson, January 14, 1865, LRNMS, M-234, Roll 552; Vigil testimony in *Condition of the Tribes,* 355.
5. Crocker to Harlan, January 16, 1865, in *Official Records,* Series I, LXVIII, 571–72.
6. Erastus Wood to Crocker, January 15, 1865, in *Condition of the Tribes,* 214.
7. General Orders 1, January, 1865, Fort Sumner Records, DNM, USACC.
8. Pearce, *New Mexico Place Names,* 28, 119–20; Twitchell, *Leading Facts of New Mexican History,* II, 273–74; Santa Fe *Weekly New Mexican,* January 27, 1865.
9. "Abstracts of Purchases for Captive Indians," in *Condition of the Tribes,* 283–85; Frank Reeve (ed.), "Albert Franklin Banta: Arizona Pioneer, Part II," *NMHR,* 17 (July 1952), 214–15; Lansing B. Bloom, "Bourke on the Southwest, Part IV," *NMHR,* 10 (January 1935), 5; Haines, *History of New Mexico,* 435; Board of Survey, January 26, 1865, "Fort Sumner Papers," UA.
10. Contract between Andres Dold and William Bell, January 2, 1865, War Department Quartermaster and Commissary Contracts, U.S. General Accounting Office [GAO], RG 217, NA.
11. Report of William P. Galloway to Major McCleave (n.d.), in *Condition of the Tribes,* 298–301.
12. Contract between William Bell and Jose Gallegos, January 2, 1865; Crocker to Cutler, February 1, 1865, Fort Sumner Records, DNM, USACC.
13. Crocker to Cutler, *ibid.*
14. Steck to Dole, February 4, 1865, LRNMS, M-234, Roll 552.
15. Knapp to Dole, February 4, 1865, *ibid.*
16. E. W. Eaton to Cutler, February 8, 1865, *ibid.*
17. General Orders 5, February 8, 1865; Abstracts of the Court Martial Proceedings Against Captain P. G. D. Morton (n.d.), Edwin J. Edgar to Jennings, March 27, 1865, LRNMS, M-234, Roll 553.
18. Calloway to McCleave, February 25, 1865, in *Condition of the Tribes,* 298–301.
19. Boards of Survey, February 10, 16, 27, 1865, "Fort Sumner Papers," UA.
20. Carleton to McCleave, March 9, 1865, LRNMS, M-234, Roll 552.
21. Cutler to McCleave, February 20, 1865, *ibid.*
22. Morning Report, Post Returns, February 20, 1865, Fort Sumner, RMP, M-617, Roll 1241; Special Orders 8, March 11, 1865, in *Condition of the Tribes,* 243; Heitman, *Historical Register,* I, 655. Twitchell, *Leading Facts of New Mexican History,* II, 400, 412.
23. Carleton to McCleave, March 10, 1865; to Wallen, March 11, 1865; to Asa B. Carey, March 16, 1865, in *Condition of the Tribes,* 165, 168, 219; Heitman, *Historical Register,* I, 246.
24. Special Orders 32, March 14, 1865, in *Official Records,* Series I, XLVIII, 1174; McCleave to Edgar, March 14, 1865; McCleave, Special Orders 42; Fort Sumner, March 30, 1865, Fort Sumner Records, DNM, USACC.
25. Steck to Charles E. Mix, March 12, 1865, Carleton to Steck, March 16, 1865, LRNMS, M-234, Roll 552.
26. Carleton to Steck, March 16, 1865, *ibid.*
27. Steck to Dole, March 25, 1865, *ibid.*
28. Cutler to Bell, March 25, 1865, Fort Sumner Records, DNM, USACC.
29. Carleton to Usher, March 30, 1865, in *Condition of the Tribes,* 311.
30. "Abstracts of Purchases," in *ibid.,* 286–89.

31. Contract between William H. Moore and J. C. McFerran, April 15, 1865, Contract File, QMO; "Abstracts of Purchases," in *Condition of the Tribes,* 289–90.

32. George Gwyther to O. M. Bryan, March 16, 1865; McCleave, Special Orders 52, March 26, 1865, Fort Sumner Records, DNM, USACC; Return of March, 1865, LRNMS, M-234, Roll 552; Pearce, *New Mexico Place Names,* 67.

33. M. Hillary to Theodore Dodd, September 6, 1866, in *Annual Report of the Commissioner of Indian Affairs, 1866* (Washington: Government Printing Office, 1866), 150–51.

34. J. G. Knapp to Dole, March 30, 1865, LRNMS, M-234, Roll 552.

35. J. M. Edmunds to Dole, May 22, 1865, *ibid.*

36. Francisco Perea to Dole, April 6, 1865, *ibid.*

37. Dole to Usher, February 18, 1865, RBOIA, M-348, Roll 14.

38. Santa Fe *Weekly New Mexican,* April 14, 1865; Carleton to McCleave, March 9, 1865, LRNMS, M-234, Roll 552.

39. Carleton to McCleave, April 26, 1865, in *Condition of the Tribes,* 225.

40. "Report of the Special Board on Tribal Reorganization," in *ibid.,* 308–11.

41. Steck to Dole, April 30, 1865, LRNMS, M-234, Roll 552.

CHAPTER 6

1. Delgado to Dole, July 16, August 20, 1865, LRNMS, M-234, Roll 552; Bloom, "Historical Society Minutes," 274; Haines, *History of New Mexico,* 293–94.

2. McCleave to Cutler, May 3, 25, 1865, Fort Sumner Records, DNM, USACC; Carleton to Thomas, May 8, 1865, in *Condition of the Tribes,* 226.

3. Bailey, *The Long Walk,* 201.

4. McCleave to Captain Fritz, May 9, 1865, Fort Sumner Records, DNM, USACC; McCleave, Sp. Or. 57, May 9, 1865, *ibid.*

5. Pearce, *New Mexico Place Names,* 3.

6. Santa Fe *Weekly New Mexican,* May 19, 1865; Pearce, *New Mexico Place Names,* 147.

7. McCleave, Sp. Or. 62, May 19, 1865, Fort Sumner Records, DNM, USACC.

8. Return for May, 1865, LRNMS, M-234, Roll 552; Carleton to Wallen, May 3, 1865, in *Condition of the Tribes,* 183.

9. "Abstracts of Stores," in *Condition of the Tribes,* 290; Bloom, "Historical Society Minutes," 275; W. H. Bell, Register of Letters Sent and Received, DNM, USACC, RG 393.

10. Pearce, *New Mexico Place Names,* 104; Santa Fe *Weekly New Mexican,* January 31, 1864, July 21, 1865; Carleton to Attorney General, July 20, 1865, in *Condition of the Tribes,* 230.

11. Bristol to McCleave, June 2, 1865, Fort Sumner Records, DNM, USACC.

12. McCleave's endorsement on Bristol to McCleave, June 2, 1865; McCleave, Sp. Or. 66, June 3, 1865, *ibid.*

13. McCleave, Sp. Or. 68, June 8, 1865, and Sp. Or. 71, June 13, 1865, *ibid.*

14. McCleave to A. A. G., June 15, 1865, *ibid.,* Carleton to Major William H. Lewis, June 19, 1865, in *Condition of the Tribes,* 227–28, 302–04; Post Returns, June, 1865, Fort Sumner, RMP, M-617, Roll 1241.

15. Testimony before the Doolittle Committee, June and July, in *Condition of the Tribes,* 323–59; *Who Was Who In America* (Historical Volume; Chicago: A. N. Marquis Co., 1963), 455; Donald Chaput, "Generals, Indian Agents, Politicians: The Doolittle Survey of 1865," *WHQ* 3 (July 1972), 269–82.

16. Carleton to Doolittle, July 25, 1865, AGO, M-619, Roll 561.

17. Frances McCabe, Report of July 9, 1865, Pl. Ex. 365, Docket 229, Navajo Claims Data File, Arizona Historical Society [AHS]; Julius C. Shaw to Ben Cutler, July 10, 1865, Pl. Ex. 366, Docket 229, *ibid.*

18. Cutler to Lewis, June 22, 1865, in *Condition of the Tribes,* 228–29.

19. Return for June, 1865; McCleave to Cutler, July 6, 1865, LRNMS, M-234, Roll 552; Santa Fe *Weekly Gazette,* July 1, 1865.

20. McCleave, Sp. Or. 76, June 27, 1865; McCleave to Cutler, July 3, 1865, Fort Sumner Records, DNM, USACC.

21. McCleave to Carleton, July 14, 1865, in *Condition of the Tribes,* 312; Bell, July 8, 1865, Register of Letters, DNM, USACC.

22. Carleton to McCleave, July 18, 1865, LRNMS, M-234, Roll 552; Carleton to McCleave, August 9, in *Condition of the Tribes,* 233–34; McCleave, Circular, August 16, 1865, Fort Sumner Records, DNM, USACC.

23. McCleave, Sp. Or. 86, July 17, 1865, Fort Sumner Records, DNM, USACC; Edward E. Hill to Gerald Thompson, January 6, 1972; Sidney W. Smith, *From the Cow Camp to the Pulpit* (Cincinnati: The Christian Leader Corporation, 1927), 231. J. Evetts Haley, *Charles Goodnight, Cowman and Plainsman* (Norman: University of Oklahoma Press, 1949), 127–53; Charles Kenner, "The Origins of the 'Goodnight' Trail Reconsidered," *Southwestern Historical Quarterly,* 77 (January 1974), 390–94.

24. Cutler to Bristol, August 9, 1865, Fort Sumner Records, DNM, USACC.

25. Contract between Andres Dold and H. M. Enos, July 28, 1865, Contract File, QMO.

26. Transcript of a Power of Attorney for James H. Carleton, July 20, 1865, Albert Case Benedict Collection, AHS.

27. Santa Fe *Weekly New Mexican,* May 26, July 28, 1865.

28. Carleton to McCleave, July 24, 1865, in *Condition of the Tribes,* 230–31; Shaw to Cutler, July 24, 1865, Pl. Ex. 367, Docket 299, Navajo Claims Data File, AHS.

29. Lawrence G. Murphy to B. Taylor, July 28, 1865, LRNMS, M-234, Roll 552.

30. Return for July, 1865, *ibid.*

31. Carleton to Dole, August 6, 1865, *ibid.*

32. McCleave, Endorsement, August 10, 1865; McCleave, Gen. Ors. 28 and 29, August 11, 12, 1865, *ibid.*

33. Carleton to McCleave, August 16, in *Condition of the Tribes,* 234.

34. Consolidated Morning Report, Post Returns, August 31, 1865, Fort Sumner, RMP, M-617, Roll 1241; McCleave, Gen. Or. 102, August 25, 1865, Fort Sumner Records, DNM, USACC.

35. Report on the Indian Fund, August, 1865, LRNMS, M-234, Roll 552.

36. Dodd to CIA, September 9, 1865; to Dole, July 24, 1865, *ibid.;* Twitchell, *Leading Facts of New Mexico History,* II, 399.

37. Delgado to D. N. Cooley, September 10, 1865, in *Annual Report of the Commissioner of Indian Affairs, 1865* (Washington: Government Printing Office, 1865), 346–47.

38. Julius K. Graves to R. B. Van Valkenburg, September 12, 1865; John Pope to General Grant, October 26, 1865, LRNMS, M-234, Roll 552.

39. Theodore S. Kervet (?) to Seward, September 11, 1865, NMTP, M-T 17, Roll 3; David Brugge, *Navajos in the Catholic Church Records of New Mexico, 1694–1875* (Window Rock, Az.: Research Section, Parks and Recreation Dept., The Navajo Tribe, 1965), 85–92.

40. McCleave, Gen. Or. 33, 35, 36, 40, September 21, October 2, October 7, and November 2, 1865, Fort Sumner Records, DNM, USACC.

41. Carleton to Richard C. Drum, September 15, 1865, in *Condition of the Tribes,* 236; Shinn, "Map of the Reservation for Navajo Indians," Fortifications File, Drawer 142, Sheet 47, CE.

42. Santa Fe *Weekly New Mexican,* October 6, 1865.

43. *Ibid.,* October 27, November 24, 1865; Carleton, Sp. Or. 5, Dist. of New Mexico, October 8, 1865, Fort Sumner Records, DNM, USACC; Santa Fe *Weekly Gazette,* October 28, 1865.

44. McCleave, Endorsement, October 17, 1865; Sp. Or. 122, October 27, 1865, Fort Sumner Records, DNM, USACC.

45. Sp. Or. 40, October 29, 1865, LRNMS, M-234, Roll 552.

46. McCleave to Cutler, November 3, 1865, Fort Sumner Records, DNM, USACC.

47. Return for October, 1865; Delgado to Cooley, December 10, 1865, LRNMS, M-234, Rolls 552–53.

48. McCleave to Cutler, November 6, 1865, Fort Sumner Records, DNM, USACC.

49. McCleave, Sp. Or. 128, November 7, 1865, *ibid.*

50. McCleave, Sp. Or. 135, November 21, 1865; and Sp. Or. 140, November 28, 1865, *ibid.*

CHAPTER 7

1. Bristol, Report of Produce Raised on the Apache Farm, November 30, 1865; Bristol, Report of Produce Raised on the Navajo Farm, November 30, 1865; "Abstracts of Provisions Issued to Captive Indians by Captain Morton," February 3, 1866; Cyrus H. DeForrest, Statements "C" and "D," February 6, 1865, AGO, M-619, Roll 561; Bristol, "Report (in continuation) of Produce Raised," December 31, 1865; DeForrest, February 8, 1865, *ibid.*

2. McCleave, Sp. Or. 146, December 12, 1865, Fort Sumner Records, DNM, USACC;

McCleave, Gen. Or. 48, December 6, 1865, and Gen. Or. 50, December 13, 1865, *ibid.*
    3. Lucero to Carleton, December 14, 1865, Pl. Ex. 377, Docket 299, Navajo Claims Data File, AHS.
    4. Lucero to Henry Connelly, Santa Fe *Weekly New Mexican,* January 12, 1866.
    5. Harlan to Stanton, December 16, 1865.
    6. A. B. Eaton to Stanton, December 27, 1865, Fort Sumner Records, DNM, USACC; Carleton to Doolittle, July 15, 1865, AGO, M-619, Roll 561.
    7. Santa Fe *Weekly New Mexican,* November 3, 1865.
    8. Keleher, *Turmoil in New Mexico,* 454–56.
    9. Santa Fe *Weekly New Mexican,* January 5, 1866; Jack D. Rittenhouse, *New Mexico Civil War Bibliography* (Houston: Stagecoach Press, 1961), 34–35.
    10. Pope to Grant, October 26, 1865; Graves to Cooley, November 9, 1865, LRNMS, M-234, Roll 553.
    11. Dodd to Cooley, December 31, 1865, *ibid.*
    12. Graves' Report, February, 1866, LRNMS, M-234, Roll 553.
    13. Graves' Report on the Council with the Navajos (n.d.), 1866, *ibid.*
    14. Replies of the Legislature to Inquiries of J. K. Graves, January 30, 1866, *ibid.*
    15. Bristol to Graves, February 6, 1866, *ibid.*
    16. Santa Fe *Weekly New Mexican,* January 5, 1866; McCleave to Cutler, January 6, 1866, in Santa Fe *Weekly Gazette,* January 20, 1866.
    17. McCleave, Sp. Or. 14, 17, January 30, February 3, 1866, and Sp. Or. 30, March 1, 1866, Fort Sumner Records, DNM, USACC.
    18. McCleave, Gen. Or. 1, January 13, 1866, *ibid.*
    19. Gen. Or. 8, March 13, 1866, *ibid.*
    20. McCleave, Sp. Or. 9, January 23 and Sp. Or. 10, January 26, 1866, *ibid.*
    21. Santa Fe *Weekly New Mexican,* January 26, 1866.
    22. McCleave, Sp. Or. 24, February 15, 1866, Fort Sumner Records, DNM, USACC.
    23. Santa Fe *Weekly New Mexican,* February 16, 1866; Notice of the appointment of A. Baldwin Norton, February 17, 1866; Report of Graves, February, 1866, LRNMS, M-234, Roll 553; Grant to Sherman, April 18, 1866, U. S. Grant Papers, Series 5, Vol. 109, p. 250, Library of Congress [LC].
    24. McCleave, Sp. Or. 38, March 26, 1866, and Sp. Or. 10, March 18, 1866, Fort Sumner Records, DNM, USACC.
    25. Santa Fe *Weekly Gazette,* April 2, 1866; Staab and Bro. to Cooley, April 20, 1866, LRNMS, M-234, Roll 553.
    26. A. B. Eaton to Bell, April 12, AGO, M-619, Roll 561.
    27. Santa Fe *Weekly New Mexican,* April 27, 1866.
    28. McCleave, Sp. Or. 52, May, 1866, Gen. Or. 12, May 17, 1866, Sp. Or. 53, May 11, 1866, and Sp. Or. 60, May 20, 1866, Fort Sumner Records, DNM, USACC; Santa Fe *Weekly Gazette,* May 10, 1866.
    29. Santa Fe *Weekly New Mexican,* May 25 and April 6, 1866.
    30. Charles T. Jennings to DeForrest, May 25, 1866, in Santa Fe *Weekly Gazette,* June, 1866, Bosque Redondo File, QMO; "Civilian Employee Abstract," Frank McNitt Collection, New Mexico State Records Center and Archives.
    31. Report of D. N. Cooley, *Report of the CIA, 1866,* 31.
    32. Santa Fe *Weekly New Mexican,* June 8, 1866; McCleave, Sp. Or. 67, June 8, 1866, Fort Sumner Records, DNM, USACC.
    33. Carleton to Oscar Brown, June 4, 1866; Brown to Orville H. Browning, September 3, 1866, LRNMS, M-234, Roll 553; McCleave, Sp. Or., February 6, 1866, Fort Sumner Records, DNM, USACC; Grant to Pope, May 7, 1866, Grant Papers, Series 5, Vol. 109, p. 262.
    34. McCleave, Gen. Or. 16, June 14, 1866, Fort Sumner Records, DNM, USACC.
    35. Santa Fe *Weekly New Mexican,* June 16, 1866.
    36. McCleave, Sp. Or. 62, May 24, and Sp. Or. 70, June 19, 1866, Fort Sumner Records, DNM, USACC.
    37. Vose to W. R. Savage, June 22, 1866, in Santa Fe *Weekly Gazette,* July 28, 1866.
    38. James D. Shinkle, *Fifty Years of Roswell History, 1867–1917* (Roswell, New Mexico: Hall-Poorbaugh Press, 1964), 6–7; James Cox, *Historical and Biographical Record of the Cattle Industry* (St. Louis: Woodward and Tiernan Printing Company, 1895), 306–308; Haley, *Charles Goodnight,* 119–20, 127–53; Contract between Bell and Patterson, August 15, 1866, and Contract between Bell and W. H. Moore, March 14, 1866, War Department Contracts, GAO.
    39. Santa Fe *Weekly Gazette,* July 7, 1866; Santa Fe *Weekly New Mexican,* July 7, 1866.

40. Bailey, *The Long Walk,* 209; Santa Fe *Weekly New Mexican,* July 29, 1866; Norton to Cooley, July 31, 1866, LRNMS, M-234, Roll 553; McCleave to DeForrest, July 14, 1866, in Santa Fe *Weekly Gazette,* July 28, 1866; Bristol to Porter, July 14, *ibid.;* Santa Fe *Weekly Gazette,* July 7, 1866.
41. Santa Fe *Weekly New Mexican,* July 14, 1866, and July 26, 1866.
42. McCleave, Sp. Or. 81, July 28, 1866; Gen. Or. 19, July 2, 1866, Sp. Or. 76, July 1866, Fort Sumner Records, DNM, USACC.
43. Harlan to Cooley, August 2, 1866; Norton to Cooley, August 17, 1866, *ibid.;* Sonnichsen, *The Mescalero Apaches,* 121–22.
44. Carleton, Sp. Or. 24, August 12, 1866, Fort Sumner Records, DNM, USACC; Heitman, *Historical Register,* I, 663; McCleave, Sp. Or. 84, August 16, 1866, Fort Sumner Records, DNM, USACC; Russell F. Weigley, *History of the United States Army* (New York: The Macmillan Company, 1967), 265–68.
45. Santa Fe *Weekly New Mexican,* October 27, 1866.

CHAPTER 8

1. McDonald to DeForrest, January, 1867, AGO, M-619, Roll 561; McDonald to McClure, November 17, 1866, Bosque Redondo File, QMO; Santa Fe *Weekly Gazette,* September 22, 1866.
2. Shinkle, *Fifty Years of Roswell History,* 6–7; Cox, *Historical Record of the Cattle Industry,* 306–308; J. Harris to Bell, September 24, 1866, Bosque Redondo File, QMO. Nichols to Bell, October 11, 1866; Bell to McClure, October 27, 1866, *ibid.;* Santa Fe *Weekly New Mexican,* October 13, 1866; C. L. Sonnichsen, *Pass of the North* (El Paso: Texas Western Press, 1968), 162, 171–76.
3. Graves to Cooley, September 28, 1866, LRNMS, M-234, Roll 553.
4. Cooley to Browning, October 11, 1866, RBOIA, M-348, Roll 15; Browning to Stanton, October 17, 1866, AGO, M-619, Roll 484.
5. Grant to Browning, October 13, 1866, Grant Papers, Series 5, Vol. 47, p. 189.
6. Stanton to Browning, October 31, 1866, AGO, M-619, Roll 484.
7. Santa Fe *Weekly Gazette,* October 20, 1866.
8. Butler to DeForrest, November 11, 1866, in Santa Fe *Weekly Gazette,* November 17, 1866; Santa Fe *Weekly New Mexican,* November 24, 1866; Pearce, *New Mexico Place Names,* 61.
9. Arny to Bogy, November 24, 1866, LRNMS, M-234, Roll 553.
10. Nesmith to Bogy, November 17, 1866, *ibid.*
11. Roberts and Patterson to DeForrest, November 29, 1866, Bosque Redondo File, QMO.
12. Gen. Or. 24, November 16, 1866, Fort Sumner Records, DNM, USACC; Santa Fe *Weekly Gazette,* December 8, 1866.
13. Carleton to McClure, December 3, 1866, Bosque Redondo File, QMO; Randall to McClure, November 8, 1866, *ibid.*
14. Carleton to Thomas, December 5, 1866, *ibid.*
15. John Brooke to Mason Howard, December 19, 1866, AGO, M-619, Roll 561.
16. La Rue to Sykes, December 21, 1866; Sykes to Carleton, December 21, 1866; Carleton to McKeever, December 27, 1866, *ibid.*
17. McDonald to McClure, December 22, 1866, Bosque Redondo File, QMO; Carleton to McClure, December 27, 1866, *ibid.*
18. Grant, Sp. Or. 651, December 30, 1866, AGO, M-619, Roll 561. Norton to Bogy, February 6, 1867, LRNMS, M-234, Roll 554; Norton to Taylor, March 19, 1867, *ibid.*
19. Contract between Charles McClure and Vicente Romero, December 24, 1866, War Department Contracts, GAO; Hancock, Sp. Or. 10, January 13, 1867, AGO, M-619, Roll 561; Santa Fe *Weekly Gazette,* January 26, 1867.
20. Santa Fe *Weekly Gazette,* January 12, 1867; Sykes, Gen. Or. 1, January 10, 1867, Fort Sumner Records, DNM, USACC.
21. Santa Fe *Weekly New Mexican,* January 12 and 19, 1867; Santa Fe *Weekly Gazette,* January 19, 1867.
22. Carleton to Hancock, January 20, 1867, AGO, M-619, Roll 561.
23. Carleton to Hancock, *ibid.;* Carleton to Hancock, January 23, 1867, AGO, M-619, Roll 561.
24. Comstock to Alexander, January 23, 1867, Grant Papers, Series 5, Vol. 47, 244; Santa Fe *Weekly New Mexican,* January 26, 1867.

25. Hancock to Carleton, February 18, 1867, AGO, M-619, Roll 561; Carleton to McKeever, February 2, 1867, *ibid.*
26. Norton to Bogy, February 6, 1867; Norton to Taylor, March 19, 1867, LRNMS, M-234, Roll 554; Santa Fe *Weekly New Mexican,* February 23, March 2, 1867.
27. Sykes, Memo, March 3, 1867, Fort Sumner Records, DNM, USACC; Sykes, Sp. Or. 36, *ibid.*
28. Norton to Taylor, March 21, 1867, LRNMS, M-234, Roll 554.
29. Chaves to Browning, March 27, 1867, *ibid.*
30. Chaves to Taylor, April 2, 1867, *ibid.*
31. Post Returns, March, April, May, Fort Sumner, RMP M-617, Roll 1241; Hunt, *Carleton,* 348; Santa Fe *Weekly Gazette,* March–July, 1867.
32. Heitman, *Historical Register,* I, 452; Sykes, Circular, May 15, 1867; Sp. Or. 66, May 21, 1867, Fort Sumner Records, DNM, USACC.
33. Sykes, Sp. Or. 67, May 22, 1867, *ibid.*
34. Norton to Bogy, February 6, 1867, LRNMS, M-234, Roll 554; Norton to Taylor, March 19, 1867, *ibid.;* Brown to Bogy, February 10, 1867 and March 14, 1867; Taylor to Otto, May 25, 1867, *ibid.*
35. Taylor to Otto, June 1, 1867, RBOIA, M-348, Roll 16; Otto to Taylor, June 3, 1867, *ibid.*
36. Taylor to Johnson, June 11, 1867, *ibid.*
37. Hancock, Sp. Or. 10, June 11, 1867, AGO, M-619, Roll 484; Theodore Lloyd to CIA, June 18, 1867, LRNMS, M-234, Roll 554; Hancock to Dodd, January 31, 1867, *ibid.;* Santa Fe *Weekly New Mexican,* June 23, 1867.
38. Dodd to Norton, June 30, 1867, "Annual Report of the Commissioner of Indian Affairs, 1867," *HED 1,* 40 Cong., 2 Sess. (Serial 1326), 198–203.
39. Taylor to Otto, June 28, 1867, RBOIA, M-348, Roll 16; Elijah Simerly to Taylor, June 28, 1867, LRNMS, M-234, Roll 554; Taylor to Otto, June 28, 1867, *ibid.*
40. Taylor to Otto, July 10, 1867, RBOIA, M-348, Roll 16; Taylor to Browning, July 18, 1867, *ibid.*
41. Report of a Board of Officers, August 5, 1867, AGO, M-619, Roll 484; Board of Inquiry, August 5, 1867; Davidson to Winfield Scott Hancock, September 10, 1867, *ibid.;* Post Returns, July, 1867, Fort Sumner, RMP, M-617, Roll 1241; Bragg to Porter July 9, 1867; Whiting, Sp. Or. 61, July 28, 1867, Fort Sumner Records, DNM, USACC; Getty to McKeever, August 24, 1867, AGO, M-619, Roll 484; Santa Fe *Weekly New Mexican,* July 20, 1867; Getty, Sp. Or. 53, Fort Sumner Records, DNM, USACC; Heitman, *Historical Register,* I, 240, 944–45.

CHAPTER 9

1. Bailey, *The Long Walk,* 229–30; Norton, "Report of a Council with the Navajos," July 15, 1867, LRNMS, M-234, Roll 554.
2. J. Marvin Hunter, *The Trail Drivers of Texas* (2 vols.; New York: Argosy-Antiquarian Press, 1963). II, 908–13; Haley, *Charles Goodnight,* 119–20, 127–53; Edgar C. McMechan, "John Hittson: Cattle King," *Colorado Magazine,* 11 (September 1934), 164–70.
3. Getty to McKeever, August 24, 1867, AGO, M-619, Roll 484; Virginia Hoffman and Broderick Johnson, *Navajo Biographies* (Rough Rock, Arizona: Dine, Inc., 1970), 162–85.
4. Norton to Getty, August 21, 1867, AGO, M-619, Roll 484; Getty to Norton, August 22, 1867, *ibid.*
5. Norton to Taylor, August 24, 1867, "Report of the CIA, 1867," 190–91.
6. Labadie to Norton, August 28, 1867, *ibid.,* 214–15.
7. Getty, Sp. Or. 70, August 25, 1867, Fort Sumner Records, DNM, USACC; Whiting, Gen. Or. 22, August 30, 1867; Morning Report of the Navajo Indians (Consolidated) for August, 1867, *ibid.*
8. Mix to Otto, September, 1867, RBOIA, M-348, Roll 17.
9. Hoffman and Johnson, *Navajo Biographies,* 151–53; Whiting to Hunter, September 28, 1867, Fort Sumner Records, DNM, USACC.
10. Bainridge to Lane, October 5, 1867; Getty to Whiting, October 3, 1867; Hunter to CO, Ft. Wingate, October 3, 1867, to CO, Ft. Stanton, October 3, 1867, AGO, M-619, Roll 484.
11. Whiting, Sp. Or. 27, October 6, 1867, Fort Sumner Records, DNM, USACC; Tarlton to Porter, October 8, 1867, AGO, M-619, Roll 484.

12. DuBois to AAG, October 11, 1867; Tarlton to Post Adjutant, October (n.d.), 1867, *ibid.;* Whiting to Hunter, October 12, 1867, *ibid.;* Post Returns, October, 1867, Fort Sumner, RMP, M-617, Roll 1241.
13. Whiting to Hunter, October 12, 1867, AGO, M-619, Roll 484.
14. Getty to Norton, September 30, 1867; Norton to Getty, October 1, 1867; Getty to Norton, October 3, 1867, *ibid.*
15. Comstock to Alexander, October 11, 1867, Grant Papers, Series 5, Vol. 47, p. 302.
16. Whiting, Sp. Or. 125, October 4, 1867, DNM, USACC.
17. Whiting, Sp. Or. 159, November 29, 1867, *ibid.*
18. John Dold, Proposal, November 26, 1867, Bosque Redondo File, QMO.
19. Post Returns, November, 1867, Fort Sumner, RMP, M-617, Roll 1241.
20. Grant to Carleton, December 23, 1867, Grant Papers, Series 5, Vol. 47, p. 315.
21. Santa Fe *Weekly New Mexican,* December 31, 1867; Hunt, *James H. Carleton,* 338.
22. Mix to Browning, January 10, 1868, RBOIA, M-348, Roll 17. Fuller to Taylor, December 10, 1867, LRNMS, M-234, Roll 554.
23. Mix to Browning, January 15, 1868; Taylor to Browning, January 25, 1868, RBOIA, M-348, Roll 17; Santa Fe *Weekly New Mexican,* January 14, 1868.
24. "Letter from the Secretary of War Relative to the Unsuitableness of the Bosque Redondo Reservation," *HED 248,* 40 Cong., 2 Sess. (Serial 1341), 1–8.
25. Clever to Taylor, February 19, 1868, NMTP, M-T 17, Roll 3.
26. Taylor to Browning, February 21, 1868, *HED 185,* 40 Cong., 2 Sess. (Serial 1341), 1–2.
27. Hoffman and Johnson, *Navajo Biographies,* 114–15.
28. Santa Fe *Weekly New Mexican,* March 10, 1868; Whiting, Gen. Or. 5, February 27, 1868, Fort Sumner Records, DNM, USACC; Whiting, Gen. Or. 7, March 31, 1868, *ibid.*
29. Taylor to Browning, April 9, 1868, RBOIA, M-348, Roll 17; Santa Fe *Weekly New Mexican,* April 21, 1868.
30. Hoffman and Johnson, *Navajo Biographies,* 119, 180.
31. Sherman to Grant, June 7, 1868, AGO, M-619, Roll 639; Dodd to Sherman, May 30, 1868, *ibid.*
32. Rosenthal to Dodd, May 28, 1868, *ibid.*
33. Ruth Roessel (editor), *Navajo Stories of the Long Walk Period* (Tsaile, Arizona: Navajo Community College Press, 1973), 212, 238–39, 244; Hoffman and Johnson, *Navajo Biographies,* 113–33; Kappler, "Treaty with the Navajos, 1868," *Senate Document 452,* Vol. II, 57 Cong., 1 Sess. (Serial 4254), 782–85.
34. Sherman to Getty, June 1, 1868, AGO, M-619, Roll 639; "Removal of Navajo and Ute Indians," *HED 308,* 40 Cong., 2 Sess. (Serial 1345), Marie Mitchell, *The Navajo Peace Treaty of 1868* (New York: Mason & Lipscomb Publishers, 1973), 90–106.
35. Jordan to Post Adj., June 6, 1868, AGO, M-619, Roll 639; Roberts to Sherman, June 15, 1868, *ibid.*
36. Getty to Sherman, June 7, 1868, *ibid.;* Getty to Sherman, June 7, 1868; Grant's endorsement on Sherman's report, June 18, 1868; Sherman to Grant, June 7, 1868, *ibid.*
37. Roberts, Sp. Or. 91, June 22, 1868, Fort Sumner Records, DNM, USACC; Santa Fe *Weekly New Mexican,* June 9, July 2, 14, 21, 1868; Bailey, *The Long Walk,* 232–33; "Fort Sumner Reserve," Drawer 189, New Mexico 10, Sheets 2–3, Fortifications File, CE.

CHAPTER 10

1. Information on material culture is drawn from Clyde and Lucy W. Kluckhohn, and W. W. Hill, *Navajo Material Culture* (Cambridge: Harvard University Press, 1971), 64–74.

References

Primary Sources

UNPUBLISHED MATERIALS

Arizona Historical Society
Albert Case Benedict Collection
Navajo Claims Data File

Bancroft Library, University of California, Berkeley
Papers and Memoirs of William McCleave

Library of Congress
Papers of Ulysses S. Grant

Museum of New Mexico
Photographic Archives

National Archives
Chief of Engineers. "Fort Sumner Reserve." Fortifications File. Drawer 189, New Mexico 10, Sheets 2–3. Record Group 77.
Chief of Engineers. Shinn, John B. "Map of a part of the Reservation for Navajo Indians, at Fort Sumner, N. M." Fortifications File. Drawer 142, Sheet 47. Record Group 77.
Department of State. State Department Territorial Papers, New Mexico, 1851–72. Record Group 59.
Office of the Adjutant General. Letters Received by the Office of the Adjutant General, Main Series, 1861–70. Record Group 94.
Office of Indian Affairs. Letters Received, New Mexico Superintendency. Record Group 75.
Office of Indian Affairs. Report Books of the Office of Indian Affairs, 1838–85. Record Group 75.
Office of the Quartermaster General. Bosque Redondo File, Consolidated Correspondence File, 1794–1890. Record Group 92.
United States Army Commands. Returns from U. S. Military Posts. Record Group 98.
United States Army Continental Commands. Fort Sumner Records. Letters Sent and Received, Department of New Mexico, 1862–69. Record Group 393.
United States Army Continental Commands. Registers of Letters Sent and Received, Department of New Mexico. Record Group 393.
United States Army Signal Corps. Photographic Collection of Fort Sumner.
United States General Accounting Office. War Department Quartermaster and Commissary Contracts. Record Group 217.

New Mexico State Records and Archives
Frank McNitt Collection
Special Collections, University of Arizona Library
U. S. Army. District of New Mexico. "Miscellaneous administrative papers from Fort Sumner and various other New Mexico army posts."

PUBLISHED MATERIALS

Government Documents
Abel, Annie Heloise (ed.). *The Official Correspondence of James S. Calhoun*. Washington: Government Printing Office, 1915.
"Annual Report of the Commissioner of Indian Affairs, 1864." *House Executive Document 1*, 38 Congress, 1 Session (Serial 1220).
Annual Report of the Commissioner of Indian Affairs, 1865. Washington: Government Printing Office, 1865.
Annual Report of the Commissioner of Indian Affairs, 1866. Washington: Government Printing Office, 1866.
"Annual Report of the Commissioner of Indian Affairs, 1867." *House Executive Document 1*, 40 Congress, 2 Session (Serial 1326).
"Appropriation for the Navajo Indians." *House Executive Document 70*, 38 Congress, 1 Session (Serial 1193).
Heitman, Francis B. *Historical Register and Dictionary of the U. S. Army*. Washington: Government Printing Office, 1903.
Joint Special Committee on Indian Affairs. *The Condition of the Indian Tribes*. Washington: Government Printing Office, 1867.
Kappler, Charles J. (ed.). "Indian Affairs, Laws and Treaties, II," *Senate Executive Document 452*, 57 Congress, 1 Session (Serial 4253).
"Letter from the Secretary of War Relative to the Unsuitableness of the Bosque Redondo Reservation." *House Executive Document 248*, 40 Congress, 2 Session (Serial 1341).
"Removal of the Navajo and Ute Indians." *House Executive Document 308*, 40 Congress, 2 Session (Serial 1345).
"Resolution of the Legislature of Kansas." *Senate Miscellaneous Document 34*, 39 Congress, 2 Session (Serial 1278).
Usher, John P. "Report on the Navajo Indians." *House Executive Document 65*, 38 Congress, 1 Session (Serial 1193).
The War of the Rebellion; The Official Records of the Union and Confederate Armies. 139 vols. Washington: Government Printing Office, 1891–96.
Newspapers
Albuquerque *Rio Abajo Weekly Press* (New Mexico), 1863–65.
Santa Fe *Weekly Gazette* (New Mexico), 1864–68.
Santa Fe *Weekly New Mexican* (New Mexico), 1863–68.

Secondary Sources

BOOKS

Bailey, Lynn R. *The Long Walk*. Los Angeles: Westernlore Press, 1964.
————. *Bosque Redondo: An American Concentration Camp*. Pasadena: Socio-Technical Books, 1970.
Bancroft, Hubert H. *History of Arizona and New Mexico*. New Edition. Albuquerque: Horn and Wallace, 1962.
Brown, Dee. *Bury My Heart at Wounded Knee*. New York: Holt, Rinehart, and Winston, 1970.
Brugge, David M. *Navajos in the Catholic Church Records of New Mexico, 1694–1875*. Window Rock, Arizona: Research Section, Parks and Recreation Dept., The Navajo Tribe, 1968.

————. *Zarcillos Largos*. Window Rock, Arizona: Navajo Parks Publications, 1970.
Brugge, David M., and Correll, J. Lee. *Navajo Bibliography*. Window Rock, Arizona: Navajo Tribal Museum, 1967.
Carter, Harvey L. *Dear Old Kit*. Norman: University of Oklahoma Press, 1968.
Coan, Charles F. *A History of New Mexico*. 3 vols. Chicago: The American Historical Society, 1925.
Cox, James. *Historical and Biographical Record of the Cattle Industry*. St. Louis: Woodward and Tiernan Printing Company, 1895.
Cremony, John C. *Life Among the Apaches*. San Francisco: A. Roman and Company, 1868.
Cullimore, Clarence. *Forgotten Fort Tejon*. Bakersfield: Kern County Historical Society, 1941.
Cullum, George W. (comp.). *Biographical Register of the Officers and Graduates of the United States Military Academy*. Third Edition. 9 vols. Boston: Houghton, Mifflin and Company, 1891–1950.
Forbes, Jack. *Apache, Navajo and Spaniard*. Norman: University of Oklahoma Press, 1960.
Foreman, Grant. *Advancing the Frontier*. Norman: University of Oklahoma Press, 1933.
Frink, Maurice. *Fort Defiance and the Navajos*. Boulder, Colorado: Pruett Press, 1968.
Haines, Helen. *History of New Mexico from the Spanish Conquest to the Present Time, 1530–1890*. New York: New Mexico Historical Publishing Co., 1891.
Haley, J. Evetts. *Charles Goodnight, Cowman and Plainsman*. Norman: University of Oklahoma Press, 1949.
Heyman, Max L. *Prudent Soldier, E. R. S. Canby*. Glendale: The Arthur H. Clark Company, 1959.
Hoffman, Virginia and Johnson, Broderick. *Navajo Biographies*. Rough Rock, Arizona: Dine, Inc., 1970.
Hunt, Aurora. *Major General James H. Carleton, 1814–1873: Western Frontier Dragoon*. Glendale: Arthur H. Clark Company, 1958.
Hunter, J. Marvin. *The Trail Drivers of Texas*. 2 vols. New York: Argosy-Antiquarian Press, 1963.
Johnson, Allen and Malone, Dumas (eds.). *The Dictionary of American Biography*. 20 vols. New York: Charles Scribner's Sons, 1935.
Keleher, William A. *Turmoil in New Mexico, 1846–1868*. Santa Fe: The Rydal Press, 1952.
Kelly, Lawrence C. *Navajo Roundup*. Boulder, Colorado: Pruett Press, 1970.
Kluckholn, Clyde and Lucy W., and Hill, W. W. *Navajo Material Culture*. Cambridge: Harvard University Press, 1971.
Lamar, Howard Roberts. *The Far Southwest, 1846–1912*. New Haven: Yale University Press, 1966.
McNitt, Frank. *Navajo Wars: Military Campaigns, Slave Raids and Reprisals*. Albuquerque: University of New Mexico Press, 1972.
Mitchell, Marie. *The Navajo Peace Treaty of 1868*. New York: Macon and Lipscomb Publishers, 1973.
Pearce, T. M. (ed.). *New Mexico Place Names*. Albuquerque: University of New Mexico Press, 1965.
Pearson, Jim Berry. *The Maxwell Land Grant*. Norman: University of Oklahoma Press, 1961.
Peithman, Irvin M. *Broken Peace Pipes*. Springfield, Ill.: Charles C. Thomas Publisher, 1964.
Read, Benjamin M. *Illustrated History of New Mexico*. Santa Fe: New Mexico Printing Company, 1912.
Rittenhouse, Jack D. *New Mexico Civil War Bibliography*. Houston: Stagecoach Press, 1961.
Roessell, Ruth (ed.). *Navajo Stories of the Long Walk Period*. Tsaile, Arizona: Navajo Community College Press, 1973.

Sabin, Edwin L. *Kit Carson Days.* 2 vols. New York: The Press of the Pioneers, 1935.
Shinkle, James D. *Fifty Years of Roswell History, 1867–1917.* Roswell, New Mexico: Hall-Poorbaugh Press, 1964.
———. *Fort Sumner and the Bosque Redondo Indian Reservation.* Roswell, New Mexico: Hall-Poorbaugh Press, 1965.
Smith, Sidney W. *From the Cow Camp to the Pulpit.* Cincinnati: The Christian Leader Corporation, 1927.
Sonnichsen, C. L. *The Mescalero Apaches.* Norman: University of Oklahoma Press, 1958.
———. *Pass of the North.* El Paso: Texas Western Press, 1968.
Spicer, Edward H. *Cycles of Conquest.* Tucson: University of Arizona Press, 1962.
Stanley, F. *E. V. Sumner.* Borger, Texas: Jim Hess Printers, 1969.
Terrell, John Upton. *The Navajos.* New York: Weybright and Talley, 1970.
Twitchell, Ralph. *Leading Facts of New Mexico History.* New Edition. 2 vols. Albuquerque: Horn and Wallace, 1963.
———. *Old Santa Fe.* New Edition. Chicago: The Rio Grande Press, 1963.
Walker, Henry P. *The Wagonmasters.* Norman: University of Oklahoma Press, 1968.
Waters, Frank. *The Book of the Hopi.* New York: Ballantine Books, 1970.
Weighley, Russell F. *History of the United States Army.* New York: The Macmillan Company, 1967.
Who Was Who in America. Historical Volume. Chicago: A. N. Marquis Co., 1963.
Wilson, John P. *Military Campaigns in the Navajo Country.* Santa Fe: Museum of New Mexico Press, 1967.

ARTICLES

Bloom, Lansing B. (ed.). "Bourke on the Southwest, Part IV," *New Mexico Historical Review,* 10 (January 1935), 1–35.
———. "Historical Society Minutes," *New Mexico Historical Review,* 18 (July 1943), 247–311, and (October 1943), 394–428.
Chaput, Donald. "Generals, Indian Agents, Politicians: The Doolittle Survey of 1865." *Western Historical Quarterly,* 3 (July 1972), 269–82.
Correll, J. Lee. "Ganado Mucho — Navajo Naat'aani," *The Navajo Times,* November 30, 1967, 24–25, 27.
Crouter, Richard E. and Rolle, Andrew. "Edward Fitzgerald Beale, and the Indian Peace Commissioners in California, 1851–54," *Historical Society of Southern California,* 42 (June 1960), 107–32.
Jett, Stephen C. "The Destruction of the Navajo Orchards in 1864: John Thompson's Report," *Arizona and the West* 14 (Winter 1974), 365–78.
Kenner, Charles. "The Origins of the 'Goodnight' Trail Reconsidered." *Southwestern Historical Quarterly* 77 (Jan. 1974), 390–94.
McMechan, Edgar C. "John Hittson: Cattle King," *Colorado Magazine* 11 (September 1943), 164–71.
McNitt, Frank. "Fort Sumner: A Study in Origins," *New Mexico Historical Review* 45 (April 1970), 101–17.
Reeve, Frank D. "The Government and the Navajos, 1846–1858," *New Mexico Historical Review* 14 (January 1939), 82–114.
———. "Albert Franklin Banta: Arizona Pioneer, Part II," *New Mexico Historical Review* 17 (July 1952), 200–52.
———. "Navajo Foreign Affairs, 1795–1846, Part I," *New Mexico Historical Review* 46 (April 1971), 101–32; and "Part II" (June 1971), 223–51.
Thompson, Gerald. " 'To the People of New Mexico,' General Carleton Defends the Bosque Redondo." *Arizona and the West* 14 (Winter 1972), 347–66.
Unrau, William E. "The Civil War Career of Jesse Henry Leavenworth," *Montana, The Magazine of Western History* 12 (April 1962), 74–83.

Walker, Henry P. (ed.). "Soldier in the California Column: The Diary of John W. Teal," *Arizona and the West* 13 (Spring 1971), 33–82.
Worchester, Donald E. "The Navajo During the Spanish Regime in New Mexico," *New Mexico Historical Review* 26 (April 1951), 101–18.
Young, Mary E. "Indian Removal and Land Allotment: The Civilized Tribes and Jacksonian Justice," *American Historical Review* 64 (October 1958), 31–45.

THESES

Girdner, Alwin J. "Navajo-United States Relations." M. A. Thesis. The University of Arizona, 1950.
Mehren, Lawrence L. "A History of the Mescalero Apache Reservation, 1869–1881." M. A. Thesis. The University of Arizona, 1968.

CORRESPONDENCE

Freeze, Alys H., Western History Department, Denver Public Library, to author, April 8, 1969.
Hanff, Peter E., Bancroft Library, to author, March 10, 1972.
Hill, Edward E. to author, January 6, 1972.
Starkey, Virginia L., State Historical Society of Colorado, to author, April 3, 1969.

Index

Colorado River, 2
Comanche Indians,
    noted, 4, 12, 40, 53, 56, 74, 127
    raid near Bosque, 88, 93, 120, 135,
       140–41, 145, 152–54
Comancheros, 120, 135
Committee on Indian Affairs, 89, 104
Confederacy (C. S. A.),
    noted, 94, 97, 159
    and New Mexico, 8–11
Connelly, Henry,
    noted, 58, 97, 101, 107
    supports Bosque Redondo, 24–25,
       32–34, 65, 69
Conrad, Charles M., 6
Cooley, C. E., 73
Cooley, D. N.,
    as Commissioner of Indian Affairs, 96,
       107–10, 118–20, 124, 143
Copperheads, 97
Council Grove (Kansas), 66, 88
Coyotero Apache Indians, 95
Cremony, John C.,
    at Fort Sumner, 15–17, 22, 26
Crocker, Marcellus M.,
    noted, 61, 97
    appointed post commander, 52–53
    and Navajo Fund, 54–55
    and rationing crisis, 56–60
    creates police force, 64–65,
    and 1864 appropriation, 66–67
    and reservation problems, 71–77, 160
    photo of, 52
Cronin, Michael,
    at Fort Sumner, 92–93
Cubero, 109
Cutler, Abraham,
    supports Carleton's policy, 106–8
Cutler, Benjamin,
    as Carleton's adjutant, 92–94

Datil Mountains, 101
Davidson, John W., 139
Davis, Nelson H., photo of, 30
Davis, William P., 134
DeForrest, Cyrus, 14, 42, 94
DeHague, Joseph, 99
Delgadito (Navajo),
    aids military, 22, 27–29, 47, 55, 61, 89,
       151, 156
    at 1867 council, 142–43
Delgado, Felipe,
    as Superintendent of Indian Affairs,
       83–86, 96, 107, 120
Democratic Party, 18, 32, 58, 121
Denman, H. B.,
    and contracting, 40-42, 46, 73, 76, 80
Denver (Colo.), 18

Desmarias, Miguel, 78
Detrich, Martin, 108
Diaz, Charles, 15
Dodd, Theodore H.,
    noted, 14
    as Navajo agent, 81–83, 89, 133–37, 160
    and 1865 appropriation, 96–97, 104, 120
    and Navajo transfer, 142–47
    and Bosque closing, 151–52
Dodge, Henry L., 6
Dog Canyon, 14
Dold, Andres,
    and contracting, 22, 45, 49, 73, 79–80, 94
Dold, John, 49, 54, 147
Dole, William P.,
    and Mescaleros, 18–19
    and Steck, 21, 24–25, 31–33, 38, 41,
       44, 54, 74, 79, 83
    agrees to Bosque, 36–37
    and 1864 appropriation, 61–63, 67
    and Carleton, 51, 60, 74–75
    and 1865 appropriation, 81–82, 95–96
    noted, 51, 60
Dona Ana County, 94
Doniphan, Alexander W., 4
Doolittle, James R.,
    investigates Bosque Redondo, 89–91,
       104
Dubois, John V., 146

Eaton, Amos B., 102, 108, 149
Edgar, Edwin J., 75, 119
Edgar, James C., 78
Edmunds, J. M., 81
Edmunston, Robert, 121
El Hijo (Navajo), 55
Elizabethtown, 19
El Paso, 124
Emigrant Crossing (Texas), 93
Enos, Herbert M.,
    as Ft. Union's quartermaster, 56–57
    requests investigation, 147–48
    photo of, 30
Escudilla Mountains, 101
Estrella (Mescalero), 14

Faringhy, L. O., 64
Fauntleroy, Thomas, 7
Fialon, Joseph, 19, 26, 82
Fleurant, M., 98
Fonda Hotel, 106
Fort Bascom,
    noted, 129
    military scouts near, 87–88, 145–46
Fort Canby, 27, 38, 78
Fort Craig, 89
Fort Defiance,
    and Navajos, 5–8, 157